THE FLAVOR OF WINE

SAMANTHA HOHNSTADT

Twin Quills Publishing

Cover Design by M.H. Pasindu Lakshan
Images from Samantha Hohnstadt and Public Domain

ISBN-13: 978-1-7341787-0-8

Printed in the United States of America.

THE FLAVOR OF WINE

"Wine is so multi-faceted and complex;
yet,
it's also the most simple pleasure in the world —
an easy way to bring together both friends
and strangers
over a common appreciation
for what's in their glass."

- Cortney Casey
Owner, Michigan By The Bottle

For Papa

1

Everything or cinnamon raisin?

I set my coffee down next to my notebook and picked up a plate. Tuesday mornings meant all-staff meetings in the large conference room, accompanied by bagels, cream cheese, and chit chat. I opted for cinnamon raisin to avoid being stuck with garlic breath all morning and took a seat next to a colleague. It was going to be a long morning.

We all settled into our seats and the meeting began. Every week, we gathered to review current job openings, "hot candidates", and to discuss both individual and team priorities for the week. I went through the routine and read the notes I'd prepared in my notebook the day before, barely looking up to make eye contact with anyone else. They knew me well enough by now to know that I wasn't myself. We were professional, but close. It was a tight-knit office.

I had been working at the recruiting office since April, just months after I graduated from college. Although I had just received my bachelor's degree in International Business Administration that December, one recruiting job was much better than working at a gym full-time and pulling shifts at a coffee shop to make ends meet. The more I learned about recruiting and got to know my colleagues, the more it grew on me. I was happy there. Most of the time. But that Tuesday, staring out the floor-to-ceiling windows in the conference room at the gray August exterior, I was far from it. Today was not a happy day.

I was exhausted. I'd been up most of the night, scrutinizing various details from the previous weekend over and over in my mind. Hours spent in the hospital, crying family members, dividing decisions, and endless prayers. Everything had been normal until about a week prior, when I was coming home from a vacation to Mackinac Island with a friend of mine. We were on the ferry, laughing and reminiscing about fresh memories, unaware of what had been going on at home. While we were hiking the trails, he was falling. While we tried local brews and talked about boys, he had a stroke. And then we were on the ferry, heading back to shore to drive home, and my mom called. He was in the hospital.

Two days later, another phone call: he'd had a heart attack. I was at the gym at the time, doing kickbacks and worrying about adding more weight to my next set, and he was somewhere in a hospital, suffering. He fell, my mom shared, because he had several small strokes. They didn't know when the strokes happened, only that there was evidence they had caused the fall. The fall caused a gash. The gash caused hospitalization. The hospitalization caused a heart attack. And then two heart attacks. The man would not be brought down easily.

That was Papa: my loving, stubborn, tough-as-nails, Navy/Marine vet grandfather. He rarely got sick, could stick his hand in a flame without wincing, and had been doing considerably well until the falling started. He was the indestructible one in the family: the "Ultimate Patriarch." He had served in the Korean War, survived the passing of his wife (Nana) when I was a baby, and did a phenomenal job of keeping track of my mom, her sisters, and the entire family. He brought everyone together. His laugh was one of the best parts of any family gathering. A laugh I would never hear again.

Then Friday came, and I got a call while I was at work. Normally I loved hearing from my mother. However, with the situation being what it was, my heart sank when I saw her name on my caller ID. I had a hunch I knew what this was about. I picked up, a lump already forming in my throat.

"You might want to come to the hospital, Sam."

"Is he ok?"

"All of the grandchildren are on their way...the doctors said it might be time to say goodbye."

I swallowed hard and told her I'd be on my way. He was still alive – thank goodness – but what did that mean? Time to say goodbye? How much longer did he have?

I looked over to my boss's office. The door was open, and he was sitting at his computer looking intently at the screen. I had to tell someone where I was going, and it didn't seem appropriate given how close we all were to just send an email. Somehow my legs managed to carry me across the office, and I knocked twice.

He had barely looked at me when I felt my face screwing into an "ugly cry" distortion. No one here had any idea what was going on yet. How was I going to get this out?

"My grandpa's not doing so well." I swallowed hard and felt the first tears break from the corners of my eyes. "My mom just called – I need to leave."

He didn't hesitate. My boss was a family guy; he understood. "Go. Don't worry about anything - it's ok. Just go and let me know if you need anything."

I tried to smile and squeaked out a 'thank you' before heading back to my desk to grab my purse. I couldn't look at anyone: I hate the way my face looks when I cry, and I didn't want anyone asking questions. I just can't talk when I'm upset, or else I start crying.

I had to get to the hospital as soon as I possibly could. What if I got there and it was too late? I pushed open the office door as more tears escaped. It occurred to me that I'd never actually been to a hospital apart from when my nephew was born. The atmosphere in an ICU would surely be different than it was in the maternity ward. I climbed into the elevator, made my way out to the parking garage, and fumbled with my keys to unlock the car. As soon as I shut the door and buckled up, I lost it. Turn the car on. Would he still be awake when I got there? Would he be able to talk to me? Shift into gear and drive. My mom had told me at one point they had to buckle his arms down because he insisted on pulling out the IV's. What would that look like? I couldn't imagine my poor Papa strapped down like he was in One Flew Over the Cuckoo's Nest. Out of the parking garage, down the street, onto the expressway. The exits took forever to pass.

It was a 30-minute drive from my office to the hospital, but unfortunately it felt much faster. I could hardly breathe by the time I reached the exit, I was crying so hard. I never experienced death before: I grew up with four grandparents, both parents, and close-knit friends. I had never attended a funeral. Or a burial. Oh God, a burial? I couldn't even think of how it would feel to put a family member to rest. We were a Christian family, and of course I knew I would see him again one day in heaven, but still. What about the time between now and then? What about having him around for holidays, birthdays, and weddings? My cousin was set to get married the next month and Papa was planning to walk her down the aisle...surely he could make a recovery to do so! He was going to be fine. He might even be sitting up in his cozy hospital bed, and I would get to have a conversation with him. I would get to hear his laugh one more time. Maybe. My mind was racing as I pulled into the parking lot, following my mom's directions to the correct area of the hospital. Park the car. Pull the break. Get out and head inside.

I couldn't even feel my legs as I made my way towards the lobby. I was positive my face was red and splotchy, confirmed by the look of pity I got from the woman at the reception desk. I gave her Papa's name and room information and she handed me a visitor card. It took me a moment to gather myself before heading to the elevators. Nothing felt real.

When I reached the ICU, I was buzzed inside by a woman in scrubs and she checked my visitor card. I saw no one from my family yet but followed the woman down a curving hallway. Rooms to the left and right were filled with hospital workers carrying trays and pushing carts with various instruments on them, and there were people standing with their arms crossed, sometimes crying, staring at whomever was lying in the beds. Some looked to be in more critical condition than others. I didn't see Papa and wondered if he'd be one of the critical ones or more of an "on-the-mend" one. We reached a room just around the bend and the woman stopped outside.

"Here we are." She gave me a faint smile and put her hand on my shoulder. "Take your time."

I had never witnessed anything like the emotion I felt at that moment: empty, numb, paralyzed, completely in disbelief. From the outside, the bed/machine/Papa combination was just one big, dark blur in the center of the room. The lights were dim, and there was a periodic whirring coming from one of the machines. I walked closer, entering the room and leaving the commotion in the hallway behind. It was cold. The dark blur started to clarify. My grandfather, sleeping, was still strapped to the bed. There was what I assumed to be a feeding tube attached to one machine, and a breathing tube attached to another. Every time the machine whirred, his chest lifted as he took a breath. I stood, staring, and the lump in my throat thickened. That was my Papa. That was my Papa. I couldn't move forward. This was not what "on-the-mend" looked like.

After a few moments, or maybe several – time no longer existed – my mom walked through the door followed closely by my dad. At the sight of them, I felt a fresh batch of tears slip out and slide down my cheeks. My mom gave me a half-smile and in the faint light, I could tell she was crying as well. She hugged me, and my arms felt heavy as I hugged her back. I didn't like seeing my mom cry: it meant that something was really wrong. My dad came over and put his hand on my shoulder, and the three of us just stood there, staring. I had no idea that things had gotten this serious. Strapped at the wrists, feeding tube in place, breathing machine whirring...that was my Papa.

My sister and her husband arrived a short while later, and my parents let the two of us – two of the granddaughters – spend some alone time with him. We stood, staring, and didn't say a word. At one point my sister went over and put her hand on his. It was just all so unreal. Then we headed out into the waiting room, where my cousins, one of my brothers and his wife, my aunts, and my uncle were all sitting. My step-grandmother came a short while later, and we all sat there for what felt like hours waiting for news. No one said much: we were all too numb to make conversation. We took turns crying, and I tried to stomach a coffee from the vending machine. It didn't even have a taste.

At one point, one of the nurses came out and told us it was probably time. We all went into the room one last time to say our goodbye, give Papa a hug, and take our seat back in the waiting room. Everything started to blur together. Finally, once we had all taken a turn, my mom, her sisters, and my step-grandmother decided to remove the feeding tube and breathing tube and just "keep him comfortable." There was nothing else that could be done but wait. No more holidays, no more birthdays. No wedding. No one expected him to make it through the night, let alone the weekend. A few of us went back to visit him on Sunday, and he seemed the same: sleeping, somewhat unresponsive, just lying there, breathing. One of his brothers flew up from Florida. Other far-away family members trickled in and out. Papa couldn't talk, but we knew he could tell we were there. He fidgeted a bit when he heard voices. He moved his tongue around. He made horrible wheezing noises. And there were more tears, hugs, and prayers.

He made it through the weekend. And Monday. By Tuesday

morning, my mom told me I should probably go back to work, and she'd call me if anything happened. So there I was, staring out the window of the large conference room, bagel and coffee untouched, waiting. Other recruiters and managers took a turn speaking, but I didn't hear much other than the whirring of Papa's breathing machine. The meeting ended and I had to be nudged by my colleague to snap back to reality.

The rest of the morning was routine: drink coffee, follow up on emails and voicemails, confirm interviews, start sourcing. At some point someone suggested lunch. Phone calls, an afternoon meeting, and no call from my mother. So I called her after work, just to check in. No change. Papa was hanging on – I admired him for that – but at this point it was painful just knowing he was still lying there, wheezing occasionally, waiting to die. No one wanted to admit it, but it was to the point where he just needed to be in heaven – with his family members, with my Nana – and be done with the suffering. My mom and her sisters took turns sitting with him at the hospital. I couldn't imagine being in their position, watching my dad suffer. It broke my heart.

I didn't sleep at all that night. I wanted to be back at my parents' house, in my old bedroom, if only for the comfort of it. Instead, I spent the entire night in my apartment, staring at the ceiling, occasionally peeking over at the clock. At some point my alarm sounded and I dragged myself through my morning routine. Brush teeth, wash face, make coffee, get dressed, head to work. I was halfway to work when I realized I forgot to eat breakfast and felt completely lifeless as I pulled into the parking garage. Into the lobby, into the elevator, past reception, to my desk. Another day of anticipation for a phone call. Sometime mid-morning, it came.

"Sam? It's Mom. I just wanted to let you know...he went to

heaven early this morning."

I sent my boss an email this time and slipped out. Back past reception, back into the elevator, back into the lobby, out to the parking garage, into my car. I didn't know where to go. *To my parents' house? To the hospital? Back to my apartment?*

More tears. Papa was gone. August 24, 2016.

The next few days blended into one. We didn't have the funeral and burial right away, as he was to be cremated. His reasoning: "I don't want people to see me all cold and dead before they put me in the ground." Typical Papa. It almost made me laugh when my mom told me: I could hear him saying it, giving a hearty laugh at the end. So we waited until arrangements were made and the dust had settled and relatives could come in from out of town.

It was a very hot day, and my black sweater/black skirt/black tights combination was anything but comfortable. Good. Why should I feel comfortable at a time like this? My parents, aunts and uncles, cousins, step-grandmother, and most of my siblings were there, and we drove to a small pavilion for the service. There were a few rows of benches, a small podium at the front, and several members of the Navy there to honor him. His ashes were in front, encased in a polished black box. After kind words of honor were spoken about my grandfather, the Navy played Taps, folded the flag, and presented it to my step-grandmother. It was beautiful, and most of us cried.

At the gravesite, we watched as they buried his ashes. There was a small sign stuck in the ground containing information that would soon be carved on a gravestone. I brought white roses – for

peace, for purity, for honor – and laid them down next to it. People started to leave, but I just stood there, feet cemented in place.
I wanted to hear him again. I wanted to give him a hug and smell
his cologne. I wanted him to tell me about his time in the Service
and hear the way he would always say "wursh" instead of "wash".
But I wouldn't be able to again. There he was, reunited with my
Nana, finally home in heaven. It took me a few minutes before I
was able to turn and leave, following my family away from Papa
and on with our lives.

2

For the first few weeks following my grandfather's passing, I woke up each day hoping it had all been a dream. Then I would go about my morning, and eventually see the bulletin from his memorial service still sitting on my kitchen counter. Not a dream. The memorial service had been at my step-grandmother's church, and I couldn't bring myself to throw away the piece of paper detailing the hymns and readings. So there it sat, on my counter: a constant reminder that he was gone.

After taking a few days of bereavement, I went back to work and tried to pick up like nothing happened. It was September now, and the sky was duller than ever. Those floor-to-ceiling windows were unforgiving to the weather outside, and the office felt gloomy and dim. Some days it would rain. Some days the wind would blow so hard our entire building would sway. As we were on the 26th floor, we could actually feel it moving back and forth. It made me nauseous, or maybe that was just how it felt to experience the residual pain of everything that had happened.

I had friends reach out to me from time to time, checking in to make sure that I was ok. A few cards came in the mail, I received several sympathy texts, and my coworkers periodically stopped by my desk to chat and check in on me. Just days after it happened, my parents, siblings and their spouses, and I were all gathered at my parents' house and did one last toast to Papa and the wonderful man he'd been. He was known for loving O'Doul's — a non-alcoholic beer — and though none of us cared much for it, we all clinked cans to his memory. My dad took a photo and posted it online, eliciting comments and sympathies from far-away friends and relatives on social media. That was when my friend Cleo reached out, a friend I'd known since high school.

Cleo was an exchange student from northern Germany. I met her my senior year of high school, when our paths crossed at lunch one day. The friend I normally sat with had been sick that day, so I sat in our usual spot - alone - at the end of one of the long lunch tables. The middle of that table was where the international students sat: Germany, Finland, Japan, Vietnam, Switzerland, and other countries all represented right there in our cafeteria. Cleo shouted down to me that day that I should scoot down a few chairs and sit with them, and that was it. That was the beginning of our friendship. She invited me to a cookout at her host family's house, we went shopping and out to the movies together, and though we were in different French classes, we helped each other with our homework. I was also taking German III that year, so she helped me practice my vocabulary and grammar while offering insight on German 'slang' as well. I had never bonded with a friend so quickly. When the time finally came for her to go back to Germany, she invited me over and gave me some of her things that did not fit into her bursting suitcase. Maybe we'd done a bit too much shopping.

When Cleo left, we remained friends through Skype and social media. Occasionally we would send each other ideas about visiting, coming up with crazy scenarios and trips we wanted to take together one day. She did come back to my town at one point, when I was several states away in college. Unfortunately, I was unable to make it home to see her, so we continued making plans to one day travel together. Then in 2014, I managed to secure a summer internship in Dublin. It was the perfect opportunity to finally be reunited after nearly three years apart. So, one weekend that summer, I booked a flight over to Germany and spent time a few days with her, truly appreciating the freedom and opportunities that came with travelling. It was a bit difficult to navigate in a foreign country without knowing the language, but she helped me with German phrases and everything I'd learned in high school came flooding back. It was an amazing weekend, though far too short, and one of the happiest memories from my summer internship.

And here we were, two years later, addressing the unhappiest situation imaginable. She sent me a message after seeing my dad's photo, hoping I was doing ok. The conversation quickly switched to playing catch-up, me filling her in on what it was like to graduate college and move into my first apartment, her filling me in on a year she spent in Australia working and exploring. It sounded incredible: spending some time with a family in a foreign country while working to save money, then driving off to meet new friends and explore the Outback. We messaged back and forth for a while, completely intrigued by what the other had been doing. Australia. Now there's a place I'd like to visit.

Over the next few weeks, between wedding festivities for my cousin and working, I spent hours researching companies similar to the one Cleo had described. There were some that offered an international experience working abroad in exchange offering room and board with some money on the side for food. Others were exchange programs requiring family participation: families could basically trade their children for a set amount of time to let them see the "day-to-day" life of living abroad. And then there were other live-in options, such as being an Au pair or in-home language tutor. Yet while it was fun to imagine what life would be like living and working abroad, it was little more than a distraction from everything going on with my family. I was confident that my parents would not think any of these options were a good idea, and then there were finances (not to mention my job) to consider. I put the idea on a backburner.

The day of my cousin's wedding finally arrived, and it was absolutely beautiful. I was asked to be a bridesmaid and stood at the front of the church with my sister, cousin, and a close friend of my cousin's in our matching gold dresses. At the rehearsal dinner, we'd each been given an Alex and Ani bracelet with Papa's birthstone on it, which we all now wore around our wrists. Even though his only physical presence was the photograph nestled on the seat next to my step-grandmother, we knew he was watching the ceremony. My cousin walked down the aisle in her beautiful white dress, arm-in-arm with her mother. It was tough for those of us who knew the original plan: it was supposed to be Papa. But my aunt's face was beaming and we all smiled as we watched them walk down the center of the church.

The reception was fun, though being with the extended family again was a reminder of the last time we were all together – at the memorial service – only a few weeks earlier. Everyone there felt it: a very important member of the family was missing. It was odd not to hear his laugh in the background noise. And given that he had been such an important figure to my cousin throughout the years made it all the more difficult. But we still celebrated, still toasted to the new couple, and still danced the night away. It was interesting, seeing everyone trying to be so happy and focus on something exciting after such a dark time. Family is everything. Family can pull through anything.

Once the wedding had come and gone, life returned to normal and I fell into a daily routine. Wake up, make coffee, get ready, have breakfast, drive to work, sit in rush hour (both ways), come home, eat dinner, go to the gym, shower, go to bed. Occasionally I stopped for groceries. My parents and siblings lived about 45 minutes away, so I didn't spend much time with them, and my friends' schedules never seemed to line up with mine to allow for hang-out sessions. I did have a few neighbors in my apartment complex that I'd grown fairly close with, and we'd have occasional "wine nights" and watch movies. But that was it. And I was ok with not constantly being surrounded by people: It was kind of nice to have time to myself – a sort of "cool-down" phase – after so much activity with the funeral and the wedding.

On one of those evenings, while I was sitting in my apartment watching endless episodes of Gilmore Girls, I decided to look through my steamer trunk. It was one of those thick, old-fashioned trunks made of black plastic and silver details and my mom had purchased me and each of my siblings upon graduating from high school. She wanted us to have a place to keep special mementos, from our graduation cap and gown to our school books documenting the Pre-K to elementary school years. I'd had a shoebox under my bed when I was younger with the same idea – birthday cards, notes from friends, letters, souvenirs – and had stuck it in the steamer trunk along with other trinkets from my childhood. That evening, I pulled it out from under some blankets and sat cross-legged on the floor of my bedroom to sift through its contents: play bills from my band trip to Chicago in ninth grade, notebooks full of stories I'd written in eighth grade, snow globes, my honor cords from graduation, and that shoebox from childhood. I opened it.

Under a mound of cards (11th birthday, confirmation, sweet 16, etc.) was a smaller package my grandparents had given me after a trip they took years earlier. Papa and my step-grandmother had gone to Greece, where his side of the family was originally from, to explore Athens and its history. For years, our family joked about being the stereotypical "big, loud Greeks" as every family gathering included ridiculous amounts of food and conversations that grew continuously louder. No one spoke Greek, but we loved our baklava and Papa had once shown us trinkets brought to the United States by his grandparents when they immigrated. In fact, when I was in sixth grade my school's social studies teacher required each student to choose a country for periodic research reports. Each quarter, we had to do a presentation/demonstration on different aspects of the country we chose: culture, government, religion, climate. We made giant posters and drew maps to illustrate the information, and we even had an "international feast" day where each of the 60 students in my grade brought in a popular food from their country. Unsurprisingly, I had chosen Greece and spent an entire year studying the country, checking in with Papa for help or details that would be useful in my presentation. I was proud to be part Greek.

I opened the small package and pulled out a handmade pouch with the Acropolis stitched into it. A light blue *all seeing eye* bracelet was tucked inside. I stared at it, remembering the day they gave it to me. I got light blue, my sister got dark blue. They had brought souvenirs for my brothers as well (though I couldn't remember what). I put the bracelet on and took the pouch into my living room, where my laptop was set up on a table. I took a seat and began to type: ATHENS ACROPOLIS

Google showed me thousands of results, and I started looking through pictures of the structure taken from all angles. The Acropolis wasn't the actual columned building as I'd thought: it was the hill on which the building (the Parthenon) was constructed. *Interesting.* I read more. Apparently there was an Acropolis museum separate from the Parthenon. Inside were busts and trinkets found all over the Acropolis, which was rather frustrating to the people of Greece because it interfered with the integrity of the historical sites. In fact, the idea that Greek statues were shipped all over the world to be in different museums and not in their original places was quite upsetting to many people. *Interesting.* I continued reading. In many places in Greece there were different kinds of baklava, not just the pistachio/walnut variety that Papa had always liked. Depending on the geographical area, the kind of nut used and the floral profile of the honey varied, showing the different influence from all of the occupations throughout history. *Interesting.*

Before I knew it, more than four hours had passed. I was

glued to my laptop, determined to learn as much as I possibly could about Greece.

It wasn't enough.

There were so many small details. There were so many things that I wondered if Papa had seen while he was there: the street markets in Athens, the homelessness of the population, the olive groves, the bruised economy, the traditional cuisine, the crystal blue Aegean Sea. Had he walked to the places where Socrates had taught? Had he visited the small orthodox churches? I wanted to ask him. I almost picked up the phone to call him. Greece was so fascinating; I wanted to learn more. I needed to learn more. I wanted to know as much as I could about this amazing country, where my great-great-grandfather had once lived before boarding a boat and sailing to America. My mind was racing. What if I could even go so far as to find out where he had once lived?

I knew that one of my dad's aunts had done extensive research on his side of the family, and as we were connected on social media I knew she would be open to helping me. It was nearly midnight, but I sent her a message regardless. I was exhilarated when she responded, almost instantly. She shared her login information for a family tree website, and instead of continuing her work on my dad's side of the family, I started looking up information for mom's. I knew the name of my great-grandfather and where Papa had lived when he was younger, and spent another few hours poring through the website to see if I could learn more. I didn't even care that I had to work the next day: coffee could fix that. This was too important and too exciting to stop.

And finally, I found it: the photocopied, hand-written register of who had been on the boat all those years ago. My great-great grandfather Leon Christopoulos, barely legible. The city of departure was somewhere on the island of Crete. I smiled, leaned back in my chair, and let out a breath of satisfaction. *I found it.*

Maybe it was being overwhelmed by everything I'd learned in the past few hours of research. Maybe it was the sense of satisfaction from finding the port where my great-great-grandfather's boat had taken off nearly 200 years earlier. Maybe it was the excitement of feeling connected to Papa again. Or maybe it was the fact that it was now 3:15 in the morning and I was mentally exhausted. But I was so certain of the decision. Nothing was going to change my mind.

I was going to Greece.

. . . . .

As anticipated, I had to fight to keep my eyes open the next day at work. I could barely focus. I just wanted to get home and start planning the trip. When would it be? Where would I stay? How long could I go? How would I get around? Which cities would I visit? I jotted the questions down in a notebook throughout the day so that I could try to knock them out one by one in the following days. I needed to have everything carefully mapped out and accounted for before I told anyone. Specifically, I had to leave no questions unanswered before I told my parents. They liked to know details, and I liked to appease their uncertainty.

The first time I'd ever traveled was in 2009, when my French teacher arranged for my French III class to have pen pals in France. My teacher – Madame – was old friends with an English teacher there, and the two of them assigned each French student to an English student to correspond with. Several times throughout the year, we wrote emails back and forth, getting to know the students some thousands of miles away. At the end of the following summer, those in my class who were inclined (and able) to go visit would be able to do so. As French had become my main focus in high school, I decided as soon as Madame announced the idea that of course I had to go. My parents were less certain: a 10-day trip to France meant they'd be allowing their youngest daughter to travel with other students (whom they didn't know) to a foreign country (where they'd never been) to stay with a pen pal and her family (whom they had never met). I understood their hesitation. And while it took a lot of research and careful, thorough presentation of information, along with some gentle coaching from my French teacher (whom they adored), they finally permitted me to go.

The second time I'd ever traveled was when I did an internship in Dublin: the summer I'd also visited Cleo. It was after my sophomore year of college, and I had just decided to major in International Business Administration. Rather than waste another summer staying at my parents' house, waitressing and babysitting to make a few extra dollars, I decided to look into international internships. It was months of research, navigating the details of visas and different companies offering programs abroad. I landed on Global Experiences, which for a small program fee of $5500 provided me with an internship (unpaid), housing (fully paid), and several intern excursions. Unlike most of the company's other country programs, Ireland's visa rules were different: if it was unpaid and under a certain amount of days, a visa wasn't needed. This saved me about $1200, so I started entertaining the idea of spending a summer on the Emerald Isle. The more information I gathered, the more possible it seemed. Again, I organized my information and presented it in the most concise way to my parents. Miraculously, they agreed that it would be a good idea (given my college major was International Business). My dad worked with me to develop a payment plan, and I started submitting the required information to my Global Experiences recruiter. A few weeks later, I had an interview with a social media/advertising startup, followed days later by an offer. Everything fell into place. I spent the summer living with more than twenty other interns (eight of whom shared my small apartment) and got my first taste of traveling while traveling. I spent one weekend with Cleo in Germany and another flying back to France to witness the finale of the Tour de France. By the end of that summer, I was hooked. I had a passion for travel.

The third and most recent time I ever traveled was right after my college graduation. I worked over forty hours per week my final semester, knowing that I was planning to return to Europe after graduation. At my company in Dublin the previous summer, I'd made the acquaintance of a German girl named Kristina and an Austrian girl, Theresa. We kept in touch when I got back to the United States, and I decided to celebrate my college graduation with a trip to go back and visit them. Once again, I researched everything from flights to trains between the two to how I would fund the trip before presenting the idea to my parents. I didn't even need their help financially this time: my full-time job plus part-time internship provided me the amount I needed to afford flights, food, and souvenirs. December 27, 2015 – just ten days after I graduated – my parents drove me to the airport and I was off. I spent the first week in Germany bonding with Kristina and her family, even experiencing New Year's Eve on top of a mountain in Innsbruck, before packing up and taking a train to Salzburg. There, I spent the next week with Theresa visiting Mozart's birthplace, seeing my first Ski-jumping event, and learning all about

Austrian culture. It was another phenomenal trip, and the friend-ships I'd made became stronger than ever. In fact, I remember re-turning to the United States, completely aware that my three strongest friends (Cleo, Kristina, Theresa) lived in a foreign coun-try. Distance truly makes the heart grow fonder.

So deciding to spend time exploring Greece was not a back-and-forth decision. The only thing that intimidated me in the slightest was the fact that I did not speak the language. When I was in France, the amount I'd studied in high school was sufficient to help me have a very enjoyable visit with my pen pal. Even in Germany (and Austria), I remembered enough German to get by just fine. Greek, on the other hand, was a language I had never even heard spoken in person. I may have listened to a video or two when I was doing research for my sixth-grade country report, but I had never spent any amount of time studying it. It's all Greek to me, in the most literal sense. So I added 'researching keywords and phrases' to my Greece to-do list, something I was planning to present to my parents once I'd figured out all of the other details. I was a professional by this point, by the time I'd planned what would be Trip Number Four.

As I gathered information to present to my parents, I started with locations. I would start in Athens, of course, and wanted to visit Thessaloniki (in the northern part of Greece), Chania (on the island of Crete, where my great-great grandfather's boat had taken off), and Santorini (of course: the white buildings with blue roofs were an absolute must-see). As I pieced these locations to-gether, I decided it would be best to travel in the off-season. I had learned the year before on my trip to Germany and Austria, it was always better to avoid Tourist Season to get the best rates on flights and hotels. Or did I want to stay in hotels? I'd quite enjoyed staying with my friends during past travels, so why not do so again this time?

You have no friends in Greece...yet. A detail to be worked out at a later time.

The first person I actually told about my trip was Cleo. She had originally planted the "travel" seed in my mind and here it was just a short while later, fully in bloom. Cleo was as excited as I was the moment I told her what I was planning. I filled her in on my research: where I wanted to go, how much flights cost, etc. She asked me where I was staying and I didn't have an answer: it was a detail I hadn't been able to work out just yet.

"Have you heard of Couchsurfing?"

I had never heard of Couchsurfing. I was familiar with AirBNB, which she also recommended, but not Couchsurfing. I could feel the excitement in her voice as she told me about the website, a free service that connected travelers with individuals offering a spare bedroom or couch. It seemed too simple. Where was the catch? Of course the expectation was that the traveler would bring a trinket or cultural 'something' to the host or cook a traditional dinner for them in exchange for a place to stay. But to not have to pay a cent to stay somewhere for a few days? I typed in the website and signed up the day she told me about it. Cleo gave me several websites to check out during our conversation, from finding places to stay to discovering local events wherever I'd be visiting. It was such an eye-opening conversation. I had no idea those kinds of resources existed.

After speaking with Cleo, I set a date for my trip: November 16. It was in the off-season, but given that Greece was far enough south, I wouldn't be traveling in winter weather. Once I'd set a date, I started sending messages out on Couchsurfing. If I couldn't find a well-reviewed host in the city I was interested in, I checked AirBNB. There were a few individuals I spoke with who were very interested in hosting an American girl – some a bit too interested – and some who seemed legitimately open to a cultural exchange with someone from the United States. I spoke with one man in Athens, a Frenchman teaching at one of the area schools. He had just had a truly awful experience with a Couchsurfer who completely took advantage of the situation, a girl doing one of those 30-countries-in-two-weeks programs. Apparently she was incredibly rude and spent more time on her cell phone than she did speaking with him. When he tried to cook for her she thought he was making an unwelcome advance. The entire exchange had been a complete nightmare, and he was wary of taking another Couchsurfer for that very reason. I connected with him on Skype and Facebook, speaking only French with him for the next few days. After several discussions, I was excited that I had my first host for Athens.

Next, I researched a place to stay in Thessaloniki. There were very few resources on Couchsurfing, so I decided to splurge and paid a grand total of forty-five Euros for two nights on AirBNB. The place seemed wonderful: right in the center of Thessaloniki, overlooking the Aegean. The two hosts were sisters born and raised there, one working at a local club and the other with a degree in Psychology, looking for a job abroad. They were very warm during our first conversation, and I had no reservations as I booked my stay with them. From the photos, it looked like a beautiful apartment, and they even offered to take me out my first night there to experience the "True Thessaloniki". I couldn't wait to meet them.

My next stop would be Chania, on the island of Crete. I sifted through multiple hosts on Couchsurfing, eventually deciding on a middle-aged man with two kids and stunning reviews. He owned a brewery. He had a warm smile. He seemed like he genuinely wanted to get to know travelers and show them the best of Chania. I messaged him about the dates I wanted to visit, and he was happy to accept my request. He even said he could help me find my way to Koutsouras, the port from which my great-great-grandfather's boat had taken off. Stop number 3: done.

Finally, I searched for hosts in Santorini. This was a bit more difficult, given that most hosts on the Couchsurfing website were only on the island during the summer. I was planning to visit in the middle of November. Of the five hosts I messaged, three rejected me, one wrote me a nice declination and invited me the following summer, and the other never answered. I was disheartened. Especially when I started searching on AirBNB and found the same situation. My only option was to stay with a host who lived near the airport, charging €70 per night. I would be there for two nights, so I reasoned with myself that I had been very lucky up to that point. So far, I had found either free or relatively inexpensive hosts. I could have been booking $150+ per night hotels, and instead I had only spent €45 for eight days in Greece. So I booked the AirBNB, worked out a plan to get from the airport to their house, and started a conversation with the host about what I wanted to see during my stay. At the end, she would help me with a ferry ticket back to Athens, where I was planning to spend a few more days before returning to the United States. Santorini was set.

I checked the cities off my list as I planned them: Athens, Thessaloniki, Chania, Santorini. Then I researched another host in Athens (to visit any of the places I'd missed the first time), and found a woman offering a beautiful bedroom for €15 per night. I messaged her immediately, and she was more than happy to accept my request to stay. Was I OK with staying there while a couple from Germany was renting the other bedroom? Of course! The more international people I got to meet, the better. Furthermore, this spot was only streets away from the host I was staying with at the beginning of my trip, so if things went well perhaps I could meet them for one more dinner before heading home.

Everything was planned. I printed out a map to show my parents where I'd be visiting. I wrote a list of my hosts, their contact information, and the dates I'd be staying with them. I even had started a list of all the places I wanted to visit while visiting each host, from the Parthenon to the port where my great-great-grandfather's boat had pushed off for America. The only thing that was left to do was purchase my flight.

I spoke with Cleo again once I had all of my Couchsurfing and AirBNB hosts sorted. She seemed excited for me, asking me questions about each of my hosts and stressing the point that I should Skype/write/email with them prior to my stay. We spoke in depth about her experience with the website, the amazing individuals she'd met, and the stories her friends had shared after using the website as well. Everything checked out. And then Cleo started talking about our past plans to one day visit each other and how she wished she could see me again. And since I would be in Europe anyway...

I must have snapped. It was a "throw caution to the wind" decision, and before I knew it, Cleo and I were talking about how I could fly into Germany to visit her first. From there, I could take a plane from Germany to Greece to continue my travels. It seemed insane. It seemed like an absolute dream. And then she said the magic words that lit a fire somewhere within me:

"If you're traveling to Greece to learn your culture, why don't you do the same in Germany?"

My dad's side of the family is German. The main reason I took German in high school was because I knew my family had German roots. If I was going on a trip to discover my family's history, why stop with my mom's side of things? Why not explore my dad's side as well? Cleo was right: this was exactly what I was doing in Greece, so I could absolutely do the same in Germany. After all, my siblings and I had connected with individuals on Facebook who were located in Germany and shared our last name (not a common name, either). I knew who they were: I'd even talked to them a few times and connected with their daughter and nephew. So why not?

I sent my relatives in Germany a message while I was still chatting with Cleo. Part of me didn't expect them to respond, part of me was nervous the moment I even mentioned visiting them, and part of me was oddly relieved when they did respond. I discussed the dates I was thinking of coming, and they were more than open to meeting me. In fact, they offered to let me stay with them if need be. We sent messages back and forth for quite some time, covering everything from my trip details to how we were related (which we never quite figured it out. We only knew that my great-great grandfather was from the same city in Germany as their relatives). Finally, we decided that I would come to visit prior to my trip to Greece. I would finally get to meet my German relatives in person. It had been over a hundred years since my dad's side of the family had been in Germany, and there I was, planning a trip to bridge the two. It was incredible. It was just unreal.

Over the course of one week, I had gone from simply wanting

to visit Greece to planning an entire adventure: five days in Germany, twelve days in Greece. I would stay with Cleo, take a train to visit family, take the train back to Cleo, fly from Hannover to Athens, take a train to Thessaloniki, fly down to Chania (and visit Koutsouras), fly to Santorini, take a ferry back to Athens, and fly back to Detroit. Everything was planned. All that was left was to tell my parents, secure their approval, and purchase my flights from Detroit to Hannover and from Athens to Detroit.

When I finally did tell my parents, it didn't come out as a question. It came out as a statement. And after I shared all of my information – all of my detailed plans for this trip – their response came as a shock. My mother simply said, "Okay".

3

Once I had my parents' approval, the reality of the trip really started to sink in. It was exciting, imagining being back in Europe, navigating airports and trains, meeting so many new people (especially my family), and getting to spend time with Cleo again. Until I actually told them my plan and heard myself sharing the details, it had still just seemed like a dream. But there I was, describing where I was going and everything I had researched, giving them as many details as possible, hearing my plan unfold as I went. My heart raced the more I talked, and I could tell from their expressions that they were slightly surprised. Surprised, but happy that their daughter was so passionate about learning her family's history and willing to fly to across the world to do so. It was really going to happen.

It was already October, but I managed to find flights at a very affordable price. In my past experiences, I learned that 'earlier is better' when it comes to buying tickets. However, I'd also heard that airlines tend to knock down the price approximately six weeks prior to take-off. This serves to take care of any extra seats they have at a discounted rate to fill the flight. To my surprise, it was true: I found a round-trip ticket from Detroit to Hannover, then Athens to Detroit for the low fare of around $1300. It was with a reputable airline as well, so I felt confident when the day finally came to click "purchase". Detroit to Chicago to Munich to Hannover. Then the return trip: Athens to Munich to Toronto to Detroit. The major flight was done.

Over the next few days, I also bought my flight from Hannover to Athens, where I would begin my time in Greece. Cleo helped me purchase the train ticket for my journey from Athens to Thessaloniki (I'd never purchased a train ticket online before). I was slightly excited for it: I'd never been on a train for more than an hour before, and this would be a five-and-a-half-hour ride, even passing by Mt. Olympus. I then purchased my flight from Thessaloniki to Chania. Once there, my host told me that he would help with the ferry ticket to Santorini and then from there back to Athens, where the flight home was already taken care of. I was a bit nervous about not having the tickets arranged in advance, but I trusted he would make sure everything worked out for that leg of the journey. For everything else, the tickets were purchased. I had crossed the point of no return.

For the duration of October, I spent the majority of my free time preparing for my trip. It felt so good to have something to pour my attention into: something to look forward to in the evenings other than just going to the gym. My trip 'to-do' list had nearly doubled in size after talking to my parents, so I started working my way through their suggestions and concerns. One of their biggest concerns was with trusting my hosts. So I decided to take Cleo's advice and spend some quality time getting to know each of them better. It turned out to be hugely beneficial for the comfort of both me and my parents. I wanted staying with them to feel more like visiting a friend rather than staying with a stranger. And perhaps getting to know them better would lend the opportunity for an outing or two together to get the true sense of city and culture. I didn't want to experience the countries as a typical tourist; I wanted to experience them on a local level.

As I already knew Cleo quite well and was in touch with my family in Germany, I started with my first stop in Greece: Athens. Olivier was a Frenchman who had moved to Greece to teach and 'start fresh'. He did speak English, but I was determined to exercise my French as much as possible. The first time we Skyped, he told me I was very pretty – which scared me at first – but as I got to know him and spent time chatting with him, I learned that he was just a very forward, blunt individual. Olivier had not always had the best experience with Couchsurfers, so he was very glad I wanted to get to know him prior to going as much as he wanted to get to know me. It was very interesting to hear his past experiences: the girl on the insane trip, other Couchsurfers-turned-nightmares, etc. I was so surprised that people would take such advantage of hosts who were offering their homes for free. Maybe I was raised differently. I had always been taught that if someone welcomes you into their home – no matter how big or small or comfortable – you thank them, do something for them in return, and definitely stay on your best behavior. The assumption with Couchsurfing was that a cultural exchange would take place, so I asked Olivier if there were any American meals he wanted me to cook for him while I was there. He told me that no one had ever asked him that before, but his kitchen was too small to cook a proper meal. I decided instead to take him something and kept a lookout for any Michigan-themed trinkets over the next few weeks.

After just a few conversations (all in French), Olivier felt like an old friend. He told me which places I should look up and which I should avoid, how the weather would be while I was there, the best places to see the Parthenon, and even offered to take me to some great views of the city while I was visiting. We talked about France (of course), and why he no longer lived there. We discussed our past travels. He'd ask me how work was going, and I'd tell him some funny stories or different things going on in the office. I'd ask for details about his teaching position, and he'd share stories of his frustration with certain students and how the company he worked for would always mess up his paycheck. Regardless, he seemed happy living in Athens and working, showing travelers around in his free time.

The next hosts were a bit more difficult to chat with as I could only do so through the AirBNB website (they didn't have Facebook or Skype). It was the set of sisters living in Thessaloniki, and they seemed very excited to have an American girl coming to live with them. They told me they did have a German girl staying with them as well, a long-term guest there on an internship. I was ecstatic. Maybe we'd become friends and I would be able to practice my German with her. The two sisters – Marilena and Dimitria – were very interested in the fact that I was vegetarian, as they were also.

So along with getting to know each other better, we started sharing recipes back and forth. I was looking forward to staying with them: the pictures of their flat on the AirBNB website showed walls painted bold colors, black and white portraits, and modern furniture. They had three cats, which didn't bother me, and they even said I would be able to wash laundry there if I needed. This was an added bonus, given I was planning to pack as lightly as possible.

In order to get in touch with my next host, I had to install WhatsApp, an app for international communication that used the internet rather than a phone plan (like Skype). Yiannis was a middle-aged dad with a beautiful home in Chania, on the island of Crete. He had a five-year-old son, who only stayed with him a few days per week. I liked that he had a son and bragged about him a bit on his Couchsurfing page: it made me feel much more comfortable staying with him. The room he posted on Couchsurfing was the son's room when he came to stay: the pictures online even showed Donald Duck books on the desk. Once I started speaking with Yiannis on WhatsApp, I felt even more comfortable staying with him: he said he hosted Couchsurfers quite regularly and enjoyed taking them to his family's restaurant on the bay. We didn't talk much more beyond our initial conversation, but at least I had some information to share with my parents. They were thrilled that I was taking time to get to know my hosts prior to staying with them.

With how smoothly everything was going to that point, it was inevitable that I would have one host that would be difficult to get a hold of. The hosts in Santorini didn't have any social media pages and rarely checked their AirBNB page. Part of me had hoped they would be very responsive to my messages as I was looking forward to visiting Santorini more than most of the other cities. Every picture I'd seen of the island looked absolutely stunning: I loved the view of the Aegean, the clean architecture, and all of the vibrant colors. I couldn't wait to visit. Angelique was offering a room in her family's holiday home, a white apartment with wood accents around the borders and pictures showing pink flowers and vines covering the walls. It looked absolutely beautiful. The few discussions we did have were mainly about rides to and from the airport and the ferry schedule to Athens. Oh well. At least I had a place to stay.

My final host was back in Athens. I decided that if something didn't work out with her, I would see if I could stay with Olivier again. I had found Tamara on AirBNB, and as I had spent less money on places to stay than I was expecting I thought I'd try to find somewhere a bit nicer to stay for my last few days abroad. Tamara had told me up front that she would be hosting a couple from Germany at the same time, but there were several bedrooms in her flat. She shared photos with me of her apartment, which was right around the corner from the Acropolis museum. As she worked as a freelancer, she did mention that she wouldn't be at home much but would be happy to show me around in her spare time. She even gave me the name of some restaurants to visit and recommendations on which "lesser known" places I should check out on my trip. To my relief, she also offered to meet me at the metro station when I first arrived, so I felt very confident that the final leg of my journey would go smoothly.

I tried to message back and forth with my various hosts a few times per week, making sure there were no last-minute cancellations or surprises. Once I had established somewhat of a relationship with all of them, I felt even more excited about the trip. Cleo and I were planning what we would do together when I visited her, my family told me they were very excited to meet me, and from there my Greek hosts would take over. Everything was falling into place. By November, I had everything accounted for except the gifts I was planning to take each of my hosts. After speaking with them, I came to the conclusion that cooking a meal for them would be too difficult. Some worked, others – like Olivier – just didn't have enough room, etc. My family in Germany wanted to cook for me as they knew I was vegetarian and had a recipe they wanted to try. So instead I went shopping for knick-knacks.

My mom had once introduced me to a store called, "Art Is In Market" at a local shopping center near my parents' house. Everything inside was Michigan or Detroit-themed, from coffee mugs and t-shirts to handmade goods such as wooden cutting boards, purses, jams, and fudge. The week before my trip, I went back to Art Is In Market to find gifts for each of my hosts and was incredibly successful. I found "Detroit Brew" coffee and a small history booklet for my family, a coffee mug with "Michigan" spelled out in photographs (the 'M' from University of Michigan, the 'I' a flower, "C" was part of a wagon wheel at Greenfield Village, etc.) and a bag of Skittles for Olivier, Michigan Taffy for the sisters in Thessaloniki, fudge for Yiannis in Chania, a Petoskey stone turtle for my host in Santorini, and another bag of taffy for my final host in Athens. Cleo made it clear that she just wanted Skittles.

With everyone's gifts purchased, the only thing left to do was pack. I had decided at the beginning of my planning that I was going to pack as lightly as possible: everything had to fit in a carry-on. I'd heard horror stories of people's luggage getting lost (including my grandparents' on their trip to Greece), and as I was only planning on spending a short time in each spot, it would be easier to just have everything I needed in one small bag. It was going to be a challenge (especially given the number of gifts I was taking), but I was determined. It took me a few practice rounds to pack everything into one carry-on bag, and I had to start over from scratch when I realized that the weather in November in Greece was going to be much different than the weather in Michigan. I bought a few long-sleeve t-shirts at Target (instead of packing thick sweaters), decided on one scarf and one coat that I would wear on the plane, and only packed one fleece in my bag for days when it was cold enough for extra layers. The difficult thing was that it would still be "Michigan cold" in Germany, where I'd be for the first five days of my trip. I was going to be cold, but I didn't have room for any bulky clothing...not with the coffee mug and bags of taffy and two giant bags of Skittles crammed into my bag.

After several practice rounds, I decided on one pair of leggings and a t-shirt (for pajamas), one pair of blue jeans (which I'd wear) and one pair of black jeans, two tank tops to alternate under a thin red sweater, one fleece, four long-sleeve t-shirts, two bras, five pairs of socks, and underwear (enough to get me to Thessaloniki, where Marilena and Dimitria had said I could do laundry). I planned to wear a pair of black military-style boots and fit a pair of black and white Converse into my bag, and decided on minimal make-up (foundation, mascara), jewelry (one necklace, which I planned to wear on the plane), and toiletries (toothbrush, toothpaste, mini Castille soap). I could buy small bottles of shampoo and conditioner once I was there which freed up room in my bag for the Skittles and coffee. Any souvenirs I wanted to buy for myself would have to be small. And if worse came to worst I could leave the black boots behind. I'd bought them on clearance anyway.

I was ready. Everything was planned. Everything was organized. I bought a messenger-style purse at TJ Maxx and organized a few protein bars, an apple, my passport, my notebook and pen, my cell phone and charger (and the converter plug for the European outlets), my toothbrush and toothpaste, and my wallet inside. From my past travel experience, I had become something of an expert at streamlining everything for the airport. The boots I was wearing had a "cheat zipper" up the back so I wouldn't have to deal with laces before and after security. I wore all of my bulkiest clothing. I made sure I had everything I needed in the most convenient spot possible. I did not want to be "that person" in the security check that took too much time and made everyone else impatient.

As my flight was at 7:45pm on a Friday, I had arranged for a coworker to pick me up for work and another to take me to the airport after work, so I didn't have to deal with parking (I had the best coworkers!). My friend Leslie — who lived a few floors above me in my apartment complex — said she would pick me up from the airport when I returned, so I had no need for my car. Transportation, done.

After weeks of planning, organizing, double-checking, shopping, communicating with my hosts, and arranging all the fine details for the trip, it seemed like a dream when I woke up on the morning of take-off: November 11, 2016. The morning was chaotic, rushing around my apartment before being picked up for work, ensuring that dishes were clean, my bed was made, clutter was put away, and I hadn't forgotten to pack anything. My parents had always taught me to do a thorough 'once-over' before leaving for any extended period of time. It always felt nice to return to a clean home after a long trip.

I climbed into my coworker's little green Fiesta around 7:30am, and we were on our way. At the office, my other coworkers and my boss all had the same reaction when they saw my carry-on. Is that all you're taking? That's it? One even asked if my luggage was still in the car. Little did they know how much effort had gone into cramming everything I could possibly need for two weeks (plus gifts) into that bag! I tried explaining the I-don't-want-to-deal-with-lost-luggage idea to them due to the fact that I'd essentially be city-hopping every few days. Regardless, confusion.

The day at work was packed with sending last-minute emails, alerting the candidates I was currently working with that I would be gone for a few weeks. I shared their resumes and contact information with various other recruiters in the office so none would be "left in the dark" just because I wasn't there to continue working with them. I even had a sit-down meeting with a coworker I was particularly close with to share the Excel spreadsheet I used to keep track of all of them. My boss called me into his office at one point to see if I was ready and to let him know if I needed anything while I was gone. I had never worked with such a caring, supportive group of people. When the time finally came for me and my ride to head out, I felt completely confident that I wouldn't be returning to a disaster with my work when I returned: my fellow recruiters reassured me of that.

By 4:30pm we were in the car on the way to the airport. My colleague came inside with me, continuing on about how she couldn't believe I only had one bag for the entire trip. We had some time before I needed to be at the gate, so we decided to stop for a drink at a place called Legend Bar. It was nice to have a sort of 'trip prep' session with her, exchanging stories from our past travels, what went right/wrong, and what I might find in

Greece. She'd spent time in Costa Rica, and hearing about someone else's trip made me even more excited for my own. At 6:00pm, we hugged good-bye and I headed to the security check. Everything went so smoothly (I was very thankful to have worn the cheat zipper boots), and I quickly found my gate. The waiting began.

I pulled out my notebook and pen and began to write. I had always loved writing and wanted to make sure I could remember as many details as possible. When I was in Dublin those few summers earlier, I had even started a travel blog. Throughout the entirety of my summer there (mini trips to France and Germany included), I spent dull evenings in my apartment, curled up on my bed typing. I shared stories, photos, cultural snippets, and whatever else came to mind so that my family and friends at home could keep up with me. It was so nice to have a sort of "keepsake" at the end of the summer, and I was glad I'd decided to write throughout the internship rather than just trying to write one all-encompassing summary at the end. Having a hard copy of my trip was a nice way to 'relive' my favorite moments. And since I didn't have room in my bag to take my laptop with me this time around, I brought a small white and gold notebook instead. It would have to do.

Sitting on the hard, blue chair at the gate, I started my first entry: a brief summary of my morning, the day at work, and the airport. It occurred to me that I hadn't eaten since lunch, so I ate one of the protein bars I'd brought along. Beer at Legend Bar and a protein bar at the gate; it may not have been the best dinner, but my excitement was enough to sustain me until I could get real food at the next airport. Before long, it was time to pack up my notebook and board the plane. As I handed my boarding pass and passport to the woman at the counter, I couldn't help but think, *there is truly nothing like this feeling.*

Off I went.

4

The flight from DTW to Chicago went extremely well. I had a window seat (a personal preference), and no one was in the seat next to me. I could have easily taken a nap had it not been for the fact that it was only a twenty-minute flight. Plus, I had to be ready to get off quickly and head to my next gate as I had a very short connection.

The plane pulled into ORD and I powered through the airport. There were no issues finding my next gate despite the short time I had to get there, so I had a few moments to collect myself. I stopped in one of the bathrooms to freshen up, brushing my teeth and washing my face. On a past trip, I'd seen another woman doing these things in an airport bathroom and was amazed at how much better I felt when I took a few moments to do them, too. Then I walked back to the gate where moments later, it was time to board.

This time, I had an aisle seat in the middle section next to an older gentleman with half-moon glasses. He nodded politely as I sat down, and I quickly stowed my bag beneath the seat in front of me before settling in. Takeoff for Munich was scheduled for 9:35pm – right on schedule – so we started to make our way towards the runway. I turned on the movie system on the back of the seat in front of me and started flicking through films. Tarzan caught my attention and I hit play, realizing quickly that I forgot my headphones. *I'll ask once we're in the air.*

After five minutes of taxiing, we were back at the gate. People were glancing around wondering what was going on, and I looked up from my soundless movie to hear the announcement:

"Attention ladies and gentlemen, we are currently experiencing a delay with takeoff. Our crew is working to identify the issue and we will provide additional details as soon as we have further information. Thank you for your patience and we ensure we will be on our way as soon as possible."

I glanced back at the movie screen and continued watching. The people around me seemed very upset that our takeoff was delayed and somewhere in the background, a child started wailing. I had an hour-and-a-half connection in Munich, so I wasn't worried. Flight delays happened all the time; more likely than not we'd be en route in minutes.

Or maybe not. Thirty minutes later, the loudspeaker clicked on again. They discovered that there had been a failure with the brakes, but fortunately it had been caught and a team of technicians was currently working to resolve the issue. My heart fluttered. And if they hadn't caught that? We waited. Something interesting was going on with Tarzan and I couldn't understand what it was. I watched, trying not to get nervous. I now had one hour in Munich to get to my connecting flight: still enough time. So when another thirty minutes passed (people still complaining, children still crying), I cringed to hear the following announcement:

"Attention ladies and gentlemen, we thank you for your patience. In order to fix the issue we identified earlier our team will be disabling the brakes in order to allow us to take off. Wait, what? Then what happens when we land? They are working as quickly as possible and we anticipate take-off in approximately one hour. Please accept our apologies for the inconvenience. Free drink service will be provided to those on board. Thank you and we will provide more details as they become available."

There was a chorus of sighs and "Are you kidding me?"s throughout the plane. Flight attendants began pushing drink carts down the aisles, trying not to be affected by the complaints of the passengers. At least there was wine. I made small talk with the man next to me, who to my surprise was very chatty. As we waited for further information, he told me about his company and how they provided brewing equipment to breweries around the world. I was intrigued. He explained that he was in sales; he would periodically be sent out to meet the owners or managers of the breweries, talk to them about size and overall goals of their breweries, and share different products his company offered to help them build or maintain their brewery. He had been in Arizona for the past few days and was now on his way home, somewhere in Germany. It was fascinating, and we ended the conversation with an exchange of business cards. A short time later, the plane once again began to taxi. There was excitement and relief as people realized we were moving. I now had a zero-minute layover in Munich but if we made good time, maybe a miracle could happen.

But five minutes later we were back at the gate.

"Attention ladies and gentlemen, we apologize for the delay. Due to the nature of the issue we will be deactivating the brakes, refueling the plane, and once again departing for take-off. Please be patient as we ready the plane and we will be on our way as soon as possible. Thank you." Click.

Everyone on the plane was already stir crazy and we hadn't even taken off yet. I had been planning to meet Kristina at the airport in Munich during my layover, and now that I would be needing a different flight from Munich to Hannover I sent her a message to cancel. I was so disappointed. The last time I'd seen Kristina was the past December, nearly one year earlier. I considered her one of my best friends and now I would be missing a rare opportunity to see her.

We finally took off shortly after midnight.

There had been a screaming child somewhere on the plane during the entire delay, and once we were in the air, he finally settled down. A flight attendant brought me headphones, so I was able to pass the time watching movies and listening to music. Despite the enormous delay, the flight itself went very well. I had put in a special request for a vegetarian meal, which arrived before anyone else's. There was more free wine. The movie selection was fantastic. The only problem was the fact that I'd need to figure out a new connecting flight when I arrived in Germany. Being nervous made it difficult to get any sleep on the plane whatsoever.

I had no way to contact Cleo and Kristina once we were in

the air and I couldn't tell if they had received the messages I'd sent during the delay. When we finally did arrive in Munich, I had a handful of messages from Kristina, who was also upset that we wouldn't be meeting for coffee at the airport. I made finding the customer service desk a priority and explained the situation. I was hoping there would be a simple fix: a quick change of my ticket to put me on the next plane to Hannover. Cleo told me to let her know when I was scheduled to board the plane so that she could plan when to collect me from the airport in Hannover. What was supposed to be a very simple journey had become an enormous headache, and I felt guilty for dragging my friends into it with me.

The woman at the desk helped me to rebook my ticket for a flight to Hannover leaving in 30 minutes (at 6:50pm). I hurried to the gate and waited to board. It didn't occur to me until they started boarding that my ticket had "STANDBY" printed across the top. So it was to my absolute horror that an announcement came a few minutes later saying that the plane was full. There were no available seats for those with standby tickets. The next available flight was at 9:50pm; three hours later.

I felt a lump forming in my throat as I sent Cleo an update. We already had a very limited time together and now it was being cut even shorter by the nightmare unfolding at the airport. The woman at the service desk could clearly read panic on my face as she comforted me when I approached the desk a second time. She printed me an "apology meal" voucher for a whopping seven euros and sent me on my way.

I was furious. It was not my fault that the plane was late to arrive. It was not my fault the brakes had malfunctioned and they decided to take an extra two hours at ORD to fix the issue. It was not my fault that the woman at the service desk re-booked my ticket to a standby instead of a normal ticket. Everything leading up to this was completely out of my control. But as the frustration and growing headache and hungry pit in my stomach started to really sink in, I felt like I was being punished. And then I was given a grand total of seven euros to make up for it all. *Was this some kind of joke?*

The only decent food I could find for less than seven euros was a fruit cup. I was going to get a sandwich (€8,50) but was told that I couldn't use the voucher to partially pay for a meal. So the additional €1,50 could not be paid in cash. Fruit cups were only €6,50, so I bought one with different kinds of melon thinking the sugar would perk me up. The man at the counter seemed to agree it was a ridiculous policy and gave me a Kinder Überraschungsei (Surprise Egg) free of charge. My mood lifted ever so slightly, and I found a spot to eat. I pulled out my phone and decided to call my mother, which I'd agreed to do periodically during my trip. She didn't have WhatsApp, so I used Facebook Messenger instead. It started ringing.

I could hear the concern in her voice after I explained to her everything that had happened that day. No mom, I'm sure they're not taking advantage of me, stuff like this happens when you travel. Yes, I'm safe. Yes, I got something to eat. Yes, I know where I need to be for the next flight. I had almost considered not telling my parents about the delay situation. I had been so careful to assure them that I had everything planned out: every detail accounted for so that there was no reason to be concerned. Admitting that it was only day one and there was already a problem was not an easy thing to do.

Two hours later, I was on my way back to the gate. Two people were already standing at the service desk, yellow STANDBY tickets in hand. I joined them, and the flight began to board. I watched as people trickled by, my hope dwindling as one after another passed the counter, bags in hand. Eventually one of the attendants announced that people would start needing to check their carry-on bags because there was no more room in the overhead compartments. The line continued. Before I knew it, two of the other STANDBY passengers were ushered in and the gates were pulled shut. I didn't make it onto the plane.

By that point there were tears stinging at the corner of my eyes. I missed my original connection. The first standby plane was too full. The second standby plane was too full. And I was told to go back to the service desk to get yet another ticket for yet another plane. I was starting to doubt I'd ever get to Cleo in Hannover. There was a brand-new service agent at the desk (no doubt the woman who'd helped me before had finished her shift), and he happily printed me another ticket. As he slid the ticket across the counter, he also gave me a map of the airport (pointing out that the next gate was at the complete opposite end of the airport) and another seven-euro voucher. You have to be kidding me. He told me I had just over an hour until my next flight started boarding and recommended I check out one of the bars at the airport and use the voucher. I could barely look at him for fear of bursting into tears as I took the slips of paper from him.

It felt like I walked five miles before I finally reached the next gate, and quickly found the bar he mentioned. I was in a terrible mood. I decided to try out my German and ordered a pint and a bag of chips, and the man behind the counter smiled and asked where I was from. When I told him – aus Amerika – and continued the conversation with him, he told me my German was perfect. It was the highlight of my entire day. Fifty minutes passed, and I slumped into a chair at the gate. I assumed I wouldn't get on this flight, either, so I was thrilled when one of the attendants waved me over and ushered me through the gates. I sent a note to Cleo: FINALLY on my way! Then I filed into my seat and got comfortable.

Cleo and I had planned on having the entire afternoon to-gether. I was supposed to arrive in Hannover at 4:30pm, and there I was finally rolling into the airport around 11:00pm. The day had been a disaster. But as I made my way into the lobby, seeing her there with a giant "SAM!" sign in her hand and a massive smile on her face, I knew that everything was alright. I'd made it. I was back in Germany, back in Hannover, back with Cleo.

. . . . .

When Cleo and I were first becoming friends in high school, one of our first "hangout sessions" outside of school was a trip to JoAnn Fabrics. It was sometime in the winter, long before prom, and Cleo had shared that she was determined to make her own prom dress. She showed me pictures and the fabric scraps and bits of lace that she'd been given from her host mom, trying to explain the concept she was going for. Then the two of us spent hours in JoAnn Fabric, her picking out patterns and me trying to help with accents like silver beads and fringe. As neither of us had much sewing experience (apart from small pouches and handkerchiefs), it was destined to be a mess. But we filled a cart anyway. By the time we actually found everything she would need, we realized how expensive it would be and how much work we'd have to put into it and ended up putting everything back. That was Cleo: al-ways spontaneous, extremely creative, and determined. Even if it didn't always work out.

So it goes without saying that we were both rather surprised this crazy trip had actually worked out, and that I was actually sat there in her car, and we were actually on our way to her flat. (I'd made the mistake of calling it an apartment and she scolded me that I wasn't in America anymore. Apartments were Flats in Europe.). During the drive, she filled me in on her day, and I filled her in on mine. I felt like I couldn't apologize enough for all of the delays and for ultimately arriving nearly seven hours later than we'd originally planned. She casually waved a hand and told me not to worry; I was there now and that's what mattered.

Her flat was in a different town than the one where I'd visited her previously. Before, she was on the first floor of a house in Hannover, in a small neighborhood with a bakery (eine Bäckerei), a post office (ein Postbüro) and a bus stop (eine Bushaltestelle). Now, she was in a shared flat with two other students who fortunately would not be there while I was. This flat was in the town of Braunschweig, which instantly made me think of the lunchmeat my dad always put on his sandwiches. (I shared this fact with Cleo when we saw the first sign for Braunschweig, and she laughed. Apparently, that didn't exist in Germany.) It was right in the center of town: just outside, there was a bus stop and several small stores including a pharmacy and a convenience store. She pointed down one road and said there was an Aldi (about 10 minutes' time walking) and down another, a shop called *Lidl* (a slightly larger version of Aldi, 15 minutes away). As we parked outside her building, she pointed out the bakery she went to most mornings and some flats of her friends and acquaintances. It was incredible to see all of the different buildings, architecture varying from one to the next. The old German buildings towered above us, and I couldn't help but appreciate how close together everything was. I couldn't wait to explore.

We made our way through a small alleyway to the back of

one of the buildings, where vines and leaves were everywhere. She led the way to a large black door and we went inside, climbing creaky stairs higher and higher to reach her flat. There was no elevator; this was how she came and went every day. Her flat was nearly at the top, and I was relieved when she pulled out her keys and ushered me in.

It was quaint: there was a small kitchen to the right, a long hallway down the middle with what I assumed were the bedrooms (doors all shut) along the sides, and a small bathroom to the left. Cleo grabbed my bag from me and headed for the door at the end of the hallway. We flopped to the floor of her bedroom and began to chat. It was almost 1:00 in the morning, and we dove into conversation covering everything from boys to high school to university classes to work. Our original plan of going out for drinks had been abandoned. Instead, Cleo and I relocated to the kitchen, where she prepared Brot mit Blaubeeremarmelade (bread with blueberry jam), Nutella, and butter. I was absolutely starving: all I'd had since the flight to Munich was a fruit cup, beer, chips, and a Kinder egg. Nothing tasted as good that first piece of real, German bread.

When we'd finished eating, Cleo grabbed a bottle of white wine and we went back to the bedroom. She showed me how to use the shower and I freshened up while she pulled up photos from Australia on her laptop. Then we each poured a glass and the slideshow began. She'd spent the first three months working on a farm, earning her spot at a family's house and saving the small amount they paid her for her help. Once she'd finished working, she spent the next several months traveling around the Outback. Cleo showed me photos of "sandboarding," in which she and some friends she'd met used long snowboard-like boards to cruise down giant hills of sand. They cooked out on small stoves in the trunks of their cars (she emphasized how annoying the bugs were when they smelled the food), went snorkeling with sea lions, climbed giant trees looking for koalas, held baby Kangaroos, and swam in the most beautiful, colorful lagoons I'd ever seen. I could tell she made the most of her trip and missed it: she would pause from time to time and put her hand on her heart, taking in a deep breath and exhaling, "Oh my God, it was so amazing." I could only hope this trip would leave me feeling the same way.

We finished the bottle of wine and fell asleep watching Mordecai. It felt amazing to crawl into bed and close my eyes after such a long and trying day. And then, in the morning, to have such a great friend wake me up with a cup of coffee in hand, I felt like I was still dreaming. I'd slept long and hard and it was nearly noon.

When she pulled me into the kitchen I saw that Cleo had prepared the kitchen for a magnificent brunch. It was filled with the aroma of fresh bread and coffee, and a feast waited for us on the table: scrambled eggs, Brötchen (bread rolls) fresh from the bakery (she'd gone while I was sleeping), Blaubeeremarmelade, Soja joghurt (yogurt made with soy milk) with muesli, fruit, and more coffee. The coffee was made in a small machine something like a Keurig, but instead of plastic pods, the coffee rounds were more akin to tea bags. She poured in a cup of water, smashed the pod into the top of the machine, and hit a button. It was the most phenomenal coffee I'd ever had (or maybe I was just caffeine-deprived). She pointed out some of the other things in the kitchen, including the small fridge (the size of a dorm fridge in the US) which was shared with her flat mates, the three small garbage bins they used to separate their trash, and some of her favorite teas all stored in colorful tins. She showed me the trinkets she'd collected over the years (including a tea tin I'd brought her when I visited her in Hannover), which were displayed on a small shelf above her kitchen table. It was a quaint, but cozy kitchen.

After we spent some time brunching, it was time to get ready and head to her studio. Cleo was studying to become an architect, and she had some work to do on a project for school. Having never been to an actual German university, I was excited that she welcomed me to tag along. I took a shower while she packed up some of our leftovers, and we were off.

TU Braunschweig was only a short drive away, and we found we were the only ones there (not surprising, given it was a Sunday afternoon). The studio was enormous, with long tables stretching down the length of the room and various building materials stacked up along the walls. There were various machines on the tables, including a few that looked like giant sewing machines. Cleo walked over to these immediately. I watched as she retrieved a large piece of hard, white foam and pulled out some sketches from a folder. Then she showed me how to use the machine. As she pushed the pedal on the floor, a high-pitched hum came from the machine. The wire (which I had mistaken as thread for the 'sewing machine'), heated when she pushed the pedal, and cleanly cut the small piece of foam she pushed into it. She explained that she had to cut several foam pieces of various shapes and sizes and create a sort of puzzle box with them. Her drawings were far too complicated for me to understand, but I watched as she pushed and turned and measured and cut, creating intricate pieces for her project. After a short while, she disappeared into a closet and emerged with another foam-cutting machine. She set it up in front of me, then handed me one of her scraps.

"Try it, it's kind of fun!"

And she was right. The next several hours were spent in the studio, creating random bits out of the foam. She made coffee in a machine near the back, and at some point, we broke out our snacks and had a light dinner of brunch leftovers and fruit. Some of her classmates came into the studio and shared cookies with us as well. We talked and created, her occasionally asking me to cut a certain size cube or hold something for her while she made considerable progress on her project. It didn't take long to get the hang of the machines, and by the time we decided to leave I'd even managed to make a small owl out of the foam.

We drove back to her apartment, where we quickly dropped off our things and got ready for an evening out. Cleo and I took a bus downtown, where we walked a short way to a bar called *Relax*. It was very chilly out; there were flurries of snow starting to come down and I regretted not bringing a warmer coat with me. But we waited outside for a friend of hers (Janni, one of the classmates from the studio) and he arrived with a friend shortly after we did. The four of us went inside, discovering a smoky, dimly lit atmosphere. There were fruity flavors wafting throughout the bar (several people were smoking shisha, or hookah), and it was difficult to hear what anyone was saying because of the loud music. Cleo and her friends spoke rapid German, and I found as the evening went on I could understand more and more of what was being said. We each ordered Planter's Punsch cocktails — a combination of rum, orange juice, and grenadine — and her friends ordered a cherry-flavored hookah for the table. The Planter's Punsch was absolutely delicious: powerful, but delicious. Cleo's friends asked me about America, told me about different trips they'd taken to the United States, and told me they were glad they could practice their English. I tried speaking German with them and they told me

I had a cute accent. *Thanks, but do I take that as a compliment?*

At some point nachos and salsa appeared on the table, and Cleo ordered another Planter's Punsch. I opted for a Kirsche Weizenbier (cherry wheat beer), and we spent another hour relaxing at Relax. The name was fitting. It was well after midnight by the time we headed home, taking a bus back to the stop just outside her flat. Back through the alley, back through the mess of leaves and vines, back through the giant door. Climbing stairs had never been so difficult. When we were finally back in her flat, we finished watching the movie we'd started the night before and quickly fell asleep. Braunschweig: Day 1 was an absolute success.

. . . . .

The next morning, I woke to an empty apartment. As it was a Monday morning, Cleo had to spend some time at her university. She'd left me some bread and jam for breakfast, which I enjoyed with a coffee and some sliced Birne (pear). I took my time showering, organizing my things, and was on my way downstairs by 10:00am to do some exploring.

Though I'd known Cleo for years, I wanted to give her the same courtesy I would be giving my Couchsurfing hosts for permitting me to stay with them for a few days; I wanted to make a meal for her. She was due home around 1:00pm, so I made it my mission to head out, find either the Aldi or Lidl, and put together a proper lunch for us. I managed to find Aldi, and spent a while simply browsing and admiring all of the various German products and brands. (We had Aldi in the United States, but most of the brands were different.) One thing I noticed was the remarkable amount of Advent calendars for sale. I didn't realize it was such a strong tradition there. There was even a giant Coca-Cola-themed one: a tin semi-truck full of cans of Coke!

After buying a few things in Aldi, I decided to try my luck at finding Lidl as well. I decided to make one of my favorite meals: Greek salad (while not exactly an American food, I later learned that what I considered a Greek salad was actually a very Americanized version of the dish). As a vegetarian, it was the perfect dish to share: I decided I'd simply add Hähnchen (chicken) for Cleo. I hauled my load to the counter and needed to purchase a bag to accommodate everything: Oliven (olives), Fetakäse (feta cheese), Grüner Salat (lettuce), Tomaten (tomatoes), Sprossen (sprouts), Rüben (beets), the Hähnchen, Baguette (of course I had to buy bread), and two Überraschungseier (naturally). I walked home, groceries in hand, thoroughly enjoying the fresh air and feel of the new city. By the time I'd returned home, chopped and cooked and seasoned everything, Cleo walked through the front door and joined me in the kitchen. It was perfect timing.

She filled me in on her morning at university and asked me how I'd enjoyed exploring Braunschweig. It was strange, excitedly telling her about Aldi and Lidl and seeing the look of amusement on her face as I mentioned things like the brands I'd never heard of and neat little shops I saw along the way. I assumed I sounded crazy as the reality of the situation set it, me getting excited about things that she as a local saw on a daily basis. It was all normal to her, but to me it was just fascinating. She laughed and told me she had felt the same way when she first came to the United States and discovered stores like Meijer and Target.

It was the small details, like the unfamiliar brands at a store or the routines of day-to-day life (going to the bakery every morning, for example), that fascinated me more than any other aspect of travel. Of course, visiting the Eiffel Tower in Paris and seeing the River Liffey in Dublin were incredibly memorable, but to actually discover the locals' habits was much more appealing to me than any major tourist trap. Anything relating to daily life was. On my first trip to France, when I stayed with my pen pal and her family, I learned more about the culture than any textbook could teach me. The family ate traditional French meals (several courses, all home-cooked cuisine), took me with them to the bakery they frequented, and even took me to Chartres for a fancy dinner and a light show on the walls of one of the cathedrals. I watched French television programs and drank licorice tea before bed. My pen pal showed me her collection of French books and I made it a mission to find my own copy of <u>Harry Potter à l'École des Sorciers</u> before returning home. Prior to the trip, I'd never even thought of buying French books. I'd certainly never heard of Chartres. I would have never tried half the foods the family cooked for me, let alone find that restaurant and experience the "high gastronomy" of France. And the political banter between my pen pal's family members during meals? Definitely not something that could be learned about in a guide book. After that first trip abroad, I'd made up my mind; If I had the chance to travel, I was going to learn as much about the culture as I could from locals. The little details were everything.

And so Cleo let me excitedly share my afternoon in town before we did some research on how to reach my family the next day. As she pulled up Google maps and typed in their town (I'd agreed to meet them at the train station at a certain time), we were surprised to see they were actually further away than I'd originally thought. What was worse, I would need to change trains. This terrified me. We didn't have the same level of public transport in Michigan — in fact, we didn't have any — and having to navigate a train change by myself without Cleo there was intimidating. She said she would walk with me the next morning to the bus stop (she had classes again), and I could do nothing but hope for the best as we purchased my tickets. I felt less than confident in my ability to manage the trip, but it had to be done. I hadn't flown over four thousand miles to back down out of fear when the time came to meet my family.

After lunch, we cleaned up the kitchen and decided to visit a place called Prinzen Park. We brought tea, fruit, nuts, and Kinder chocolates with us, bundled up (Cleo lent me some winter gear), and headed out. It was only a short drive away, and before long we were trudging through the dead leaves and light snow at the park. We walked around for a bit, enjoying the cool weather and the reality of being together again, and eventually took a seat on a bench at the top of the hill. It was beautiful; there was a long, winding path through the center of the park, a few statues scattered here and there, people playing catch, and a few others walking their dogs. Cleo pulled out a blanket to warm our laps and we enjoyed our snack there on the hill. I messaged my family on Facebook, sharing the schedule for the train/bus the next day, and everything was planned out. Then it was a few more minutes of chatting and snacking before we went back to the car. Cleo said that Janni lived nearby (one of the boys from Relax the night before) and that he'd invited us to join him for dinner. We decided to walk as our parking spot was halfway between the park and his flat, so were completely frozen when we arrived. Almost the moment we walked through the door, he set about making us coffee.

We sat in Janni's bedroom listening to music as Cleo and Janni shared a cigarette (a habit I would not be adopting), and the two of them began to show me photos of past architecture projects on the computer. Our coffees quickly emptied, and Janni brought out a few bottles of Heineken. Then the three of us relocated to the kitchen, where we spent nearly an hour preparing dinner. Janni and Cleo decided to make curry, and he prepared the rice while the two of us set about chopping vegetables.

What started as an innocent "friends cooking dinner" quickly turned into a something of a disaster. After cutting avocado and carrots, Janni handed us packages of chilis and onions to chop. Cleo's eyes started watering as she sliced the peppers and though it claimed to be waterproof, my mascara was quickly running down my cheeks. The three of us could barely stand to be in the kitchen with the thick essence of onion and chili in the air. Janni even opened a window and let a blast of cold air in to try and diffuse its potency, but it didn't seem to help. When he tried to close it, it seemed the window was jammed so Cleo stood up to help as well. By that point, we all started laughing, and whether it was just the time of night or the slight effect of the beer, we couldn't stop. If anyone had entered the kitchen, they would have had quite the sight to see: three people with tears streaming down their faces, laughing so hard they could barely breathe, Cleo standing on a chair trying to shut the window, Janni with one hand also pushing down on the window, the other stirring the curry, and me with black mascara running down my cheeks, laughing and continuing to chop the vegetables. It was ridiculous, hilarious chaos.

Eventually we gave up on chopping any more vegetables and cooked what we had. The curry turned out very well, and as we'd failed to shut the kitchen window (and were therefore freezing) we truly appreciated its warmth. One of Janni's friends came over, and the four of us decided to go out to a pub for drinks. It was called Luke6, and was another dimly lit, stone-walled pub in Braunschweig. Janni and his friend ordered a round of something called a Mexicaner, which reminded me of a Bloody Mary, just in shot form. Then Cleo ordered us drinks called Touchdowns, which were extremely fruity and sweet. More Mexicaners appeared soon after, as well as another handful of guys that Janni had invited. Before I knew it, Cleo and I were surrounded by a massive crowd of architecture students and their friends. One sitting near me spoke English, and we had somewhat of a conversation about American football (as if I knew much) and Fussball (soccer – again, not a strong subject for me). After the Mexicaners, the Touchdowns, and a cider or two, Cleo and I decided to call it a night. We had to be up early the next day, so we bid everyone "Tschüss!" and found the bus stop.

It was to our great misfortune that we missed the bus by five minutes, which also happened to be the last one for the night. As a result, we had to walk nearly 25 minutes in the frigid cold but were rather unphased as we were still warm from the drinks at Luke6. In fact, rather than pout about missing the last bus, we thought it might be a good idea to skip home while singing "We're off to see the Wizard" from the Wizard of Oz. We laughed the entire way home until a car with "Polizei" stamped across the side stopped us just outside her apartment building. The officer asked us our ages, clearly under the impression that we weren't old enough to be drinking but let us off with a warning to be careful in the cold after she checked our IDs. There was nothing more sobering than being approached by a police officer in a foreign country.

When we got home, we raided Cleo's fridge and put together a midnight snack of baguette with butter, garlic cloves, tomatoes, and leftover lettuce from our salads that afternoon. We sprawled out on her bedroom floor as we ate and watched a few minutes of a movie, and I decided to take a shower so as to save time in the morning. Braunschweig: Day 2 was another success.

As the prior two days played over in my mind, I couldn't help but feel the nerves begin to set in as I drifted off to sleep. My time with Cleo was nearing an end, which meant the trip to visit my family was imminent. My dad's father – Opa – never talked much about his German roots. But from my aunt's Ancestry page, I'd discovered that his grandfather had come to the United States nearly 100 years earlier. No one had ever returned to bridge the gap.

Until now.

5

The next morning did not begin as planned.

Cleo and I had been planning on having one last brunch together. We were going to go to the bakery together (so I could see
what it looked like), make another batch of scrambled eggs, and
have adequate time to get ready before I headed out to meet my
family. It was going to be a perfect morning.

Instead, we woke up 30 minutes after we'd originally set our
alarms. Both of us had a pounding headache, and the Soja joghurt
(the only quick-grab food in her fridge) did not sound remotely
appetizing. I quickly shoved everything into my carry-on while she
made me a cup of coffee, and we had about five minutes to chat
before leaving for the bus station. She reviewed the route with me

one more time: take the bus to the Vechelde Bahnhof. Then, wait six minutes for the connecting train that would go to the Bielefeld Hauptbahnhof. My family would meet me there and help me buy a ticket back to Braunschweig after I spent the day with them. Cleo handed me my ticket and we walked to the bus stop, where she wished me luck and hugged me goodbye. The bus came five minutes late, and I climbed aboard.

With the bus running behind schedule, I had a sinking feeling about making my train on time. We passed the Aldi I'd visited the day before, and soon I was out of Braunschweig and out of Cleo's reach. I sat there, nervously listening for the voice reading off stops to say, Vechelde Bahnhof. The clock on my phone soon told me I had five minutes before my train departed, so the moment I heard Vechelde, I grabbed my things and climbed off the bus.

But I didn't see a train station.

Instead, I saw Vechelde Wahler Weg printed on a bus stop on the side of the road, and houses on either side as far as I could see. You have got to be kidding me, I thought. I got off at the wrong stop.

I saw a woman walking her dog a ways down the sidewalk, and fortunately my German was adequate enough to communicate the issue. She sighed and told me that the Vechelde Bahnhof was a 15-minute walk down the road, and I would definitely miss my train if it only left in five minutes' time. I must've looked absolutely mortified, as she quickly told me that she would walk with me to the train station. When we got there, she pointed out the different schedules, eventually turning towards me with a half-smile on her face.

"The next train for Bielefeld leaves in two hours."

I truly wanted to cry. My family would be waiting for me at

the Bielefeld Hauptbahnhof at 2:00pm and now I wouldn't be arriving until well after 4:00pm, at the earliest. The woman helped me to buy a new ticket and directed me to a Tankstelle (gas station) to buy me a coffee before heading on her way. She wished me Glück and was soon out of sight. The situation was less than perfect, but at least I had a new ticket and a hot cup of coffee.

I stood at a small table as I waited for the train. I bought a package of Ferrero Küsschen (my second favorite German chocolates after Kinder eggs) and took out my notebook. People streamed in and out of the Tankstelle, and the man behind the counter started glancing over at me every few minutes. I probably looked extremely suspicious: large bag in hand, terrified expression, small purchase. My heart was pounding. What would happen if I couldn't get a hold of my family? Would I be stuck here? Should I go to Bielefeld anyway? How could I have gotten off at the wrong stop? The man behind the counter finally came over to me after twenty minutes.

"Kann ich dir helfen?" May I help you?

I didn't know if the man spoke English or not, so I tried in German:

"Ja, bitte. Ich wollte nach Bielefeld, aber ich habe meinen Zug verpasst. Und jetzt meine Familie weiß nicht, wann ich ankommen werde." Yes please, I was going to Bielefeld, but I missed my train. And now my family doesn't know when I will arrive.

"Kannst du sie anrufen?" Can you call them?

"Nein, mein Handy funktioniert nicht. Ich komme aus Amerika. Aber ich habe ihre Telefonnummer." My phone doesn't work. I'm from America. But I do have their phone number.

I took out the slip of paper on which I'd written their number, which I'd almost thrown away. I'd written it down for Cleo, who had used it in Prinzen Park when we were coordinating times with my family. I handed the man the slip of paper and my new train ticket, telling him that someone named Jürgen would answer. The man took the slip of paper behind the counter, where he picked up a phone and punched in the number. I heard someone answer, and the two were quickly engaged in conversation. A woman came out from somewhere and asked if she could help me as well, and I nodded to the man to indicate that I'd been taken care of. She walked over to him, interrupting his conversation, and the two glanced from my ticket over to me and then he pointed at the phone. Did we have some kind of problem?

After a few minutes, the man walked back over to me, setting the ticket down on the table and handing me the phone. Jürgen asked me in English if I was ok, and what had possibly happened that I missed my train. I told him yes – I was – but the bus had been late, and I got off one stop early.

"Not a problem. This Tankstelle man said you'll be arriving here at 4:30pm so we will be at Bielefeld Hauptbahnhof then to pick you up. No worries! Enjoy your trip! See you soon, Sam!"

His voice was calm and reassuring. I smiled and thanked the man and woman behind the counter. They gave me another coffee free of charge and I bought a sandwich to take with me on the train. My stomach was starting to growl.

I put my chocolates, the sandwich, and my notebook back in my purse and headed back to the train station. It was a very small station with only a small awning, a ticket machine, and a bench, but it began to fill up quickly as the train's arrival grew closer. I noticed another girl who appeared my age standing further down the platform and took a chance in saying 'hi'. I wanted to make absolutely sure that I got on the correct train, so I excused myself as I approached her.

"Entschuldigung, dieser Zug fährt nach Bielefeld – Bielefeld Hauptbahnhof?" Excuse me, is this train going to Bielefeld Hauptbahnhof? I asked, showing her my ticket and pointing at the name and number of the train. She smiled and nodded.

Her name was Marina, and she was a Lebanese student studying medicine in Berlin. She had some time off and was visiting friends in Hannover and Bielefeld at the moment. Marina didn't speak English and I didn't speak Lebanese, so it was interesting speaking in German when neither one of us spoke it as a first language. When the train finally arrived, we sat next to each other to continue chatting, exchanging contact information and connecting on Facebook. She had a fascinating story; there was a program in Berlin that was associated with her university in Lebanon, and due to a series of very fortunate events, she'd landed the position of her dreams. I was amazed; moving to Germany to work had been a dream of mine since the first time I visited Hannover. And here someone was, doing just that. Lucky.

She got off at the Hannover station and we promised to keep in touch. I still had nearly an hour on the train once she left, so I had my sandwich and spent a bit more time writing. I got to thinking about the trip, which seemed like a crazier idea every time I stopped to think what I was actually doing. This was family, yes. But it wasn't family like at one of our reunions in the United States: family that my grandparents knew or who had known me since I was a baby, but I didn't remember ever meeting them. This was family that my parents, aunts, uncles, grandparents – great grandparents, even – had never even met. I wondered if they'd like me. I wondered if they'd even recognize me when I arrived (regardless of having seen me on Facebook). I wondered if they'd have family information that would help us connect the dots. Maybe they'd even have some similarities to me and my American family. I had printed out pictures from the Ancestry website to share with them, thinking we might find the connecting piece(s). My great-great grandfather was Friedrich Wilhelm: would they know him? Was he a direct relative of theirs? Or did we need to push further back? I was nervous and excited and anxious all at once, and the feeling grew bolder and more overwhelming as the train drew closer to Bielefeld.

When we finally did reach Bielefeld Hauptbahnhof, I climbed down the stairs from my train's platform and emerged on the main floor. The moment I separated myself from the crowd, I heard it:

"Sam!"

I turned around and there she was: my (aunt?) Elvira with a huge smile on her face. She ran over to me and put her arms around me. Jürgen followed, and as I stood there hugging the two of them on the platform, I instantly felt it: home.

It was such a strange emotion. When I came home from college for the first time, it was four months after I'd originally moved into my dorm. During my time away, I'd dyed my hair, gotten my conch pierced (a unique type of ear piercing), gotten my first long-term job, made a ton of new friends my parents would never meet, and learned how to take care of myself in a city nearly 1000 miles away from my home in Michigan. When I came home that first time – when I first walked through my parents' front door – despite all the changes, despite being a different person than I'd been four months earlier, my parents hugged me like I was the prodigal daughter. There was a warmth in their hug and a sense that I was more welcome in their house than ever, despite whatever they'd missed or whatever was going on back at school. I had never felt so loved as I did in that moment.

That was the feeling I got hugging my "aunt" and "uncle" for the very first time. It was so overwhelming, I almost started crying. The gap had been bridged.

They smiled and hugged me some more and the three of us made our way to their Volkswagen. It was a 40-minute drive from the Hauptbahnhof to their home in Preußisch Oldendorf, and the entire ride was spent in conversation. They wanted to know all about my trip so far, how I'd met Cleo, and what we'd done in Braunschweig. As they were friends with most of my relatives on Facebook, Jürgen and Elvira also asked about my family members - who was in my immediate family? Who was the woman who did all the research on Ancestry? Why did we all live so far apart (Michigan, Minnesota, Wisconsin) if we were family? It felt like I had known them my entire life, and here we were just discussing family members. The whole situation was incredible.

They had decided to cook a vegetarische (vegetarian) German dish for me, so we stopped at Edeka (similar to Lidl) once we reached their town for some groceries. The dish was called Blumenkohlgratin – cheesy cauliflower – and Elvira and I walked around the store collecting everything she needed. I was amazed at the amount of cheese and meat there was! And then, as we walked down one of the aisles, she pointed out a beer called Rote Erde. She seemed to really like it, so I offered to buy them some for cooking dinner. She laughed.

"No need, that's Jürgen's beer. He makes it at home: we have plenty."

So, my 'uncle' made and sold his own beer; I don't know why

I was shocked. I knew plenty of people who brewed their own beer at home, but to see it for sale at an actual store was amazing. Elvira explained that he and a friend had started the business as a hobby, and it was starting to take off since they were well-connected and fairly well-known in their town. She assured me I could try it that evening if I wanted.

We hauled our groceries back to the car and were on our way. It wasn't long before we reached their house, a beautiful white stone home with solar panels on the roof. We parked in the back, where a vine-covered archway separated the house from the backyard. Jürgen grabbed my carry-on bag and I followed him and Elvira inside.

The entryway was a narrow hallway, with shoes lined along the wall and coats hanging just above them. There was a stairway in the back and a hallway to the left leading into the kitchen. I took my boots, coat, and scarf off and followed my aunt and uncle into the kitchen. It was a large room, with a white wrap-around counter with matching cupboards off to one side, more cupboards and the refrigerator on the other. Ahead, a solid wood table with wooden benches on either side was decorated with a fruit bowl and a blue plaid table runner, and a black and white cat peeked out from underneath. Off to one side of the table was a white stone fireplace that matched the exterior of the house, and on the other side was a door leading to the yard. Jürgen set my bag under one of the stools at the counter and asked if I'd like a coffee. *Of course, Danke!*

I sat at the kitchen table taking it all in: the warmth from my family, the coffee, the fire. It was all too good to be true. Moments after I sat down, a small 6-year-old came bopping into the room and stopped at the end of the table, staring at me. He was tall for his age, with round glasses and disheveled caramel-colored hair, holding a Nintendo DS in one hand. His eyes were wide and excited.

"Mutti, wer ist sie?" Mama, who is she?

Elvira smiled as she brought over a box of Kekse (cookies) and sat down across from me at the table. She started speaking rapidly in German and I heard my name mentioned once or twice. I picked up bits of what she was saying – aus Amerika, Deutschland und Griechenland, and the magic word – Familie. She told him to introduce himself and he instantly started acting shy. After much prompting from his mother, he looked at the ground and took a step towards me.

"My name is Marlin and I am six years old."

It was the most adorable thing I'd ever heard. I couldn't help but smile as my (cousin?) radiated pride at having spoken English. He bopped back out of the room and Elvira smiled. She told me that their three kids – Marlin, Meret, and Madita – studied English in school but only Madita (the oldest, currently at university) spoke it very well. Apparently, she'd spent time abroad and was now nearly fluent. Meret (thirteen), came into the kitchen shortly after Marlin left and introduced herself as well. I could tell she was unsure of me, this stranger from America coming to visit her family. I would have felt the same way at her age.

Jürgen set about making dinner, and I retrieved the Detroit coffee and the book I'd brought for them. We continued talking, drinking coffee, and eating kekse until another someone knocked on the door. It was the third and final family member I'd connected with on Facebook, Aren. He was half-German, half-Hungarian and hadn't seen Jürgen or Elvira for nearly six years. He was close to me in age, very tall, and hugged me as soon as he introduced himself. Jürgen thanked him for coming over and the two of them took their place with me and Elvira at the table. I showed them the photos I'd brought of my great-great-grandfather and his family, and they pulled out a family album as well. There was a genealogy written in the very front, which Jürgen traced with his finger in search of Friedrich Wilhelm. Another knock on the door.

An older gentleman with snow white hair and glasses came through the back door, tall enough that he had to duck under the molding, carrying a covered plate. Jürgen explained quickly that it was his father, who conveniently lived next door, and welcomed him into the kitchen. Elvira uncovered the plate – chocolate hazelnut cakes made by Jürgen's mother – and the now five of us resumed the conversation. According to Jürgen's father (Christian), they knew that years ago one of their relatives left Germany to go to the United States. He had left for economic reasons: he wanted to try and establish a new life in America. No one had ever heard from him again or had any idea what became of him, until now. Christian explained that no "Friedrich Wilhelm" was in his direct line as it traced back, but it was very possible that he was a cousin of his grandfather or even Aren's great-grandfather. He said he would take a look at the official records (which were located in the church there) and perhaps we could finally find the connecting piece. That was enough for me. I was beyond content after having spoken with them; after having met someone who knew something of family's history in Germany. If we could find the exact connection, how incredible would that be?

We continued our conversation, and eventually Jürgen and Christian left to find some Rote Erde beer for us to try. Elvira set about making dinner, and Aren and I dove into a very political conversation spanning everything from gender equality in the workplace to what I thought of Donald Trump. He had some very strong opinions on certain issues and explained them to me in comparison to how things worked in Germany. I was intrigued: I had never learned half the things he told me about in my International Relations class in college. He seemed to know more about the American government than I did, so I was relieved when Jürgen and Christian returned, beers in hand.

Rote Erde was a light beer with a few citrus notes and was absolutely delicious. Elvira called Marlin and Meret into the kitchen and dinner was served. I sat between Elvira and Marlin, with Jürgen, Meret, and Aren sitting across from us (Christian had left for the evening). We spent quite some time enjoying the Blumenkohlgratin (the cheesy cauliflower), further discussing our family history and the city where 'our family' began. Aren and Jürgen were convinced that they would be able to find the proper records and said they would also reach out to my aunt (with the Ancestry account) for any lost information. The time simply flew by. I learned about their experience with American culture (they'd once visited New York and attended a Broadway performance), I heard all about Aren's apprenticeship in the dairy industry, Meret's adventures in England with her soccer team, and Madita's time abroad. They asked me about my aunts and uncles, and all sorts of questions about my niece and nephew (whose pictures had been posted on Facebook by my siblings). It felt so exciting and oddly normal to be there with all of them, as if it were just another typical family gathering with my relatives back in the U.S. No one could have ever guessed that it was the first time we'd ever met. I almost forgot, myself.

My train had originally been scheduled to leave at 7:00pm, but Jürgen and Elvira asked if I'd like to stay a bit longer since our time had already been cut short by my earlier train mishap. After all, we were having such a nice time enjoying great beer, great food, and excellent conversation. They also thought it might be better for them to drive me back to Cleo rather than trust my not-so-phenomenal navigation skills. So, I stayed until 9:00pm before we decided we should leave, as it was nearly a two hours' drive to Hannover. Cleo told me she was now visiting her parents there, and since we'd be going to the Hannover airport the next day I should just meet her at their house. My family and I finished our dinner, cleaned up the kitchen, and took a few photographs to remember the evening. Then I reluctantly said my 'goodbye's and Jürgen and I were back in the car, heading off to Hannover.

We talked a bit on the way, listening to classic American rock music (Jürgen's favorite). I tried to stay awake to no avail. I was so tired: it had been a very long, very eventful day and the hum of the motor lulled me to sleep. Jürgen woke me up when we arrived at Cleo's parents' house and walked with me to the door to meet her. Then he gave me a hug, wished me *viel Glück* on my upcoming adventure in Greece, and assured me I would see them again.

I watched as my uncle backed the car down the driveway and pulled away. It took me a few minutes to break my gaze: half of me was in disbelief of what had happened that day and the other half was still asleep. *I did it*, I remember thinking as Cleo wrapped her arm around me and walked with me into the house. *I finally met our family.*

6

"So, you had a nice time?"

"Absolutely! It was so great to meet them all, I just can't be-lieve it actually happened."

"And now tomorrow you will be on your way to *Greece*!"

"I know!"

Cleo and I sat at the kitchen table, discussing everything that had happened that day. She couldn't believe that I'd managed to get off at the wrong stop and missed my train in Vechelde. She laughed when I told her that I stood at a table in the Tankstelle for two hours but was glad that the people there were willing to help me get a hold of my uncle. I told Cleo about Marina from Lebanon, all about meeting my family, the information Christian shared with me about knowing "one of them" had gone to America, what the Rote Erde beer tasted like, and how it had just felt like a family visit rather than a first-time meeting. She made us tea and we continued talking until it occurred to us that we had to be up very early the next morning. My flight from the Hannover airport was scheduled to take off at 8:30am, and in order to have time for breakfast in the morning (we did not want to miss another breakfast together) and arrive to the airport two hours early (as was always my policy), we needed to be up at 5:15am.

Her dad, who'd been doing some work in his office, came out and hugged us goodnight. He promised that he wouldn't let us sleep through our alarms (again). We climbed the stairs to Cleo's old bedroom and fell asleep nearly as soon as our heads hit the pillows. It felt like Christmas Eve; I lay there in bed, knowing full well that I needed to be up early, and my heart was pounding in anticipation of the next day. I would be in Greece: the number one country to visit on my bucket list. In less than 24 hours, I would be back on a plane, traveling around on my own, discovering the ancient ruins and historical museums, finally meeting Olivier in person, and on to the next adventure.

. . . . .

The buzz of the alarm woke us up at 5:15am sharp. Cleo headed downstairs to start making breakfast, and I took a shower and carefully packed up my things. It was easier now that I had a bit more room in my suitcase (as the coffee, the book, and the giant bag of Skittles had now been given away). Before heading downstairs to the kitchen, I did one last check to make sure everything was properly arranged in my purse to accommodate another day of airports and flights. Then I grabbed my bags and went to join Cleo in the kitchen.

We had my favorite breakfast of Brötchen with Frischkäse (cream cheese) and Nutella, and Cleo made us each a cup of coffee. I reviewed my itinerary with her, and she joked about my ability to get to Greece successfully:

"Just make sure you don't get off at the wrong stop. You don't want to end up somewhere else!"

We were on our way to the airport in no time. It was so hard to say goodbye once we arrived; Cleo and I didn't know the next time we'd see each other. It had taken forever for us to get from high school to our first weekend in Hannover, and another two years for me to come back to Braunschweig. But we both knew that we'd stay friends no matter what: we'd Skyped and emailed in the past and if nothing else, that would sustain us until the next trip. I turned around a few times as I made my way through airport security, tears starting to form in the corners of my eyes. There was nothing like catching that "last look" of a dear friend.

When I made it to the gate, I realized that I had a bit of time before boarding began. I stopped at the Duty-Free shop and bought a magazine (in German, for practice), some Studentenfutter (a type of trail mix that I'd grown particularly fond of), and some keychains for my coworkers back home. Then I sat at the gate, once again situated in a hard, blue chair, and pulled out my notebook to write. Germany had without a doubt exceeded my expectations. I leaned back and closed my eyes, thinking of everything that had happened in the past few days: the delay in Chicago, the panic in the Munich airport, being reunited with Cleo, the hilarious evening making curry, and meeting my family for the very first time. How had everything already come and gone? What was I going to experience next?

When the time came to board, I sat next to a man who refused to make eye contact with me. Fortunately, it was only a short flight to Munich, and Lufthansa provided me with a full-size Milka bar and a strong cup of coffee. I raced through the Munich airport to find my next gate, trying not to let memories of my 5+ hour delay just a few days earlier ruin my mood. There were very few people waiting at the gate, which I found with ease. From Munich, it was only a two-hour, twenty-minute flight to Athens, and I was in an aisle seat. It was ideal. The flight attendants handed out caramellos – small, fruity, hard candies – prior to take off. Halfway through the flight they served us lunch, which for me was a truly awful vegetarian pasta. I ended up eating a few Ferrero Küsschen instead. Then I slept for the duration of the flight, waking up just in time to feel the plane shake as it made contact with the runway.

It was now 2:45pm and I was finally in Athens. My heart was racing: I'd made it. Inside the airport, I found a seat and called my mom – again via Facebook – and filled her in on the trip thus far. She told me she was glad to hear my voice and thrilled that I was having such a great time. Apparently, I had really worried them with my standby situation in Munich, so I decided to wait to tell her about missing my train in Vechelde until I was home safe and sound in the United States. One "parent panic" was enough for this trip. She told me that she knew I'd have a good time once I got there, and that flights were always the worst part of traveling. And travel is never perfect, you always just have to make the best of it because it is such a once-in-a-lifetime experience. As I knew my mom liked to 'keep tabs' on me (even though I was thousands of miles away), I took a few minutes to review my plan for the next few days with her. I'd be spending the next two days in Athens with Olivier, then heading to Thessaloniki via train. Two days later, I'd fly to Chania, on Crete. That's where I'd see where the boat took off for America, in Koutsouras. Two days later, off to Santorini on a ferry, and another two days later I'd be on my way back to Athens. Then on the 27th, my friend Leslie would meet me at the Detroit airport just after 10:00pm. I'd go to their house the next evening for dinner, after a day back at work, and fill them in on the trip then. *Everything is timed out perfectly, mom. But of course I'll keep you posted as I go.* She told me she loved me and to have a blast, and then we hung up. After hearing myself share the plan out loud, a new excitement rushed through me.

The plan was to meet Olivier at Syntagma Square at 4:00pm, which was a forty-five-minute bus ride from the airport. I headed to the bus station just outside the airport and bought a ticket for bus 'X95'. There was an old couple behind me who heard I was also going to Syntagma, and they chatted with me in thick Scottish accents as we waited for our bus. There was something oddly comforting about knowing I was among other tourists who were also not entirely sure of where they were going.

When the bus arrived, I was separated from the old couple as we found empty spots on the bus. I was glad to have been near the front of the crowd; by the time the bus took off, there was hardly any room to move let alone sit down. The bus made several stops on its way to the main Square, and miraculously even more people managed to squeeze in. By the time we finally reached Syntagma, I was nearly pushed off the bus because it had become so crowded. But it was my first time in open air in Athens and nothing was going to damage my mood. Syntagma Square was beautiful; it was a huge, open area with a fountain in the center, a few trees in planters here and there, and stairs leading down to the train station on opposite sides of the Square. The entire thing was paved concrete, people hung around groups (some on foot, some hanging around near bike racks) and there were dogs and pigeons everywhere. I noticed a few very ritzy-looking individuals dressed in full suits, and not too far away were homeless people holding cardboard signs, sitting beside tin cans. It was the most diverse collection of people I'd ever seen in one place. And then all around the Square were various shops and cafés: some with tables set up outside and some with large racks of souvenirs for sale on the sidewalk. I had some time before I needed to meet with Olivier (or so I thought), so I found my way to a small coffee shop for my first cup of Greek καφές (kaf-ace, coffee). On the plane, I had started a list of Greek words that I thought might come in handy: Καλημέρα (kaliméra, good morning), Καλό απόγευμα (Kaló apógevma, good afternoon), Καληνυχτα (kali-nychta, good night), παρακαλώ (parakaló, please), and of course ευχαριστώ (efcharistó, thank you). I was quite proud of my list, and when I said my first efcharistó! at the café, the owners seemed delighted. I knew a grand total of five words in Greek and apparently I pronounced them well.

After relaxing in the café for a few minutes, glad and some-what in disbelief to finally be in Athens, it occurred to me to check the time. At first, I thought I still had 45 minutes before meeting with Olivier. But I was wrong. I had negative 15 minutes to meet him (I blamed the poor sleep on the plane). I slugged down the rest of my coffee, grabbed my carry-on, and ran out to the Square. Then I crossed the street with a parade of people, and soon found myself running down into the train station to look for him. *Way to go. Way to make a first impression fifteen minutes late.*

The train station was musty and not very well lit, so I pulled out my phone and tried to find Wi-Fi. Not knowing if Olivier was still there – or where I might find him, for that matter – I felt my palms beginning to sweat as I searched for an open network. I needed to message him and see what side of the Square he was on. People passed me left and right, undoubtedly thinking that I couldn't be a local and was very possibly lost. Fortunately, I heard a voice shout out my and turned around just in time to see Olivier walking towards me from a nearby stairway.

"Sam! I was so worried, I thought you were lost!"

"I'm so sorry, I got the time mixed up, I didn't mean to be so late. Je suis tellement désolée."

I apologized over and over again. He must've been waiting for me for a while! He laughed and told me it was nothing. We gave each other the standard French bises (kisses on the cheek), and then he took my bag, motioning for me to follow him. Apparently, we needed to hurry as the next train was leaving in a matter of minutes. He helped me purchase a ticket, which a machine spat out at me after feeding it a few coins. Then we were on our way.

Olivier was exactly as I remembered him from Skype: tall, with disheveled black hair, glasses, and a slender figure. He was wearing a black peacoat with a scarf, jeans, black loafer-style shoes, and had a black backpack slung over one shoulder. He smiled as we headed towards the train, and it felt like I was just meeting up with an old friend I hadn't seen for years. What's more, we spoke completely in French. It actually felt more comfortable to be speaking French in person than it had over Skype, so I think Olivier was slightly surprised (he even told me once or twice that my French accent was excellent, and 'not at all Ameri-can'). I was so happy to be using the language I'd spent nearly nine years studying. *Speaking French in Greece*, I remember thinking as

Olivier and I boarded the train. *This is going to be amazing.*

It wasn't long before we pulled up to his stop. I hopped off after him, and we walked a short distance to his flat. We passed several small cafés and bakeries, car shops, and other businesses that had storefronts along the street. They were all connected: it reminded me of the buildings in Braunschweig, some rising four to five stories above the stores, stretching the length of the street. Occasionally a loud bike would zoom by, standing out above the noise of the other traffic. People shuffled past us quickly, mumbling and speaking in different languages. They didn't even seem to see us. As I noticed streets jetting off to the left and right in no particular pattern, I wondered how the people even knew where they were going. The streets of Athens were bustling.

Olivier's flat was just around the corner from an automotive supply shop, and as we rounded it he pushed open a large door with bars on it. *Please don't be indicative of what's inside!* I followed him in, and we made our way up several flights of stairs. Just like Cleo, he lived near the top, so my legs were on fire by the time we reached his flat. It was very small. There was a small hallway that doubled as the entryway, full of his shoes and coats and a few bags of fruit. To my right was a small kitchen the size of my bathroom back home. As I peeked inside, I saw dirty dishes piled on either side of the sink, rags hung about, and a few questionable oranges sitting on the counter. There was no table, and he had pushed a small chair against the wall that appeared to be serving as extra counter space. Not to mention the smell. Then to my left, there was a small bathroom with several noticeable differences from what I considered 'the norm'. His shower had no curtain, and there were no cupboards beneath the sink. *Where did he keep everything?* And then — most surprising of all — was to see that the toilet tank was separate from the bowl, connected to the wall above it with a chain hanging down to flush. *It's so different than ours!*

We walked down the small, cluttered hallway, past the kitchen and bathroom doorways, and into the main room. His dresser - to the left - was covered in clothes, books, and more bags of fruit. Just past it - on the floor - was a mattress with one blanket and a pillow the size of my purse. To the right, a few shelves loaded with books (was that an apple core sticking out?) and a small desk with his laptop balanced on top. An air mattress the size of a pool floaty leaned against one wall, and at the far side of the room was a door opening onto the balcony.

"Not much of a view, but it's home," he said. I tried to control the look of shock on my face.

I had never considered myself to be 'high maintenance'. On past trips, I had dealt with my fair share of less-than-perfect living conditions and in college I'd lived with some very messy room-mates. But this was almost too much to take in. I'd Skyped with Olivier from the other side of that laptop and had apparently thought the flat looked cleaner than it was. Or maybe I'd thought he was just in his bedroom. As I looked around, there was more and more that bothered me: the moldy fruit strewn about, the dirty plates on the floor and desk, the streaks of dirt on the air mattress, and the dingy look of the blanket on that mattress on the floor. I'd once spent a summer in Portland sleeping on the car-pet in my apartment – not even on an air mattress – but I kept it spic-and-span so that I didn't even mind. I literally just had a pillow and a blanket on the floor: that was it. In Olivier's flat I didn't even want to take off my shoes. Lord knows what would crawl out from under this mess. I almost considered offering to clean for him.

Olivier set my bag down and offered to make us tea. I wondered whether the mugs would actually be clean, but he emerged from the kitchen and handed me one before I had much time to think about it. I gave him the Michigan mug and the bag of Skittles I'd brought him from home, and we continued chatting. He told me he would sleep on the air mattress and I could sleep on the actual mattress - with the dingy blanket, great. But I thanked him and told myself to consider it a nice gesture that he was giving me the more comfortable option. He grabbed a bag of oranges from the entryway and picked through them, selecting a few and tossing one my way. He said that he knew where to buy the best fruit in Athens: there was a street market he'd show me sometime during my stay. I'd noticed he seemed to be a huge fan of fruit: there were bags of oranges and apples sitting in at least three different places around his flat.

We headed back out into the city after our tea and oranges, back into the busy streets of Athens. He wanted to give me the 'lay of the land', so he said that we wouldn't be getting back on the train. It would be completely on foot, which sounded like a great idea.

First, we walked past the base of the Acropolis – l'Acropoli, in French – and the museum situated there. I made a note to come back and visit it, trying to remember the directions. From there, we went past the Venetian Theater, where we eavesdropped as a group of Chinese tourists listened to a tour guide:

"...statues from the Theater were taken away from Athens in two boats in order to be copied for museums. One of the boats sank in a storm on the Aegean Sea, and the statues rested on the seafloor for two years before they were recovered..."

It was starting to get dark as we made our way to the ritzy Thissio District, an area that Olivier explained as being only for the very old and very wealthy. I could see why: it was absolutely beautiful and didn't quite seem to match the surrounding areas. One after the next, ornately decorated restaurants opened into well-lit outdoor seating areas. Canopies adorned with vines and fairy lights enclosed the dining areas, and soft music was playing from somewhere inside. Waiters walked towards us, displaying menus to lure us in, and Olivier kept his head down and pulled me along. He said they did that on purpose: the moment they mentioned a food and you gave any indication that you were interested, they began to charge you. I instantly stopped making eye contact with them. In front of the restaurants, I noticed there were quite a few stray cats walking around, and even saw a dog or two roam by in search of food. People dressed in fancy clothes made their way into the restaurants, and others dressed in rags sat on the opposite side of the street, blankets of trinkets stretched out in front of them. It was such a unique atmosphere, unlike any I'd ever experienced, just as it had been in Syntagma Square. This was Greece.

Olivier and I continued on, eventually turning off the main street and up a long, flat stone staircase leading us to the top of a hill high above the city. By that point it was completely dark out, and the lights of the city below contrasted sharply against the dark sky and the stars above. We could see the Parthenon in the distance, display lights casting shadows on its ancient columns. Off in a different direction, another large hill with a white stone building on top was illuminated by the lights below. And then there was the Aegean – inky black and blue in the dark – stretching off into the distance. Olivier said it was his second favorite view in the entire city; another day, he would take me to his first (the view from the white stone building).

I thanked him for bringing me to see such an incredible view of the city, and we spent several minutes just standing there, taking in the beauty of it all. Other people were standing and sitting around as well, staring off into the city. Some tried taking pictures, others smoked cigarettes, and one young couple was getting fairly 'handsy' for being in a public place. After a few minutes of taking it all in, we realized how hungry we were and went on our way in search of food. I told Olivier that I wanted to take him to dinner for being such a wonderful guide and asked if he knew of any traditional Greek restaurants nearby. At first, I thought he might lead us back to the Thissio district, but instead we headed down the stone stairs and off in the opposite direction. We walked for what felt like miles, down narrow streets with shops of all kinds on either side. Some shops were already closed for the night, their garage-like doors pulled down revealing tons of graffiti. A few bars were open with vibrant lights and loud music coming from within, and Olivier pointed out one particularly interesting one that had black cats and a witch on a broomstick posed just above the door. From the dark, narrow streets to not knowing where we were going to my growling stomach, I was beginning to feel uneasy. And just when I was about to say something, Olivier turned the corner and stopped.

"Le voilà!" *We made it!*

There was music coming from inside; two men were sitting on a small stage playing guitar-looking instruments, singing their hearts out in Greek. As we walked inside, I noticed instantly the ambiance from the white cloth-covered tables and the dim, flickering candles. On the walls were huge, vibrant murals of Greece showcasing the different landmarks and of course, the gods. It was fairly crowded for how empty the streets had been outside, and some of the people were even singing along with the musicians. A waiter in a vest and tie took us to a table near the back, and a bread plate with hummus appeared on the table shortly after. Olivier picked up a wine list as he casually explained that he'd brought Couchsurfers to this restaurant before. They'd always seemed to enjoy it, so of course he had to share it with me as well.

I can see why, I thought. Even the menu was fancy, completely bound in leather. I was glad to see that it was in both Greek and English, so I eagerly started looking through at all of the delicious options. Olivier made a few suggestions, and – knowing that I was vegetarian – advised against certain dishes like *Moussaka* that probably wouldn't be a good choice. He ordered the dish for himself so I could at least see what it looked like, along with a plate of French fries. Per his suggestion I ordered *Horiatiki* – a Village Salad – with a side of *Gigantis Plaki* (a dish of giant kidney beans with tomato sauce and spices). My step-grandmother had once told me that the Village Salad was one of Papa's favorites dishes in Greece. It was essentially chunks of cucumbers, tomatoes, olives, sometimes peppers, and a big chunk of feta cheese, all drizzled in fresh, Greek olive oil and sprinkled with herbs. It was a beautiful salad, made entirely without lettuce. Papa hated lettuce. It was the perfect dish for him, and I'd decided prior to coming that I had to try it.

Olivier also ordered half a liter of white wine to share, pointing out that since I wasn't eating meat it would be better to pair white wine with whatever I ordered. I didn't point out that I preferred red. *Whatever you say, Olivier. Tonight, you're the expert.*

It was the most amazing meal; the feta on the Horiatiki was the size of a deck of cards, the beans and spices were delicious, the wine was amazing, the homemade hummus was drizzled with fresh olive oil, and even the bread was perfectly fluffy on the inside, with a flaky crust on the outside. I was in heaven. With the music in the background and soft candlelight on the tables, I couldn't have asked for a better introduction to Greek cuisine.

Olivier and I talked for a while, enjoying our food and getting to know each other better (I felt certain people thought we were on a date). He elaborated on the story of how he'd come to live in Athens from his home city in France, and I told him about Papa and everything that led me to plan a trip to Greece. Then he shared different stories from past Couchsurfers. I never knew how popular the website was; I'd never even heard of it until Cleo shared it with me. Olivier admitted that he was quite surprised that more Americans didn't know about it. *Flights to Europe must be so expensive, how can everyone afford to stay in hotels when they get here?*

When we finally left, it was pitch black outside with only a few street lights and the glow from the restaurants lighting our way. Despite it being near the beginning of November, we could see the dark outlines of Christmas decorations hanging about the city, on lamp posts and storefronts and even on park benches. As we walked through the streets, slowly making our way back to his apartment, I noticed there were still several stores open. And to my complete surprise (and delight), we came across a Starbucks.

I didn't hesitate for a second. "Olivier, je dois y aller. Il faut que j'achète quelque chose." *I have to go inside. I have to buy something.*

I had worked at a Starbucks (within a Target) for nearly four years when I was in college. And while I had never actually enjoyed the taste of their coffee, I still felt a connection to it and wanted to go inside. At one point during my years as a barista, someone brought in a mug to return because they'd received it as a gift but already had it. It was one of the You Are Here Collection mugs: a collection of mugs sold by Starbucks featuring different states, cities, and even countries around the world, packaged into neat little green boxes. As I continued through school, I traveled around the United States from time to time, even doing an internship in the Portland/Seattle area. As I did so, I started to collect more of the mugs. It became an impulse: see a new You Are Here Collection mug, buy it. Price didn't matter, length of time in the location didn't matter (I once spent 2 hours in the Atlanta, GA airport and that was enough to feel an obligation to buy the mug). As long as I'd visited the city/state, I bought the mug. By the time I'd left for Germany, I'd collected over 20 mugs. So there, in the Starbucks in Athens, I pulled a "Greece" mug off the shelf. But then I saw mugs for the other cities I would be visiting later in my trip: Crete, Thessaloniki, and then Athens. *Did I really need all of them? Or just Greece? Or just the cities? How would I take them all with me?*

Sensing my dilemma, Olivier stepped in. As he knew I'd be coming back to Athens for a few days prior to returning home, he said that I could buy them all and leave them at his flat until I returned. He would 'babysit' them for me so that I could travel without worrying I'd break them as I made my way around the country. It was perfect: I'd just meet up with him before heading back to the airport and he'd bring the mugs for me. By that time I would have more room in my carry-on from giving away more gifts, so I'd surely find a way to fit the mugs inside. With a plan in place, I couldn't have been happier as we walked back to his flat, giant Starbucks bag in hand.

We made it home eventually, after passing the Roman Agora

and a few other structures that were difficult to see in the dark. Olivier rambled on in French, and as we took a different route home I was far too drawn into our surroundings to pay him any attention. Before I knew it, we were climbing the stairs back up to his flat and the reality of the mess came flooding back. That 'couldn't be happier' feeling I'd had just moments earlier walking out of Starbucks vanished as he opened the door to his small, dirty apartment.

I'd tried to put it out of my mind during our evening out. Olivier was so kind, showing me the best views and the different districts and that wonderful restaurant; I couldn't let him know that his living situation made me want to lose my dinner. I decided to take a shower, thinking maybe it would help me clear my mind and find a fresh perspective on the not-so-fresh flat. Olivier had some papers to grade, so he busied himself as I grabbed my things and headed into the bathroom.

Somehow the situation got worse. That's right, there's no shower curtain. And there's no floor mats? And he doesn't have an extra towel (though would I really trust it anyway?). How can someone live like this? What would my mother say? It was a challenge to take a shower with no shower curtain. To make matters worse, there was also no wall mount for the shower head: it was just a hose coming out of the tub with a shower head attached on the end. I squatted to avoid getting water everywhere, aiming the shower head at the wall. I could only imagine the sight as I attempted to wash my hair with one hand while holding the hose in the other. I wondered how Olivier ever managed to take a proper shower. At one point – and to my absolute horror – I actually dropped the hose and water went everywhere, coating the bathroom from floor to ceiling. The t-shirt I'd decided to use as a towel was rendered useless, so once I finished trying to wash myself, I pulled my pajamas on (still soaking wet). I was just thankful my top wasn't white. The entire situation was just laughably miserable.

"Tu n'as pas de rideau de douche?" I asked when I re-entered the main room. *You don't have a shower curtain?*

"Je dois me cacher pendant que je me douche?" *Do I need to hide while I shower?*

He laughed and turned back to his laptop, and I couldn't tell if he was sarcastically telling me off or just making an honest joke. As I'd learned, he was blunt, though sometimes still quite difficult to read. I let the thought pass and looked down at the mattress – my mattress – adorned with that awful blanket. *You didn't pay for this*, I reminded myself. *Just be glad you have somewhere to sleep.*

I crawled onto the mattress and pushed the pillow aside, instead rolling up my scarf to rest my head on. Olivier closed his laptop, opened the door to the balcony (it was rather warm in his flat), and flung his air mattress onto the floor. I thanked him again for such a great first evening in Athens, and he told me there were much better things to come. Before long, it was lights out, and he was snoring.

From my bed, I looked out the balcony window at the stone wall of the building next door. I had never felt more thankful in my life: thankful for the clean bed – and the shower curtain – I had back home, thankful for the family I had living near me in Michigan (Olivier's family was a few countries away), thankful for the chance to have seen Cleo, thankful for Olivier's excellent skills as a tour guide, and thankful for whatever lay ahead in the coming days of my trip. (I had to focus on something other than the smelly mattress beneath me and the loud snoring a few feet away.) He could have easily said 'no' when I first reached out to him on Couchsurfing; after hearing some of the past experiences he'd had with Couchsurfers, I wouldn't have blamed him. I could've had to pay for an AirBNB or even a hotel in the city for the next few days. But there he was, offering me the comfortable (though smelly) mattress and making sure I saw the best Athens had to offer.

As I drifted off, I smiled. That was enough for me.

7

I woke up the next morning feeling very well rested. Apart from the slight kink in my neck (from using a scarf instead of a pillow) and the dull headache I had (from the wine the night before), I was ready to take on my first full day in Athens. Olivier had to teach from noon until eight o'clock that evening, so we decided it would be the perfect morning for a "cultural tour". We got ready quickly, and I finished tying my shoes just as he propped the air mattress back up against the wall.

"On y va?"

"On y va."

Let's go: out the door, down the stairs, and out into the crisp, city morning air. Our first stop was only a short walk away, far from any tourist traps. It was a bakery called Attika, and I remembered passing by it the day before. Olivier told me he'd been learning Greek and could manage ordering us breakfast, so I chose piece of traditional Spanikopita (Spinach pie) and a coffee. He ordered what looked like a puff pastry with pizza toppings on it and a coffee as well. We sat outside for a few minutes and he told me what he had in mind for the day. I listened, thoroughly enjoying my Spanikopita. It was the best thing I'd ever tasted: layers of feta cheese, butter, and spinach in warm, flaky phyllo dough. It became a very fast favorite in Greece.

He wanted to show me another view of the Parthenon, a few places around the heart of the city, and would leave me at the Archaeological Museum when we were done. Then he would go to work, and I'd be free to continue exploring the city. At 9:00pm, he would meet me back at Syntagma and we could go somewhere for a late dinner. The plan was set.

We started by walking a fair distance to the Prison of Socrates. When we arrived, I saw that it was essentially a cluster of cells carved into a large, stone wall with bars fixed into the rock around the opening. Olivier tried explaining the history. Socrates had been captured and unjustly sentenced to death, and spent time there waiting to be executed. He had a friend named Crito who tried endlessly to convince him to escape, and had even bribed the guards, who were ready to turn their backs. Socrates could not be convinced to leave, stating the famous, 'Two wrongs do not make a right' saying and telling him he had to stay and die to prove his innocence.

"Quelque chose comme ça..." *Something like that.*

Groups of people crowded around the bars, taking pictures of the stone prison. Olivier shook his head and told me that all of those pictures were just merde – shit – because there were too many tourists around and they all were getting in each other's way. He pulled me along up the side of the hill, rising higher and higher above the city. We passed Socrates' University – what looked like ten flat stones stuck in the ground – and finally, a tomb at the very top of the hill. I tried to imagine what it must have been like thousands of years earlier, when the great philosophers actually walked the same paths that we were on then. Olivier mentioned that some people had claimed to see paranormal activity on those hills, saying they'd seen the ancient philosophers coming out of the shadows and telling late-night visitors to run or shouting words of warning from behind the prison bars. Though I had never been one to believe those kinds of stories, it was a weird, somewhat eerie feeling to think about the things that took place on those hills, knowing that little had been altered for so many years.

After seeing the tomb, we climbed a few rocky slopes (very difficult to do in Converse) and saw the most spectacular view in all of Greece. It was more beautiful than the one we'd seen the night before, and I had to sit down because we emerged at the top so close to the edge. The Parthenon was off in the distance, surprisingly more alluring than it had been in the dark. People were climbing up the winding stairs to experience it up-close, just a trail of ants in the distance. Olivier pointed out his flat, a few places we'd be visiting, and the restaurant we'd been at the night before. Everything looked so different in the daylight. Different, but still amazing.

He gave me time to take as many pictures as I wanted, then offered to take one of me with the Parthenon in the background. As I smiled, I couldn't help but think I wish I could show this to

Papa. He'd be proud.

From there, we retraced our steps, back to the streets we'd walked the night before. The graffitied garage doors were now open, revealing tourist trap after tourist trap full of cheap, useless trinkets. Olivier took me into a random office-looking building, where we took an elevator to the roof for another spectacular view. I could tell, from the way he looked out at the city while showing me all of his favorite spots, that Olivier truly loved living in Athens. Showing visitors around wasn't just a way to entertain them, but a way for him to see it all again, over and over. And according to him, because it was such a big, diverse city, there was always something new to see. It was a quality I came to admire about Olivier: he had the innate ability to appreciate everything for what it was completely and wholeheartedly. Whether it was the hustle and bustle of the city, the food we ate (or the fruit), or something new he hadn't noticed before, he was instantly taken over by amazement and it read very clearly on his face. I finally understood why he enjoyed hosting Couchsurfers so much.

During the rest of our time together that morning, he took me through a meat market (with literal animal corpses hanging upside down for sale), a fish market (to experience "the true smell of the Aegean"), and then a fresh produce market. Naturally, I enjoyed the latter the most. The market seemed to stretch for miles, lined with colorful stalls selling everything from apples and oranges to apricots, tomatoes, and herbs. One stall had several large bins full of different colored olives, and I lingered a moment to look at the various kinds. The vendor instantly held one out to me, and remembering Olivier's advice about the waiters from the night before, I turned him down. We left with a small bag of mandarin oranges (his favorite, I'd learned) and continued on our way.

A short distance ahead, there was a street vendor at what looked like a sort of hot dog cart. However, instead of hot dogs he was selling large, round, pretzel-like pastries covered in sesame seeds. Olivier told me they were called Kalouri, and he often bought one for breakfast on his way to work. I bought one for each of us (€0,50/piece) and we continued walking, talking, and enjoying our morning in Athens. There were some students demonstrating something outside of the Athens Polytechnic University, and Olivier told me it would be best for me to ignore them: they were just protesting something, as students always did. I took note and averted my gaze, not giving it a second thought. We soon reached the Archaeological museum, where he bid me À plus. *See you later.* I walked up to the large, front doors and frowned.

To my misfortune, there was a little sign posted on the door informing visitors that they would be closing at noon for renovations. I looked at my phone: 11:45am. I wasn't due to meet with Olivier again until 9:00pm. *What am I going to do for nine hours?* The plan had been to spend at least two or three in the museum and continue on from there. I spun around, but Olivier was already out of sight. Fortunately, I had my oranges and my map, so I set off towards Syntagma Square. Since that's where we were meant to meet later on, I decided to start there and branch off so as not to get lost. I headed back down the sidewalk, and back past the university.

The atmosphere had changed entirely.

It hadn't been twenty minutes since we'd first walked past the Polytechnic University, but something felt off. The students who had been handing out brochures at the demonstration were now clearing off their tables. There were some angry-looking adults throwing dirty looks at them. The streets seemed slightly less crowded in general, so I picked up my pace and tried not to make eye contact with everyone. I heard a few people shouting in the distance, and my eyes started to water. *I'm not crying, I thought. Am I allergic to something?*

I threw away the rest of the orange I'd been eating just in case and continued on. I turned down the wrong streets a few times, but eventually found my way to Syntagma. When I had stopped at the small café the day before, I'd noticed a restaurant off to one side offered free Wi-Fi. It was called Piatsa, and it was easy to pick out with its large, vibrant sign. I crossed the Square, stopping at one of the tourist traps to buy a few postcards on the way (I'd made it a habit to always send a few when I travelled). Once inside Piatsa, I was seated in the upper level, on the balcony overlooking the square. I ordered a glass of red wine and my new favorite Horiatiki salad, then took out my notebook to write. As I sat enjoying my lunch, I noticed the carefree atmosphere in the Square changing beneath me. Large, black vans started blocking off the street leading off to the Polytechnic University: the street I'd walked down only moments earlier. Out came a fleet of men, also in black, some holding large, plastic shields. What is going on? The waiter returned after fifteen minutes and I asked what was going on. He looked from me to the Square and back again and informed me that it probably wasn't a wise idea to come to Athens on November 17th. Years before – in 1973 – students at the Polytechnic University had been protesting the dictatorship and the military regime, pleading instead for democracy. The protest started just days before (on the 14th) and escalated to the point where the government actually sent a tank through the university's gates (on the 17th). The waiter grew more animated as he talked, and I could tell it was something he was very passionate about and that the entire ordeal really struck a note with him. He went on to explain that over twenty people were killed over those few days, and November 17th has been an observed holiday ever since. It was a day to commemorate those who fought against the military regime and those who had lost their lives, and there is always a demonstration after the commemorative services end. When I told him how recently I'd been near the Polytechnic University, his eyes widened, and he told me I was very lucky to be safe in Piatsa: apparently the demonstration had already started and would soon be in full force, parading to the United States Embassy. I must have had a look of panic on my face: he quickly told me not to worry. As long as I stayed off the streets for a while (particularly around Syntagma and the Polytechnic University), I would be safe.

He disappeared, and I turned to look back out over the Square. Sure enough, there was a massive parade of people coming down the street from the university, passing the black van barricade, and marching down another street. I watched as they went on their way, horrified that I had been just moments away from getting swept into it all. It was difficult to break away my gaze, let alone enjoy my lunch. The Horiatiki salad was similar to the one I'd had the night before, but with more olives and less feta (which I found I preferred). The wine, however, was far better, and I was thankful for something to take the edge off after my conversation with the waiter. I wrote down as much as I could remember of what he'd told me, making a note to research the next few cities on my journey to make sure there were no other giant protests I might get sucked into. I continued eating and writing, sipping on my wine and periodically glancing back down to the protesters. I hadn't been paying much attention to the rest of the restaurant or who was in it, so I was surprised to hear chairs sliding inside. I turned to see who it was.

At least a dozen police officers had come into Piatsa and were taking their seats around a large table inside. My attention shifted from the Square to the policemen, then back to my half-eaten lunch, and I felt my appetite fizzle out. *I have no idea what to do. Stay? Go? Ignore them? Am I safe?* As if on cue, the waiter returned to my table. He explained that the group of policemen were just there on break, but that they advised I stay inside for a short while longer to be safe. I nodded and sat in disbelief, barely making eye contact as he spoke to me. I had never been so terrified in my life. I didn't know much about the political climate in Greece, but I knew that a giant demonstration, police barricades, and protesters on their way to the United States Embassy did not amount to a very welcoming environment for a US citizen. All I had was this new knowledge from the waiter and the general sense that Greece was struggling financially as a country.

The waiter returned once more a few moments later with another glass of wine and a small piece of fancy chocolate cake.

"For your troubles, this is on the house."

He set the glass and the plate down on my table, and I watched as other tables were given the same courtesy: free desserts and drinks to encourage us to stay in safety. I could see the same unsure, confused looks on some of the other customers' faces. I had no desire for chocolate cake. I just wanted to get as far away from the Square as possible. I'd even go back to Olivier's messy flat rather than stay in the danger zone. However, I was safe there on the balcony, so I finished my wine and continued writing.

In total, I stayed at Piatsa for over four hours. The waiter finally came back and told me it was safe to leave, if I wanted, so I paid and rushed off in the opposite direction of the Polytechnic University. I had considered going to the Acropolis museum but arrived just minutes before they closed. Instead, I followed my map, exploring some of the sights outside the busy city center. On the way up to one of the city views, I followed a stone path leading off in a random direction and decided to follow it.

By that point, my emotions had been through enough in one day that the thought of wandering away from civilization to find a spot to breathe was extremely appealing. After walking for about ten minutes, I found a bench situated under a tree, looking out over Athens. The sun was beginning to set, hovering just above the Aegean Sea on the other side of the city. I sat on the bench for nearly an hour, just soaking it in. It was the most beautiful sunset I'd ever witnessed: stripes of yellow, red, and orange sank lower and lower into the Sea, eventually disappearing altogether. Satisfied and finally relaxed, I stood and continued along the path, visiting the Sundial of Meton, the Altar of Zeus Adoraios (basically a big rock formation), the Hill of the Muses, and the Pnyx Monument. I lingered at each, fully reading the inscriptions to learn about their significance.

I still had roughly two hours until I had to meet Olivier, but as I had been walking for some time I decided to slowly make my way back to the Square. I wandered back past the Thissio district, where I got turned around and had to ask for directions back to Syntagma. I stopped into a few stores, bought a package of dried apricots (a new favorite snack of mine) and went on my way.

By that time, there were police everywhere. Syntagma Square had basically been shut down, but I saw lights were still on in Piatsa and made my way back over to it. My feet were throbbing after spending so much time walking: I just needed somewhere to sit and relax. I considered finding another restaurant nearby and wait for Olivier there, but I knew the Wi-Fi worked at Piatsa and at least the waitstaff was friendly. I sat on the first floor this second time around and ordered a coffee while I waited for him. There was a large photo album/informational book on Syntagma Square propped up on the counter, so I flipped through it while I enjoyed my coffee. Within moments, Piatsa was full of policemen (again) and one of them caught my eye.

"Where are you from?" he asked. I shuddered. Why is he asking?

"America," I said. Then, even though I knew the answer, "What's going on?"

"We're here for you," he said, then smirked and turned back to the group. He's trying to make a joke and I'm downright terrified. I should try to laugh or I'm going to burst into tears.

He gave me the same information as the waiter had just a few hours earlier, and said they were just keeping watch through the night to make sure the Square stayed safe. He recommended I 'sit tight' for a bit, as the demonstration marched to the United States Embassy because they thought America meddled in the way the political system functioned there. While Greeks were typically a fairly accepting people, it wasn't a great day to be an American traveling in Athens, especially alone. *Wonderful.*

I closed the book and focused on the postcards I'd purchased earlier instead. I filled three for my family members while I waited for Olivier and felt a huge rush of relief when he finally arrived. He ordered a coffee as well, informing me that we'd be meeting a friend of his at another Greek restaurant shortly. Then he asked me about my day and I filled him in: the museum being closed, being stuck in Piatsa, the stone path with the bench, and all of the policemen. When I told him I thought I was allergic to the oranges because of the reaction I'd had earlier, he pointed out that I'd been in front of the university when I felt it; it wasn't allergies, it was tear gas. Apparently it was a common method used by the police to break up protests.

We left Piatsa a short while later and met up with his friend Marlena for dinner and drinks (it was now nearly 10:00pm in the evening. I was starving). Olivier ordered a gyro, I ordered a sautéed vegetable dish covered in feta served with a side of pita bread, and Marlena ordered some kind of Moussaka. She looked familiar to me: the spitting image of someone I'd gone to college with. We became fast friends – talking French the entire evening – and the three of us eventually relocated from the restaurant to an underground bar called *Six Dogs*. Olivier and Marlena were thoroughly disappointed to find it closed and decided to show me a rooftop bar instead. Some of Marlena's friends met us there – two Frenchmen, another from Brazil – and we enjoyed more wine, great conversation, and the fresh air above the city. We didn't stay long, which I was quite OK with given that we'd attracted a very drunk girl from Canterbury bugging each of us for a piece of gum. She flitted from one person in our group to the next, not sensing the annoyed looks being thrown her way. Fortunately, a friend of Marlena's was arriving from the airport around 1:00am, and we had to walk back to meet her at Syntagma Square. We finished our drinks, said goodbye to our new friends, and went on our way. By the time we got there, the police were gone and the Square had returned to normal. Marlena's friend met us just as we found a spot to wait, and the four of us walked back to Olivier's flat to drop off her suitcase. The two girls were on their way to a party and would pick it up in the morning.

Once they'd gone, Olivier set about working on his laptop and I braved the shower again. Maybe it was because I was so tired, or maybe it was because I was literally in tears from the throbbing blisters on my feet, but the shower didn't seem nearly as daunting the second time. I didn't drop the hose, my t-shirt towel was dry until I needed it (because I hadn't dropped the hose), and when I finally crawled onto the mattress, I didn't even mind its musty smell as I drifted off to sleep. I was exhausted, but I was safe.

. . . . .

The morning came far too quickly. I woke to hear footsteps and outbursts of laughter coming from the entryway; Marlena and her friend had come back to retrieve the suitcase. They were still in the clothes they'd been wearing the night before, slightly disheveled but chatty nonetheless. Olivier looked over at me and laughed.

"I think Sam will be a bit slow today." They laughed.

I didn't care; I let my head fall back onto my scarf-pillow, pounding from the night before. A few feet below, my feet – also pounding – hurt so badly that I had to close my eyes. I was hesitant to even look at them; blisters this early on in a trip did not make for an enjoyable time.

Marlena and her friend waved goodbye and Olivier disappeared into the kitchen. I got up, blisters ripping as I put weight on my feet, and headed into the bathroom to brush my teeth. I had brought along a small bottle of Ibuprofen, which I took with a mug of tea Olivier brought me. Then he grabbed a bag of oranges, took one out, and handed the bag to me. I pulled one out and dropped it instantly. *Maggots.* I'd just get something at the bakery.

He had the same schedule as the day before (working noon to eight), so we headed into the city for another morning of exploring. At Attika, we ordered a few mini Spanikopita – one regular, one just feta cheese, one filled with olives – and coffee. It tasted phenomenal, especially given the rough morning I was having. Olivier realized he forgot to wear a belt, so we quickly went back to his flat before continuing on. I was glad; I dug a few bandages out of my carry-on thinking maybe they would help with the blister situation and was relieved when my freshly bandaged feet still fit into my shoes. We were off.

Halfway between the flat and Syntagma Square we passed by the Temple of Zeus. I was surprised to see that it wasn't actually situated on a hill like it was in the Disney movie Hercules. Instead, it was in the middle of a flat, grassy clearing. Olivier waited while I took pictures, and we continued on to the National Garden. It was magnificent: there were goats and turtles in large, wooden enclosures (I felt certain they could escape if they tried), and parrots, swans, and other kinds of birds in the trees above us. The middle of the garden was lined with palm trees, and orange trees were everywhere. Olivier explained that oranges were one of the major foods grown in Greece; he'd never cared for them until he moved there. *I've noticed. But you really shouldn't eat them when they're full of maggots!*

Olivier decided to show me the famous Λυκαβηττός – Lycabettus – the hill with the white building on top he'd shown me my first night in Athens. It was quite a trek. First, we had to work our way up a gently sloping hill, past housing and fruit gardens, and too many stray cats to count. Then we reached the base of the hill, by which point my feet were already numb from pain. I was thankful that someone had taken the time to fashion a sort of path out of wooden boards on the way up, each shoved into the side of the hill as it rose steeper and steeper. I was out of breath by the time we reached the top, and my legs felt like rubber. But we'd made it, and it was completely worth it.

Olivier was right; this was a far better view of the city. The white church there – the Chapel of St. George – was surrounded with vendors selling everything from beverages to bracelets. I bought Olivier a soda and chose a lemonade for myself (which turned out to be an alcoholic beverage... at 10:30am). We stayed at the top for a while, and I bought a few bracelets for my friends and family at home. They were the perfect size; any souvenirs I took back had to fit into a very small amount of space in my carry-on, and the bracelets were tiny.

While we sat enjoying our beverages, Olivier explained that Mount Lycabettus was connected to a few different stories in Greek mythology. Some thought it once served as the home of wolves (lycos meaning 'wolves' in Greek). But traditional mythology said that Athena had once dropped a limestone on her way to help build the Acropolis, creating the hill. He said a past Couchsurfer had done the research (not him) so I could believe whatever I wanted.

It was something I'd come to love about Greece; there was a reason for everything and everything had a story. For each monument, each hill, each stone, there seemed to be a back story (truth or myth). I'd done a research paper on Greek mythology when I was in high school, and spent hours studying those places and characters. As Olivier showed me around, the memories of writing the paper came flooding back, and I tried to remember which god went with which location. I personally did not believe in Greek mythology, but it was interesting to imagine a society living their entire lives in pursuit of 'pleasing the gods' and seeing the different monuments and temples they had erected in their honor. I was literally walking the paths that an ancient civilization had walked: the stories connected to each location were proof of that. Mount Lycabettus included.

We had a short time before Olivier had to be at work, so he took me to a café he claimed was his favorite. It was located in a very steep downtown area, with narrow streets and high, white buildings. I would have passed by had I been on my own, as the entryway was tucked back away from the street between two large stores. As we pushed inside, he said that we were now in the 'wealthy student' area, and many of the restaurants and stores there were very expensive.

"But this one is not too much, and you must pay your tour guide." He laughed.

Olivier ordered a Souvlaki (a sort of chicken gyro) and I ordered a vegetarian pita wrap. It was fantastic; I hadn't realized how hungry I was until we started eating. And it felt absolutely wonderful to be off of my feet. He told me that from the café, we would go back to the Archaeological museum, where he would once again leave me before heading to work. Later, he would meet up with me at Syntagma again and we could figure out the ferry tickets from Chania to Santorini.

We did just that. After we paid for our lunch (a grand total of €9,00 for the two sandwiches), we made our way back down to the main street. As we walked along, the burning sensation I'd felt in my eyes the day before grew stronger and stronger as we neared the Polytechnic University. Tear gas, not allergies, I remembered. Olivier pulled his scarf over his nose and pointed at evidence of the previous day's demonstration: chunks taken out of the sidewalk, streetlights destroyed, street signs cut in half, and most shocking: a car that had been completely burned out. Then he pointed through the gate of the university, and we saw the giant memorial for those who were killed in 1973, now covered with ribbons and flowers. It was an unforgettable sight.

I bought two Kinder eggs for us as we walked towards the museum (he told me I was obsessed). We stopped at a post office on the way so that I could buy the stamps I needed to send my postcards to America, and I dropped them into the large, yellow box for pickup. When we finally arrived at the National Archaeological Museum, Olivier walked up the steps to the large front doors with me to make sure it was open. It was, so we said goodbye and I pushed inside.

It was the museum I had most been looking forward to visiting in Athens. There was so much to look at; I didn't know where to start. I picked up a map, paid my €8,00 entry fee, and started with an exhibit off to the left. As I went through the museum, I noted familiar names at the bases of the sculptures: Dionysus (god of wine), Apollo (god of music), and of course, Zeus (god of the sky). For being so old, most of the statues and sculptures were beautifully preserved. A few others looked like nothing more than chunks of rock with a few letters carved into them.

I walked through another exhibit – Odysseys – and read about the ancient peoples' adventures at sea. The exhibit, which included both statues and music, highlighted three different themes: The Journey (to grow as a civilization), Ithacas (the homecoming of Odysseus and prosperity in the country), and the Exodus (the great achievements of human minds). As I walked through the room - which was cast in a bluish green glow - I read about the mythology they believed accompanied them on their sea journeys. There were statues of the Sirens and of Poseidon, and giant plaques discussing the fates of sailors lured to sea. It was incredible, and from the lighting to the music, I nearly felt like I was there with them, at sea.

Another exhibit demonstrated the different styles of Greek sculpture, showing how much of the cultural influence actually came from Egypt. Side by side, Greek and Egyptian statues looked quite similar and the plaques in front of them outline the differences and the similarities. It was absolutely fascinating, and I spent several hours walking through the different exhibits, each more intriguing than the next. At one point I even found a beautiful statue of Aphrodite (goddess of love and beauty) being confronted by Pan (god of shepherds). I laughed, seeing that she was threatening him with her sandal. Situated between the two was Eros (Cupid), trying to protect her from Pan's advance. It was interesting, seeing the ancient Greek attempt at humor. *Pan, you dirty old man.*

After visiting the National Archaeological Museum, I decided to walk to the Acropolis. I wanted to climb the stairs and explore the Parthenon itself, but as my feet were now stinging with each step I thought it might be better to save that for the last part of my trip, when I would return to Athens. Hopefully by then my feet will be fully healed. Instead, I went to the museum there, which was full of statues and artifacts from the Acropolis. I walked through slowly, working my way from floor to floor. I was very thankful they were connected by long, sloping ramps instead of stairs. As I explored, I took careful note of the intricate details. Clay bowls, figurines, and utensils were concealed behind glass the length of one ramp. Another held bits of larger statues that had broken off but were too precious to dispose of. On one floor, large pedestals supported busts of philosophers, their names carved on the front in neat, perfect letters. On another, a large sculpture of Athena surrounded by mythological creatures. I remembered what I'd learned about Greeks being upset that their historical sites had been excavated and wondered what they thought of museums such as this. I took a few pictures until one of the workers scolded me and told me photography was not permitted. I was thankful he let me keep my camera, but I noticed he kept an eye on me as I continued through the museum.

It was such an immense learning experience. Greece had been fortunate on many occasions to receive assistance from other countries. Over the years, the influences from those countries had made their way into the various aspects of Greek culture: history, theater, architecture, food, and even religion. I lingered in front of the different posters, soaking in as much information as I could. Several hours passed, and I finally left and went back to Syntagma. On the way, I stopped in and out of stores to look for souvenirs. I made a note to stop back into the Pandora boutique when I returned to Athens to buy the 'All Seeing Eye' charm for my mother. Every time I'd traveled, I'd brought her back a charm for her bracelet. This trip was for Papa – for her father – of course I had to bring her a charm from Greece.

I arrived to Syntagma Square around 6:30pm and stopped into a store called *Publique*. It was a six-floor entertainment store that reminded me of a giant Barnes & Noble. Each floor had a different focus: children's books, CD's, fiction, nonfiction, movies, etc. I found a copy of my favorite book – <u>The Little Prince</u> – but decided to wait to buy it until I returned to Athens. The less I have to carry around with me, the better.

There was a café on the top floor, where I was planning to rest for a while, but it was far too crowded. Instead, I made my way back out to the Square and – unsurprisingly – back to Piatsa. The man inside waved me in like family, and I took a seat upstairs at a table inside. By the time I sat down, I was so hungry I was dizzy. Olivier and I had gone to the little café several hours earlier, and I was sure I'd walked at least five miles since then. I ordered a coffee and another kind of salad from the menu, along with an extra side of pita bread. I sent out a few messages on Facebook, then spent some time writing and organizing my things. It felt good to have established a sort of "home base" at Piatsa. I knew how to get there from anywhere in Athens, the workers there knew me, and I knew it had good, affordable food (and wine).

Olivier appeared shortly after 9:00pm and ordered a coffee while I told him about my day. He said he didn't care for the museums as they were always far too packed with tourists, but was glad to hear that I had thoroughly enjoyed them. We walked back to his flat (my feet throbbing once again), where I showered and changed my bandages. While getting ready for bed, I realized I was out of toothpaste. So I took a chance and asked if I could borrow some of his. It wasn't my first choice, but it was the only option.

"Je ne l'utilise pas," he said. *I don't use it.*

"Excuse-moi?" Surely I'd misheard him.

He told me that there was body wash on the shelf, which he used instead. According to his logic, "If it can clean your body, it can clean your teeth." I didn't even have a response.

As we sat down to order my ferry tickets, I began to feel uneasy. In the off-season, the ferries did not go from island to island: that was only in the summer. It was going to be very difficult to find a route from Chania to Santorini, and any that I did find went first to Athens, then back out to Santorini. Olivier pointed out that in total, I would be spending more than thirteen hours on a boat one way. I grew very frustrated, and he tried making me Mousse au Chocolat to make me feel better. *No, I do not want to use a dirty spoon to eat your Mousse au Chocolat out of your dirty bowl!* I almost said it out loud. I knew that I was very tired, and therefore very cranky. I just want to buy my tickets and go to bed.

I snapped a bit as I pushed the bowl away, and he suggested finding flights instead. I had no other choice; I put in my credit card information into the website for a flight (€400,00) and received an email from the airline saying they would let me know once my payment was confirmed. I couldn't imagine what it would be like to be stuck in Chania if things didn't work out. I sent my hosts in Chania and Santorini messages asking for advice on ferry tickets just in case they had some sort of information I couldn't find online. As I fell asleep that night, I could only hope that the booking went through...preferably sooner rather than later.

8

If I had considered myself cranky the night before, it was nothing compared to how I felt the next morning. I woke up extremely early, shivering uncontrollably as Olivier had opened the balcony door the night before to let in some fresh air. I was thoroughly freezing, and my legs were painfully sore; hiking Mount Lycabettus and all the walking I'd done had really taken a toll on them. I shook and shifted uncomfortably on the mattress. I considered pulling Olivier's dingy blanket up over me but the thought of it covering any part of me was too disgusting. Instead, I grabbed my fleece from my carry-on, snuggled into it, and tried to get back to sleep.

I was thankful that the day ahead held a six-hour train ride. I couldn't wait to see the countryside, pass by Mount Olympus, and possibly catch a few hours of sleep en route to Thessaloniki. Olivier had told me that the culture in northern Greece was quite different than that in Athens, so I was looking forward to experiencing whatever the North had to offer.

At 7:30am, I woke up a second time to the sound of Olivier typing away on his laptop. He'd shut the balcony door, which I appreciated greatly as I got up from the mattress and started collecting my things. I was so excited to continue on my journey to the next city. That night, I would be sleeping on an actual bed. I thought of the cozy-looking bedroom Marilena and Dimitria had posted on their AirBNB page, then down at the mattress I'd been sleeping on for the past three nights. *Definitely ready to move on.*

Naturally, we stopped one last time at Attika, where I got my Spanikopita, a coffee, and two Kalouri for the train. From there we continued on to the metro station, where Olivier began to review the route I needed to take: metro to Larissa Station (one of the major stations in Athens), then Larissa Station to Thessaloniki. We boarded the metro together, sharing last thoughts and light conversation, and were soon at his stop. I thanked him again for letting me stay at his flat and for giving me such a great tour of the city. We agreed to go for dinner when I was back in Athens so that I could pick up my Starbucks mugs, and before I knew it he was hugging me goodbye and giving me les bises. Then Olivier was gone, off into the hustle and bustle of the crowd.

I was on my own.

The stops flew by, and I watched as people got on and off the train. Some made eye contact, some kept their heads down, and some were deeply engaged in conversation with those around them. There were girls wearing heavy makeup, green coats, and thick-heeled black boots laced all the way up (Olivier had pointed out that these were the troublemakers), young couples huddled close together, and men in suits undoubtedly traveling for business. I could've stayed on the train longer, just observing those around me; it was quite the collection of people. The metro rolled into Larissa Station, and I made my way onto the platform.

It was nothing like the train stations I'd been to in Germany. There was a large indoor waiting area, with a small cafeteria down one hallway and ticket booths down another. A woman was sitting in front of the bathroom door holding a metal dish, which held a few paper notes and some coins. Olivier told me that the women who cleaned public bathrooms often did this, and while payment wasn't necessary it was expected. I made my way to the ticket booth and double-checked my ticket with the woman behind the glass. She motioned outside and confirmed the platform and number of my train. I had an hour and a half before it arrived, so I decided to buy a snack and catch up on writing while I waited. As the large glass doors of the waiting area opened and closed, pigeons snuck inside in search of food. I watched as they scurried about at peoples' feet, begging for food in an almost dog-like manner. The people in the waiting room were as different as those I'd seen on the metro: all ages, all kinds of clothing, all different nationalities. More green coats and thick-heeled boots.

When my train finally did arrive, I half expected a conductor to step out and say, "All aboard!" (Admittedly I was rather disappointed when that didn't happen.) The train – covered in graffiti like most of Athens' public transportation – simply slowed to a halt and flung open its doors. I triple-checked my ticket before climbing aboard. Right platform, right train. Here we go. My confidence in my abilities was low. Inside, the train was exactly how

I'd expected it to look: a long, thin hallway with rooms off to the right, benches on opposing sides covered in blue fabric. As I made my way down the hallway and saw the people inside, I felt like I'd just stepped onto the Hogwarts Express. People shoved past me, and I eventually tucked into one of the rooms and took a seat. Someone had stowed their luggage on the bench across from me, but I didn't care; we'd begun to move and I needed to find a seat. A few moments later, two twenty-something guys came inside and took their seats as well. We exchanged smiles as they sat down, one pulling out headphones and the other, a book. I leaned my head back and closed my eyes.

The ride went fairly quickly. I spent more time writing, ate an entire bag of pistachios and one of the Kalouri, bought a water from the restaurant car, walked in on a man using the bathroom, and eventually even managed a few hours of sleep. We arrived in Thessaloniki forty-five minutes late, so I started to worry about my next host abandoning me. Initially, Marilena had agreed to meet me at the bus stop at Aristotelous Square shortly after my train arrived. Now that I'd arrived so late, I hoped she hadn't already left, and I texted her that I was on my way. (I'd already decided that international texting charges were sometimes worth it.) She told me which bus to take from the train station, and I rushed out of the station, jumping on board just moments before it took off into the city.

It wasn't long before the announcement sounded: Aristotelous Square. My heart was beating rapidly as I looked around, trying to catch a glimpse of Marilena. I'd seen her photos on AirBNB and picked her out from the crowd instantly. She was a tiny human being, coming only to my chin (myself only being around 5'4"). Marilena had brown hair pulled into a messy bun with bangs, a bulky brown jacket with large pockets on the front, a dark skirt with vibrant leggings underneath, and boots that came up just below her knees. Her purse was small and colorful, and she had dark sunglasses pushed on top of her head. She waved at me and I ran over to her, glad to have made it to my next destination. She told me the trains were usually quite timely, but not to worry – she'd had experience with them running late as well. We powered through the streets, her asking me about my day and me explaining how much I had enjoyed Athens. For some reason I assumed she'd been there thousands of times given it was the most popular city in Greece, but she said it had actually been years since she'd gone. She was busy there in Thessaloniki, working most nights and trying to be a good host to AirBNB-ers that came to stay. As we walked through the streets on our way to her flat, she told me she had to work that night but that I could either come visit her or spend some time exploring. Later, I could meet her roommate out on the town. Apparently Dimitria and the German girl were very excited to meet me as well.

Their flat was a fifteen-minute walk from Aristotelous Square. From the outside, it resembled Olivier's (though I prayed the inside was different): a high, white stone building connected to several others the length of street, and a heavy door with bars on the outside. A few cats scattered as she walked up the steps and held open the door, taking my bag as I went inside. After climbing three flights of stairs, Marilena smiled and motioned towards a door.

"This is us!"

I was mesmerized the moment I walked through the door. The first thing I noticed was the glowing, whimsical element filling the room: every light had a red bulb. The furniture was exactly as it had been in the photos – mismatched but modern – and a wood-burning stove was flickering off to my right. They had three cats, each of which prowled into the room to see who the newcomer was, and who I could only assume to be Dimitria emerged from another room to meet me as well. Like Marilena, she had brown hair pulled up into a messy bun (though hers slightly darker in color). Her eyes were large and kind, and she hugged me as soon as I was within reach. Over her shoulder, I could see a few book-shelves against the far wall, and there was a piano situated in the corner. From the red glow and bold décor to the warmth of the stove and the piano, I could tell I was going to get along very well with these girls. They were artsy, just like me.

Marilena showed me to my bedroom (also accurately repre-sented by the photos), where she gave me a few minutes to get my things organized. I let my bag drop to the floor and sat down on the edge of a fresh, queen-sized bed. As I fell backwards onto the comfortable blanket, I couldn't help but think This is perfect. I looked around the room, noticing small details that Marilena and Dimitria had prepared for their guest. There were fresh towels folded on a vanity bench. I don't have to use my t-shirt anymore! On the vanity, there was a map of Thessaloniki with a few places to visit marked with a highlighter. There was even a small bar of soap and travel-sized shampoo and conditioner set out for me to use.

Off to one side of the room, there was a curtain hanging floor to ceiling. I walked over and pulled it aside, revealing the doorway out onto the balcony. I pushed it open. Outside, I found a small iron table and chair on top of which there was a small vase of flow-ers. It would be the perfect place to write. I could already imagine spending a few hours looking out over the city below, enjoying a bit of fresh air. I knew I was going to like Thessaloniki.

I could have easily laid down and fallen asleep right then and there. Instead, I went back out into the main room, where Marilena was pulling her boots back on to head to work. Dimitria started to ask me about my time in Athens and what I was hoping to see in Thessaloniki, truly fascinated that I had come all by myself to discover my roots. She offered to make us a cup of tea before I headed out into the city. Down a hallway, she pointed out the bathroom (doubling as their laundry room) and reminded me that I could wash my clothes if needed. When we reached the end of the hallway, she opened the door to the kitchen. It looked as if it had come straight out of a magazine. The wooden cupboards were painted bright blue, clear jars of herbs, tea, and other ingredients lined the counters, a bright yellow teapot sat on the stove, and fresh bread and fruit were set out on the wooden table. There was a giant wooden box just inside the door, and Dimitria lifted the lid to reveal dozens of jars and boxes of tea.

"Floral, green, or black?"

We sat at the table while she brewed us a floral tea and told me a bit about herself. She was currently taking some classes and would eventually like to move to the United Kingdom, traveling as much as she could in the little time she had free. Eventually she wanted to be some kind of psychologist and move away from Greece. She asked me if I'd traveled before, and I told her about my internship in Dublin, some of the places I'd visited around Europe, and the reasons behind my trip to Greece. She seemed genuinely interested, especially when I mentioned that my great-great-grandfather's boat had taken off from Koutsouras. She told me she'd been there once and was surprised it was included in my trip. Compared to most of the other cities on Crete, it was not usually a tourist destination.

After talking for a while, she had some homework to do and I decided to find a place for dinner. Before I left, she helped me get my laundry started and said she would finish it while I was out. I felt a bit guilty, but she said she was more than happy to do so as I was her guest. I remembered the taffy I'd brought for them and retrieved it from my bag, and she thanked me before suggesting a few places for dinner. She went into my room and returned with the map, pointing to a one of the highlighted spots.

"They have very good vegetarian food here," she said. She reminded me that she and Marilena were trying to fully transition into vegetarian (and eventually vegan) lifestyles and had found several places in the city with great options. I was thrilled. I could usually find something in any restaurant, but it was always nice to have a larger selection. And if they'd already tested it out, there was experience to back up her suggestion.

Dimitria set about doing my laundry, and I headed off into the city. I walked down Dragoumi, following my map to the place she'd suggested. It was beginning to get dark out, so I was drawn off course by a side street decorated with fairy lights and brightly colored lanterns. A large, wooden door was just around the corner, off to the right. It had large, high windows, with vibrant dishes and other knick-knacks on display. But it wasn't a store. It was a restaurant. I looked over the menu posted outside: Takadum. It was written in both Greek and English, and after seeing an entire page dedicated to vegetarian options, I made my way inside. I can always try Dimitria's restaurant tomorrow.

The interior was completely Bohemian: even more colorful than the outside. There were strands of bright purple, pink, and blue beads hanging from the ceiling. A tall ladder was off in one corner, covered in multi-toned blankets. It had colored, dimly lit lights casting a wonderful ambiance around the dining area. I was glad to see it wasn't too crowded given the hour (I'd noticed Greeks didn't adhere to the standard 5:30pm dinner time), so I was quickly taken to a table. The waiter motioned for me to follow him upstairs, where there was another, smaller dining room. The furniture reminded me of Marilena and Dimitria's flat: bold, mismatched, but modern. No two chairs looked alike. Mine was a dark burgundy color, and my table was bright blue with speckles like a robin's egg. I ordered a *Choriou Salad* – a traditional Greek salad with a hard-boiled egg – and a glass of red wine. It was such a great way to start my time in Thessaloniki: the food was delicious, the atmosphere was exciting, and I had a comfortable, warm bed and a clean shower waiting for me back at the flat. I smiled to myself and set about enjoying my dinner.

As I ate, I pulled out the map Dimitria had given me and looked over the highlighted spots. I had the rest of that evening and the entire next day to explore, and then would be flying to Chania the following morning. Less than 48 hours to explore Thessaloniki: it had only been a few hours, but I already wished I had more time. There were so many possibilities! There was a table of women nearby speaking a mixture of Greek and German, so (fueled by my wine) I thought I'd ask them for their advice.

"Entschuldigung, können Sie mir helfen?" *Excuse me, can you help me?*

It felt strange to be speaking German again after having spent the past few days speaking French with Olivier. But I loved it. Any opportunity I had to use my foreign languages gave me a small sense of pride after having spent so much time studying them. The women smiled and told me I was *so süß* (so sweet) for asking. They were more than happy to offer suggestions, telling me that I must visit the White Tower and statue of Alexander the Great, the Archaeological Museum of Thessaloniki, and the Upper Town, where I would be able to see the Byzantine Wall and its towers. It was great information; I wrote everything down and was glad to have a general plan for the next day. I thanked them, receiving a round of *Bitte schön* (you're very welcome) from the table. Then I paid, gathered my things, and headed out. Dimitria had mentioned she might want to meet me out that evening, so I made my way back to the flat.

It didn't take me long to find their building. When I knocked, Dimitria ushered me inside and started asking what I thought of the restaurant. I told her about Takadum and she lit up, telling me that it was another one of her favorite spots. I saw that she had finished my laundry, as it was now hanging on chairs in front of the wood-burning stove to dry. She was fantastic, and I could tell we were going to be fast friends.

Moments later, another girl appeared from the bedroom next to mine. She was about my height, with shoulder-length blonde hair and a pale complexion. There was a nose ring in her septum and she was wearing spike earrings, a red and white striped shirt, and black jeans.

"I'm Lena," she said, smiling. "I hear you were in Germany?"

Lena had been in Thessaloniki for several months on an internship, and originally came from Berlin. She'd had difficulty finding a flat to rent and had decided instead to check AirBNB, where she found Marilena and Dimitria. She loved it there. A friend of hers was visiting from the UK, and she called him out of the room to join us. Steve had saved up as much money as he could, quit his job, and was on a sort of <u>Eat, Pray, Love</u> adventure, traveling around visiting friends and spending a year on the road. He'd already visited several other countries before coming to Greece, where he met Lena. They'd spent the last few weeks together, but he said he was about ready to move on. The next day, he would continue his journey.

"Where will you go?"

"I'm flying into Budapest, and then I'm just going to get on a train and see where it leads me."

Dimitria made more tea and the four of us sat in the kitchen for a while, talking about culture and adventure and our life goals. It was amazing how comfortable we all were with each other, openly discussing anything and everything that came up in the conversation. Everyone had so much insight and such different perspectives: Greece, Germany, the UK, and America, all represented right there in that little kitchen. It was the most incredible feeling, to be so quickly and warmly accepted by these new friends, despite the fact that we were all from such different places.

Marilena had suggested we check out a popular bar called *Blue Barbel*, where there would be live rock 'n roll music that night. After spending a bit longer in the kitchen, we all got ready to go. Steve decided to stay behind as he had an early morning, so Dimitria, Lena, and I headed out for a 'girls' night'. As Dimitria pulled the door shut, a small group of people passed us on their way down the stairs.

"Hey! Where are you all going?" a small, dark-skinned woman with long, dark hair in the front asked. Behind her, an Arabic man stood off to one side, with a small, Caucasian, brown-haired woman on the other. It turned out to be a few of Dimitria's friends, on their way out as well.

"We're going to the Blue Barbel, for the music."

"No, come with us instead! We're going to Hydropólico."

It took us all of two seconds to change our plan, and soon the six of us were parading down the street, enjoying good company and the fresh night air. As it turned out, the small brown-haired woman (Lillian) was also an AirBNB-er, originally from North Carolina. She was older than the rest of us – in her thirties – and explained that she was traveling around Greece as a celebration of finishing her master's degree. She'd just arrived from Athens a few days earlier, so we had a wonderful time comparing experiences. She even gave me a few recommendations of things I simply had to see when I returned. While in Athens, she had stayed in another AirBNB, and after I told her about Olivier's flat, she gave me a hug and said it was exactly the reason she would never do Couchsurfing. She'd had a similar experience once in England and could never bring herself to try it again. I just smiled, praying that my host in Chania would be different.

The other two individuals in their party were a couple and were long-time friends of Dimitria and Marilena. They lived in the flat just above them and had taken their idea to host AirBNB-er's. I thought of my 'apartment' back in the United States and couldn't imagine ever hosting a traveler. *There is literally nothing worth seeing in walking distance of my apartment. Maybe the Tim Horton's on the corner?*

We reached Hydropólico, and when we opened the door to go inside, a waiter came out and told us there was no room for any more customers. We could wait, but it would've been quite some time before we got inside. One of Dimitria's friends suggested another place, *Mr. Jones*. So off we went. Thessaloniki in the dark was just as beautiful as it had been when I first arrived, if not more so. There were a few landmarks here and there – various churches and statues scattered throughout the city – which we tried unsuccessfully to photograph as we walked. Lillian pointed out the Arch of Galerius, the Hagia Sophia Cathedral, making a comment that there was nothing like them in her small town in North Carolina. I nodded and said the same for mine.

We reached Mr. Jones and went inside. It was a very dark, very smoky tavern that was packed with twenty-somethings (plus Lillian). Lena and the couple from upstairs ordered beer, Dimitria - who didn't drink - ordered a cup of tea, and we two Americans ordered mulled wine. It was absolutely delicious. Mulled wine I'd had in the past did not have the actual cinnamon sticks or star anise in the glass. I liked it; it was spicy and reminded me more of a fruity chai tea than a glass of wine. Dimitria procured a bag of Ruffles from her bag, and I was surprised to see that they were ketchup-flavored. (I made a note to look for them back in the United States.) It was a bit difficult to hear each other with the loud music in the background, so we left shortly after our first round of drinks. I was just thankful for the fresh air.

From Mr. Jones, we re-traced our steps to a place that Dimitria said had the best vegetarian souvlaki. On the way, she and her friends shared some of their past AirBNB experiences. The couple from upstairs had hosted nearly sixty people in the past few years: an older gentleman from the UK traveling for business, a handful of college students taking a break on their semester abroad, a couple of Asian women who tried to bring home one of the stray cats and keep it as a pet, and a family from Australia who had a baby ("That never stopped crying," the woman added). Apparently Marilena and Dimitria had housed their fair share of AirBNB-er's as well (though no children), and some of the stories they told were unbelievable. They'd hosted very rude guests in the past, from people stealing the books from their shelves to others just being horribly unappreciative. Some just hid in their rooms all day – "Wasting everything they could see in the city!" Dimitria exclaimed – and then some wouldn't even talk to them. Lillian and I were both in shock. Did people on AirBNB really take their hosts for granted that often?

We continued on, and at some point, the refugee situation in Europe came up. Dimitria told us all about how awful it had been in Greece and created quite the struggle for locals. The people there really did want to help when there were refugees looking for shelter and food, but when they helped one, more would come.

"And you can only give so much," she added.

Lillian excitedly shared that she had done a research project on the refugee crisis, a comparison of the situation in 1923 to the that of the present day. I wasn't aware of the severity or size of it all now and had no idea what had happened in 1923. I realized that as a non-European who neither saw it up close nor studied the issue, I couldn't fully understand it. Lillian agreed, and the simple walk to the souvlaki place evolved into a hugely informational political conversation. I felt myself wishing I knew more; I couldn't very well 'chime in' to a conversation when the only exposure I had to any of it was what I'd seen on the news.

When we reached the souvlaki place, there was a pack of the dark-coat, thick-heeled boot-wearing, heavily eyeliner-ed girls waiting at the counter. We moved around them and ordered our souvlaki: chicken-filled for Lena and the couple upstairs, veggie-filled for me and Lillian (also a vegetarian), and a very odd-looking

French fry-filled one for Dimitria. As soon as we were outside and out of earshot, I asked my host about the girls we'd just seen.

"Are they students here?"

"No, likely not. Most of them don't actually attend school. When you see the young people dressed in that fashion, they are usually either communists or anarchists. It's best to stay away from them," she explained. Olivier hadn't gone into detail of why they were troublemakers, only that I should avoid them. It was interesting to me that the young people had such a strong reputation and were such political activists. I was about to say something when Lillian spoke the thought running through my mind:

"You don't see that in the United States. At least not where I live."

I had to agree with her: apart from a select few who occasionally protested at specific political events, there weren't many young people where I had grown up that spent their time and effort outwardly displaying their disdain for the government. None walked around handing out pro-anarchy pamphlets in the streets, and there wasn't any kind of uniform "dark coat, thick heel" fashion that suggested anything political. In that moment I felt very thankful to live where I did: where there weren't such individuals or annual street riots involving tear gas. Of course there were times when I wished I lived in a more culturally diverse place or wished that I could travel just three hours and be somewhere other than the US (or Canada), or even to a more culturally diverse city in the United States. But overall, I realized I lived in a much safer, more politically sound place. Even despite the ongoing Trump vs. Hillary election campaigns.

We continued walking and talking, eventually arriving home

shortly after 2:00am. Lillian and I hugged goodbye (she was leaving the next morning for Italy), and the couple waved as they headed upstairs behind her. Once inside our flat, I remembered that I would get to have a proper shower (and dry off with an actual towel) and then drift off to sleep in that big, wonderful bed. After a day of travelling, more walking, and experiencing another new city I was thoroughly exhausted and could think of nothing better. My clothes (including my pajamas) were still drying by the fire, so after my shower I had to pull on the clothes I'd been wearing all day. But it didn't matter. Nothing mattered but the warmth and comfort of that lovely bed.

I decided I rather liked Thessaloniki.

9

It took me a few minutes to remember where I was when I woke up the next morning. There was sunlight and a faint breeze coming in through the balcony door, and I could hear music coming through the wall from Lena's room. I just lay there, soaking it all in, extremely well rested and excited for the day ahead. I wanted to enjoy the feeling as long as I could but didn't want to waste the day in bed, either. *This place is too perfect.*

My clothes had finally dried, so I pulled on my jeans and one of the long-sleeved t-shirts, thankful for fresh, clean clothing. My feet were healing, my legs were no longer painfully sore, and I had thoroughly washed my hair the night before for the first time since Germany (not counting the failed attempt at Oliver's flat). It was the perfect way to start the day. As I packed my clean laundry back into my bag, I came across the extra set of keys Olivier had given me for his flat. I sent him a quick message, and he seemed unconcerned:

"Ne t'en fais pas, tu peux me les donner en revenant, ma chérie. Pour les tasses." *Don't worry, you can give them to me when you get back, my dear. For your mugs.*

I headed out around 8:45am, straight for one of the bakeries we'd passed the night before. It wasn't a far walk, just a few blocks down Dragoumi and left on one of the main streets of Thessaloniki, Egnatia. The bakery was called Γατίδης Fresh ("Gatídis" Fresh), and the moment I walked inside I was greeted with the smell of warm bread and sweet pastries. One of the bakers peeked over the counter as a little doorbell jingled.

"Kaliméra!" Good morning!

I wanted to buy a piece of Spanikopita for breakfast, but without Olivier's help I wasn't sure how to order. I pointed, told the woman what I wanted (and held up one finger, for one), and added a "Parakaloú!" to be polite. I had mastered the few words I knew. She smiled, I gave her a two-euro coin, and she handed it over the counter. *This is what I'll miss most about Greece*, I thought as I took a bite. There was just nothing like it in the United States.

From the bakery, I walked along Egnatia for quite some time, following my map to the statue of Alexander the Great. As I walked along the main street, I passed by a few churches (on my left), and saw multiple clothing stores, bakeries, banks, and other small boutiques to my right. The sidewalks were much more crowded than I was expecting, but when I realized most of the traffic was concentrated around the churches it occurred to me that it was a Sunday morning, after all. Of course people were out and about. They were on their way to mass.

I finished my breakfast just as I made it to the university, glancing down at my map as I turned right onto Agelaki. A few moments later I passed by the Macedonian Museum of Modern Art and the Museum of Broadcasting, a giant space needle-looking structure, the Museum of Byzantine Culture, and the Archaeological Museum of Thessaloniki. (Per the German women's suggestion the night before, I was planning to come back that afternoon to explore the latter two). I saw the monument in the distance. There on the far side of a park, with its silhouette dark against the blue Aegean, was the majestic statue of Alexander the Great atop his horse, Voukefalas. I slowly made my way towards the statue, enjoying the sunny weather as I walked, and tried to remember everything I'd learned about him in school. His father was the king of Macedonia, a role he took on when his father was assassinated. He studied under the direction of Aristotle, gaining the knowledge he needed to create alliances, exercise incredible military tactics that allowed him to be successful in major battles, and brought a great deal of Macedonian influence to Greece. I could even remember the photo that was printed on the first page of my sixth-grade history book. It was none other than Alexander the Great, leading his army into battle. The name was fitting: he was an incredibly great king.

The park opened to the back of the monument, which looked out over the Aegean Sea. It was situated on a large, concrete platform, and there were eight upward-facing spears with giant shields on them just ahead of him. There were no words to describe its magnificence. Voukefalas was reared onto his back two legs, and Alexander the Great's cape was flying behind him. Warning visitors to Thessaloniki that this was his territory, I thought. Or maybe he was welcoming those visiting from the southern parts of Greece. Either way, there was a look of pride and courage on his face.

In front of the statue, there was a long promenade that stretched as far as the eye could see, along the length of the coast. People were walking, running, and biking, getting their Sunday morning exercise. I tried to imagine what it would be like to take a daily run in such a beautiful place: that view was absolutely incredible and would certainly keep me going. A few ships were off in the distance, balancing on the thin line separating the blue of the Sea from the light blue sky. I took a seat on one of the concrete steps leading up to the sculpture.

I had always been one of those people who actually enjoyed history class in school. There had been students in my classes who complained that it was a waste of time - What's in the past is past. You can't change anything about it now! – but I always found it interesting. The history of a place and its people gave clues to why the present was as it was and could even give hints of what was yet to come. When I was in eighth grade, my history teacher was one of the most passionate teachers I'd ever had. Not only did he teach the subject, but he spent most of his free time learning it as well. Nearly every class period involved a reference from something he'd seen on the History Channel, and his classroom walls were covered in posters depicting WWII articles, Civil War weaponry, and various American war machines. He was completely devoted to his subject. Near the end of the year, our entire grade – two eighth grade classes, fifty-four students in all – even took a trip from our home in Michigan to Washington D.C. It was my first taste of being up close and personal with history that I'd studied. Not only did we visit some of the major government buildings, but we also saw monuments, explored Mount Vernon (home of George Washington), explored a battlefield or two, and saw a play in Ford's Theater where Lincoln was assassinated. When we visited Arlington National Cemetery, I had been asked to be one of four students to lay the wreath at the Tomb of the Unknown Soldier. The entire trip, I found myself repeatedly thinking This is where it all happened. I am actually standing where our Presidents stood. It was such a bizarre concept to me. Being there, seeing the exact spot where the Declaration of Independence was signed, gave me a great sense of appreciation for the country's history. So there, at the base of Alexander the Great, I was overcome with the same emotion.

After a short while of sitting, enjoying the view, and taking pictures, I went off in search of food. I didn't realize it was already after noon, and my stomach was growling. I walked along the promenade, passing by the White Tower, and made a note to make that my next stop after finding something to eat. And then I saw the beautiful green and white siren luring me over, drawing me in with the promise of fresh coffee.

Starbucks.

I laughed to myself at the newly discovered mythological humor, then headed in the direction of the coffeehouse. It wasn't too far from the White Tower – maybe two minutes, walking – and I was soon pulling the door open and stepping inside. Typically I wouldn't have gone into Starbucks with so many small, local cafés in the area. But I hadn't looked at much else in the Athens Starbucks (I was too focused on my mugs) and wanted to see if the menu and bakery items were much different than the ones in

America. I was disappointed that there were only a few different tarts and muffins, and the coffee menu itself was identical. I bought a blueberry and bran muffin (which admittedly looked much fresher than our muffins normally did), a small coffee, and a package of trail mix. It wasn't a meal by any means but would tide me over for a while and give me the chance to sit down. I sat at a table near the back, glad to be off my feet, and spent some time writing, enjoying my snack, and people watching out the window.

When I finally did make my way to the White Tower, I was glad to learn there was only a €2,00 entry fee. Inside, there was a winding stairway around the outer wall leading upwards. On each floor, a different period of Thessaloniki's history – and specifically, that of the White Tower – was represented. Some floors contained light displays, others had pillars standing to create a life-sized timeline, and one even featured a video playing on a giant screen. I stopped on each floor to walk through the exhibit but was disappointed that nothing was in English. The pictures themselves told a great story though, so I was able to follow along. Over the years, the White Tower had become an iconic symbol of Thessaloniki. I overheard two women talking, and learned that it had once been called the "Blood Tower" because it was originally red. But of course they changed its name when it was whitewashed sometime in the 19th century. It had once been surrounded by thick walls and served to defend the harbor and monitor trade, but now was only a museum for tourists (and locals) to learn more about the city. The inner stairway led up to the roof, from which the entire city was visible. This country has no shortage of gorgeous views, I thought, and took out my camera. I would come here every day if I lived here. There was a large group of kids there on a field trip, darting about and making it difficult to get a good picture. I was glad when one of their mothers offered to take a photo for me and shooed them out of the way.

Over the next two hours, I purposely let myself get lost. Marilena and Dimitria told me there was so much to see in Thessaloniki; you never really knew what you were going to find. I thought I had seen a street market from the top of the White Tower, which I found easily once I was back on ground level. It wasn't anything like the one Olivier had shown me in Athens, as this one was had far fewer fruits and vegetables and more home-made wares like purses, jewelry, and carvings. I considered buying a Grecian dress but realized I would barely be able to fit it into my carry-on if I did. And I have four mugs to somehow fit in as well. Can't forget about those! From the market, I continued to wander through the streets, popping in and out of stores between the promenade along the coast and Egnatia, eventually making my way back to the Archaeological Museum I'd passed by earlier. It cost me €8,00 to enter and was completely worth it.

I spent the next few hours looking through centuries of Greek history, learning about the civilizations preserved behind the glass. I learned more about the gods and how a surprising amount were actually borrowed from the Egyptians (as the museum in Athens had suggested). I passed through rooms full household items, renovated tapestries, and various colored pottery. One exhibit explained the burial process (possibly my least favorite topic), and another, the afterlife. In that particular exhibit, there was a skeleton lying under a glass case that had two coins on top of its eyes. I learned that this was a common practice for the ancient Greeks. In fact, it was necessary in order for them to go to the Underworld. According to Greek mythology, in order to actually get in, they had to cross two rivers. One of which was called Styx, and the only way to cross it was with the help of Charon, who was the ferryman. It was believed that putting coins on the eyes or in the mouth of the dead would satisfy the payment to Charon for crossing that river. If the coins were not buried with the dead, they would be stuck on the wrong side of the river, and their souls would torment those still on earth as ghosts. Some said the coins were put on their eyes so that they could see clearly in the Underworld; others said one was put in the mouth so that they could speak in different tongues when they arrived. Regardless, it was a common practice. I found it absolutely fascinating and remembered how I'd felt the same intrigue years back, writing my paper in high school. At the time, I could have never imagined I'd one day be visiting museums and seeing everything up close and personal. And yet there I was.

Another display I found particularly interesting was that which described the ancient Greeks' schooling. One of the main ways they learned to read and write was through the use of a scalpel-like tool and wax. It was like an ancient Etch-a-Sketch: wax was poured over a flat board, and letters or symbols were carved into it with the sharp edge of the scalpel. Then to "erase," they would simply drag the flat end of the scalpel back over the wax to smooth it out. I can only imagine children in America using sharp tools to carve letters into wax. We hadn't even been allowed to use 'the pointy scissors' in school until the second grade.

The museum continued outside (an additional €4,00), where an enormous display of busts, pillars, and sarcophaguses was set up in a garden. They were ornately decorated with images of the gods. One that was particularly grand even had Dionysus surrounded by grapes, goblets of wine, and what I assumed were the muses carved out with intricate details.

I left the museum after another hour of walking around, surprised at how few others there were but appreciating the old society and its history nonetheless. My next destination was the Upper Town, on the opposite (north) side of the city. My stomach was growling again, so I decided to stop for food on the way at the actual restaurant Dimitria had suggested the night before. I made my way back to Egnatia and continued into the city, turning north when I hit Dragoumi. I tried coordinating with my map to find her highlighted spot marking the restaurant but was soon horribly lost. Now none of the streets I passed were on the map, so I retraced my steps to Dragoumi.

Forty-five minutes passed (this time, getting lost was not done on purpose), so I finally stopped in a bakery just to get something – anything – to tide me over. I bought an orange and something called a kristini (a hard, breadstick-like snack covered in pepitas). I also bought a bag of nuts and continued trying to find my way back. Eventually I stumbled upon Aristotelous Square, where my time in Thessaloniki had begun. At least I know where I am on the map. I traced the route with my finger: it couldn't be possible to get lost if I stayed on Venizelou and followed it all the way to the wall. There was a bright yellow line on my map, showing where the wall was, and it intersected with Venizelou about two kilometers north. I can't possibly miss it. So I set out once again, determined to see the Upper Town and the Byzantine wall.

It took me another forty-five minutes, but I managed. I was so hungry I didn't even feel it anymore, determined to find the Wall. The streets had begun to get steeper and steeper, rising higher above the city. Soon I could even see the Aegean over the rooftops. The buildings were brightly colored compared to the gray and white hues down in the heart of the city. One was blue; its neighbor, orange. And the cats – black, white, calico, tabby – were just everywhere. Kittens scurried out from under stairways as I walked by, others balanced on the ledges separating back-yards, and then some simply wandered around in the street. The kittens were the most heartbreaking to see, looking up at me with big, hungry eyes. No wonder Marilena and Dimitria have three as pets. I wouldn't be able to say 'no' either!

I spent some time exploring the Upper Town, even seeing the ancient Byzantine wall as I wandered further north. I felt satisfied. I had seen exactly what I set out to find, and it was time to go back to the flat to relax (I had long since given up finding Dimitria's res-taurant). On the way back, I passed by a church, where an enor-mous fruit stand was set up outside offering everything from ap-ples and mangoes to some brightly colored fruits I had never even seen before. I bought a few apples and continued on my way. My hosts had told me there was a small grocery store on the corner near their flat, so I stopped in and picked up ingredients to make a salad, another kristini, and a bottle of red wine. I also stopped at a small pastry shop across the street, where I decided to treat myself to the most delicious-looking piece of baklava I had ever seen. I also bought one for Marilena, and a sort of lemon yo-gurt/pudding dessert (we'd passed it the night before and Dimitria mentioned she loved the lemon pudding). It was only 7:15pm, but I was ready to be done for the day. I'd seen so much over the past ten hours, but nothing felt rushed and I didn't feel cheated in any way. I was experiencing Thessaloniki exactly as I'd hoped I would:

if the day had completely ended there, I would have been perfectly happy.

Of course my hosts had a different, much more exciting plan. They told me to take my time and relax, but they were taking me out that night to see the real nightlife of Thessaloniki. Marilena had the night off, and after hearing of our failed attempt to visit Hydropólico the night before she was determined to take me to some of her favorite spots. (She was the self-proclaimed expert, as she worked in one of the bars downtown.) As tired as I was, I agreed, and we decided we'd head out shortly after 10:00pm.

Until then, I needed to unwind. I charged my phone, checked my email multiple times for any update from the airlines, and was horrified to learn that my flights from Chania to Santorini and from Santorini to Athens were still unconfirmed. What's taking so long? I wasn't sure what to do, so naturally I called my mom and talked to her for a bit. She could always talk me out of a panic, which she once again managed to do despite being thousands of miles away.

"Don't worry, sometimes it takes a few days for ours to go through when we book flights, too. Don't let it ruin the fun few days you've got ahead of you. You're going to have a blast!"

Whatever you say. I poured a glass of wine and let the issue slip from my mind.

I sat on my balcony for a long while, enjoying the salad I'd prepared to have with my wine. It felt like I was in a movie, with the city beneath me and the Aegean in the distance. I spent an hour or so writing, editing and uploading my photos, and simply absorbing the view. When I finished eating, I washed my bowl and relocated to the kitchen with Marilena, Dimitria, and Lena. We all shared the baklava (which was absolutely fantastic) and the lemon pudding as I told them all about my day. I loved talking with the three of them. They were all so interesting in their own ways, and I wished we were all traveling together so I wouldn't have to say goodbye to them in the morning. I asked them about their flat, how they came up with the idea to paint the kitchen so vibrantly, what made them put the red light bulbs in all of the lights, etc. and they seemed very happy that I liked it so much. Marilena had spent some time studying art, and was passionate about bold, bright colors and their effects on human spirit. Even her sense of fashion screamed artsy and I couldn't help but wonder if I'd be able to pull off similar outfits back in the United States. Then culture took over the conversation (as usual), and we got to the topic of naming order in Greece. Women are typically named after their grandmothers (either their mother or father's mother, depending on whether they are the first or second daughter), and sons after their fathers' father. I told them the only significance in my name was that my grandmother, mother, and I all shared the same middle name. As I told them, it didn't sound quite as special as carrying on the first name of a grandparent. But then I was met with a round of, "Aww, so sweet!" and couldn't help but smile.

After spending a little while longer at the flat, Marilena, Lena, and I went back out into the city. They'd told me that there were "street bazaars" that popped up from time to time, and Marilena had noticed one earlier that day and wanted to show it to us. It turned out to be mounds of junk — old shoes, broken equipment, other random bits people had salvaged — organized on blankets in the small alleyways between buildings. The three of us stayed close together, as it definitely felt like something I wouldn't have sought out (or felt safe walking through, for that matter) on my own.

Afterwards, we found a small, red and white-checkered diner with a classic American diner feel. We ordered red wine, fried mushrooms, a sort of carrot falafel with tzatziki sauce, and home-style potatoes with a tomato/yogurt dip (a true feast for three vegetarians out on the town). When the food came, the waiter also brought over fresh pita bread. We talked a bit more, and absolutely devoured the food. Despite having been vegetarian for some time, I had never had such incredible, greasy food.

Lena had to return to the flat as she worked the next day, so when we'd finished at the diner Marilena led me to her favorite bar, *Pakav*. It wasn't far and were there in no time. Pakav was a loud rock 'n roll bar that was 'self-service'. No waiters came to the tables; everything had to be ordered at the bar. Marilena and I tried several different wines and beers, and lost track of time as the night went on. At one point disappeared, returning after a few moments with a shot of clear liquid.

"I'm not a huge fan of tequila..." I reasoned.

"Not tequila – ouzo!" she exclaimed as she clinked her glass with mine, downing it in one smooth motion. Her face showed no sign of struggle. I tried to take mine as smoothly but felt certain my face looked as it would if I'd stepped on a nail. *That is the worst thing I have ever tasted*, I thought, *at least ten times worse than tequila!*

The rest of the night was a blur. Despite my offer, Marilena refused to let me pay for our drinks at Pakav. We walked the short way back to the flat, laughing the entire way about heaven knows what, and finally returned home around 2:00 in the morning. It had been such a fun evening – such a fun entire day – and I couldn't believe my time in Thessaloniki was already almost over. All I could manage before crawling into bed was to wash my face and brush my teeth, and I slipped into a deep sleep as soon as my head it the pillow.

. . . . .

I was very surprised when I woke up the next morning feeling completely fine. It took me a few minutes to remember the events of the previous day, but even as I stood up to get ready, there wasn't even so much as a dull headache. Then I remembered all of the deliciously greasy vegetarian food we'd had at the diner and was glad we'd thought to order food with our drinks. I had far too busy of a day ahead of me to be tending to a hangover. I was going to Chania.

I started the morning as I had the day before, in search of a bakery and fresh Spanikopita. It had become my favorite food since coming to Greece, and I couldn't wait to try making it at home. I took the last of my apples from the fruit stand the day before and headed out. It was roughly 7:00am and my flight would be taking off at 10:30am. I had plenty of time to find the bakery, a coffee, pack my bag, and still get to the bus station by 9:00am. My hosts had convinced me that the airport was only thirty minutes from the bus stop, and it was so small that I really didn't need to be there two hours early. This went against my "two-hour early rule," but I trusted them. I would rather spend more time in Thessaloniki, even if it was only an extra hour.

On my way down the street, I saw another fruit stand. Having just eaten my apple, I thought it might be a good idea to get another to take with me for the day. As I approached, the man behind the register smiled and nodded to me.

"Kaliméra!"

I responded with my best "kaliméra," and the man instantly

started talking to me in English. *Was it my accent? Can he tell I'm not from here?*

As I picked over the apples, he asked what I was doing in Thessaloniki. I lied and said I was visiting my cousins. He asked me what part of America I was from – I told him Ohio – and he went on about how he was originally from Connecticut. His family, on the other hand, was originally from Greece, but his parents had emigrated to the United States before he was born. He grew up loving the American culture but had to move back to Greece to help his family with their business. That endeavor had since fizzled out, so now he was working at the fruit stand, dealing with Greek farmers and meeting people from all over the world. It was an interesting conversation – who would've thought, another American right there in Thessaloniki! – but I had to get back and pack my things in time to make the 9:00am bus. The man pointed me in the direction of his favorite bakery, which I found a few minutes later. Fresh Spanikopita had just come out of the oven, and I happily ordered one with my "point-and-say-please" method.

When I got back to the flat, I packed everything into my carry-on (now roomier having given Marilena and Dimitria the taffy) and made sure my purse was organized. Then I took a picture with my hosts, hugged them (and Lena) goodbye, and made my way to the bus stop. Marilena had reviewed the directions with me several times: I was to take Dragoumi all the way to Mitropoleos (a ten to fifteen-minute walk) and buy my ticket at the small booth I would see there.

"You can't miss it. The booth is right next to the café called Todaylicious."

After a final round of good-byes, I was on my way. I found the ticket booth with ease and purchased my €2,00 ticket to the airport. I watched as different busses passed by, some nearly bursting, there were so many people on board. The bus for the airport came shortly after 9:00am, and I watched as the doors opened and people actually fell out. It was too crowded. Some of the people waiting with me at the bus stop even made a move as if they were going to board, but seeing how full it was, they stayed on the sidewalk. Once again I found myself thinking, *I don't know what to do…* then, *what if all of the busses are that full?* Since I'd missed the 9:00am bus, I went back to the booth and asked when the next one would come.

"Fifteen minutes."

I felt my heartbeat start to quicken and wondered how I managed to have such bad luck. I would now have less than an hour in the airport, so I was a mixture of nervous and upset, but still excited to be going to Chania. I stopped into Todaylicious to kill some time and ended up buying a warm Kalouri. I thanked the woman at the counter, took my second pastry of the day, and headed back outside to the bus stop. It arrived ten minutes later, and I made my way on board.

I was so relieved to have found a spot on the correct bus. Once the doors pulled shut, I was squeezed through the cluster of standing individuals, feeling very uncomfortable with how crowded the bus was. It didn't seem to bother some of the people around me: they stood, headphones on, hand on a ceiling bar for balance. Others – like me – were looking around nervously, concerned about the amount of people packed like sardines on the bus. I hoped the airport was close and wouldn't make many more stops on the way. But it continued: each time it pulled up to another stop, there were moans as more people tried to fit on board, suitcases in hand. At some point, I was sandwiched between two large suitcases in the aisle, with three people squeezed into the two-person benches on either side of me. It was miserable. I wondered if this was normal for a Monday morning in Thessaloniki.

When the bus finally did pull up to the airport, everybody spilled out and headed on their way. I heard a woman shouting up ahead of the crowd and was able to make out the clear warning:

"Everyone check your pockets! This man's wallet was stolen!"

I watched as a man in a brown corduroy coat returned to the bus, double-checking his pockets. The woman who'd shouted was with him, and I saw another couple join them a few moments later. A man in a leather coat also turned around and headed back to the bus, hands patting the outside of his jacket. They all had suitcases with them, and I couldn't help but think, that really stinks! I couldn't imagine anything being stolen, let alone while traveling. I only had about forty-five minutes until my departure, so I turned and started walking towards the airport. Out of nowhere, an uneasy feeling started to set in about the woman's warning. How did the man not notice he was being robbed? Are pickpockets really that good? I stopped and looked down at my purse, a black and white Vera Bradley messenger bag I'd found at TJ Maxx a few months earlier. I'd kept it zipped and securely tucked under my arm for most of my trip (especially on the train from Braunschweig to Bielefeld and whenever I was in a crowd), but I couldn't help but think, *What if....?*

I almost didn't even check. Part of me wanted to believe I was just being paranoid about the possibility of someone having targeted me, but part of me needed to be sure. On closer look, the zipper wasn't completely shut. I yanked it open and shuffled my things around: notebook, apple, ticket, charger, phone, passport. It wasn't there. I feverishly began checking the other pockets, thinking maybe I'd shoved it in somewhere other than the main pocket after buying my Kalouri from café. But it was nowhere to be found. I felt my breathing get short and heart rate soar.

My wallet was gone.

10

When I was six years old, I fell through the ice.

I had been out ice skating with my family on a lake near our house. While my siblings and cousins were enjoying their hockey game, I started to get too cold and wanted to go home. My dad told me to skate back to shore and wait for him at the small pagoda there, which I did without hesitation. On the way, I unknowingly skated over a thin spot. I remember hearing the ice crack beneath me before plunging into the frigid water. It was the most terrifying experience of my life; even as I tried to pull myself out, the ice around the hole gave way. I screamed for my dad. There was a brief moment – submerged up to my neck in the icy cold water, weighed down by my brother's hand-me-down hockey skates – that I couldn't breathe from the shock. I was nearly paralyzed with fear.

It was the closest I had ever come to feeling as I did in that moment. Everything was gone: my credit cards, my driver's license, the €260 I'd taken out of the atm the day before. *How am I going to buy my bus ticket? What will I do for food? How am I going to make it another six days without any money?* My heart was pounding, and I felt I might be sick. *Do I get on the plane? Do I go back to Marilena's? What do I do?*

I ran back to the bus and joined the small group of people gathered outside. They all undoubtedly read the look of panic on my face, and asked if my wallet was gone, too. I nodded, and the bus driver shook his head.

"I'm sorry, miss," he said in a thick Greek accent, "there isn't much we can do. This isn't the first time something like this has happened."

The man in the corduroy jacket shook his head in disappointment, then turned and started walking towards the airport. The others followed. I was frozen on the spot, unsure of what to do. The bus driver told me to go to the police at the airport and tell them what happened: maybe they could help me in some way.

The bus pulled away and I looked down at my phone: 9:50am, just forty minutes until departure. I hurried inside of the airport and felt tears starting to form in my eyes. *This has to be a nightmare. I'm going to wake up back in the flat in a few minutes and start the day over. Come on Sam, wake up.* Unfortunately, I wasn't sleeping. I ran into the bathroom and dumped my purse onto the counter, reviewing its contents. My wallet was nowhere to be found: the only money I had were a few coins totaling €0,20. Thinking maybe I had shoved my wallet into my carry-on, I checked the front pockets. Then I unzipped the main compartment and dug through my clothes. Nothing. I looked up at myself in the mirror. My face was red and splotchy, burning from nerves and emotion. How could I let this happen? Without thinking, I called my mom. Frantically. She seemed sleepy when she answered, but I was too upset to consider the time difference. Between sobs and giant gasps of air, I told her what had happened. She told me to calm down and asked me to repeat myself. I could barely get the words out the second time before I heard her concerned words.

"Ok," she said slowly in her best 'I'm-panicking-but-going-to-try-and-solve-this' mom voice. "Are you sure you didn't misplace it? You're sure it's not in your bag?"

No, mom. Believe me I've torn through everything. "Yes, I dumped everything out. I'm sure."

"Is there anyone there who can help you? Does anyone speak English?"

I explained to her that I hadn't talked to anyone because I didn't know what to do first. I didn't know if anyone spoke English. I didn't know who you talked to in a situation like that. This was not a situation I'd ever been in before, and definitely one I never planned to be in again.

"Ok try to calm down. Take a drink of water if you can. Then find someone who works there and tell them what happened. I'm sure there's someone there who can help. There's not much I can do from here though, I'm sorry. Are you ok? Are you going to be ok?"

I felt like sobbing and wanted to tell her that no, I certainly was not ok. I was in a foreign country all by myself with no money and no credit cards. Someone in Greece had truly made out like a bandit that morning. Because they *were!* I felt paralyzed with panic, more scared than I'd been in years, and doubted if I should even still get on my plane. I lied.

"Yeah, I'll be ok."

She told me to keep her posted and we hung up. I couldn't waste any more time. I needed to find help, figure out what I should do, and possibly still get on the plane. I went back to the front lobby and found a concierge. Hoping she spoke English, I told her that my wallet had been stolen, but I had a flight leaving in less than an hour, and did I need to find the police, and what should I do, and could I still get on the plane. She looked at me with concern as I rambled and put her hand on my shoulder.

"Sweetheart, wait, one thing at a time! What happened?"

I could barely focus on the words coming out of my mouth as I told her what had happened. She asked if I still had my passport, and I handed it to her. She smiled and said I at least had that going for me – I would be in much worse trouble if that had been stolen as well. It was the smallest of comforts to me given the situation. She helped me to print off my boarding pass, then escorted me to the airport police. A tall man with dark hair introduced himself as Max and ushered me into a small office. He pointed at a chair and told me to sit down. By that point, I knew that I was visibly shaking, terrified. He asked me to talk him through what had happened that morning. It didn't take long for me to start crying once I started talking, this time the words sinking in as I went on. The officer's expression grew more and more concerned as he listened. I had no money, I was alone, I was in a country where I didn't speak the language, and I was flying to a place where I was Couchsurfing. I half expected him to give me a, "You should know better" look when I mentioned the Couchsurfing, but instead he straightened up a bit and smiled.

"Oh, that's very fun. I've hosted Couchsurfers before!"

He tried to lighten the mood by asking me about my experience so far (before that awful morning), keeping the conversation upbeat while he set about making phone calls and faxing documents. Apparently, he'd been hosting in Thessaloniki for a few years, which he did primarily to help improve his English. Meeting people from other countries was just a bonus.

He showed me how to dial their special phone for international calls and told me that I should start canceling my credit cards. He would make some phone calls for me and see what he could do. Then he asked me if I knew my next host's phone number. I gave him Yiannis' phone number (which had been saved in WhatsApp), and he called him to explain the situation. Max started speaking rapidly in Greek and I set about finding phone numbers for my cards. I looked them up on my smartphone and dialed them one by one, canceling the few I had. *Oh, I hope that whoever stole my wallet hasn't made any purchases yet!* When I spoke with the customer service representative for my first credit card, they offered to send me a replacement card. But the small amount of hope this gave me quickly faded as they told me it would take roughly a week for the new card to reach me. By then, I would already be back to the United States (fingers crossed), so I would have to wait until I was home to access any of my money. Next, I called my bank and canceled my debit card. Unlike the credit card company, they informed me that I did have a few options to get a new card as soon as possible, in less than a week. The woman on the phone explained that MasterCard had a mint in Germany, so they would be able to send a replacement to me – even in Europe – in just a few days. She told me to call back when

I was at my next location (I'd briefly explained I was traveling and didn't have the exact address yet) and they would send me the new card within three days. She even offered to give me a phone call when it arrived to the UPS store in Chania. I felt slightly better.

When Max hung up with Yiannis, he said that I should reach out to my family and see if there was any way they could send me money through something called 'Western Union'. I had never heard of it before. He explained that it was an international money transfer service, and people could send me money to be picked up as cash at any Western Union location. Apparently Yiannis had told him that there was one near his house in Chania, and he would be happy to take me when I arrived. I felt a flood of relief as he went on, explaining my options. I thanked him for his help and wished I had something to give him.

"Don't worry; it's my job. It's why I love what I do."

I picked up the police phone and dialed my mother again. I knew she was worried and wondered what I'd been thinking when I called her from the bathroom. It was 3:00 in the morning there - there was nothing she could do! At least now there were options, and the amazing possibility of this "Western Union". The phone only rang once, and she answered. I told her I was at the police station, I had my boarding pass, my credit cards were canceled, and the policeman had contacted Yiannis. There was a plan in motion. If she could send me money, I could have it that evening (next day at the latest). And what's more, in just a few days my bank would have a new card delivered to me in Chania. She sounded as relieved as I felt, and I almost started crying again from all of the stress and emotions I'd gone through in such a short period of time. She asked me how much I needed, and said she'd find a Western Union as soon as possible. I looked up to see Max tapping on his watch and realized that I had only fifteen minutes until my flight. I said goodbye to my mom, told her I loved her and would call her later, and headed off to my gate. I thanked Max again for all of his help, and he wished me good luck as I handed over my passport and boarding pass. It had been the most eventful thirty minutes of my life.

I made my way onto the plane and was off to Chania.

. . . . .

I sat in my seat, watching the people around me stow their things and get situated for the flight. There was an odd sense of calm; it felt like nothing had just happened and I was simply on another plane, taking off as usual. Or perhaps it was the feeling that by this point, things were now far beyond my control. It would do me no good to spend any time worrying. A few minutes after everyone was settled, the flight attendants walked down the aisles, preparing for takeoff.

"Caramello?"

She handed me the small basket of hard candies, wrapped in their blue and silver foils. I took a few and put them in my purse. When I zipped it closed, the image of a hand reaching in and pulling out my wallet popped into my mind. Had it been on the bus? At the bus stop? I pulled my purse closer to my body, feeling more protective of it now that my wallet had been stolen. *At least I have my passport.*

The plane taxied to the runway and took off. The calm left me as the plane pushed higher, gaining speed. My stomach dropped as it always did during takeoff, which normally was a feeling I loved. It was a feeling of excitement and anticipation of the impending adventure. This time, however, it was different. It was the feeling in the pit of my stomach that normally told me I'd just done something very wrong. It was how I felt when I'd gotten into my first fender bender; the same feeling as when I'd gotten my first D on a test in college or that one time I learned I'd have to pay $1800 for a car repair. It was a feeling of absolute dread, uncertainty, and regret. I didn't know Yiannis beyond the few conversations we'd had on WhatsApp and the short conversation he'd had with Officer Max at the airport (which was all in Greek – how did I know I could trust what they were saying?). *How would he know I'd arrived at the bus stop by his house? Wait, how am I going to take the bus from the airport? I have no money for a ticket! Will I be able to message him to come get me at the airport?*

I wished I'd thought of that back in Thessaloniki; maybe Officer Max could have asked him to meet me at the airport instead of at the bus stop. To distract myself, I pulled out my notebook and started writing. The flight was around an hour and twenty minutes, and as much as I would've liked to sleep through it, I knew waking up to the situation would be awful. It was better to put off the arrival as long as possible. It would be a rush once we landed to find Wi-Fi and contact Yiannis about the bus ticket.

I felt calmer as I wrote and thoroughly enjoyed the little Terkelin pastry they handed out halfway through the flight. But despite these distractions, the landing still came far too quickly. We arrived to the tiny airport in Chania around noon, and a shuttle came to cart us across the tarmac. My stomach growled. It had been a few hours since my Spanikopita and the Kalouri, and any remaining energy had undoubtedly been burned through the stress of the morning. I wondered if the woman sitting next to me on the shuttle could hear my stomach begging for food.

We pulled up to the entryway and soon dispersed throughout the airport. I watched as some people were greeted with smiles and hugs from family members, some smoothly snatched their luggage from the baggage claim and continued down another hallway, and the rest lingered around likely waiting for lost luggage or someone to pick them up. I pulled up the Settings app on my phone and tried to connect to the Wi-Fi. Not currently available. It was the airport's own Wi-Fi network – aptly named, "Chania International Airport 'Ioannis Daskalogiannis' (CHQ)" – and yet it wasn't working. *Maybe it's because I'm too far from the main hub. Maybe I need to find the main lobby.*

I went down a flight of stairs and entered into a giant open area with a few rows of chairs, a small café, a service desk, and the exit to the outside world. There were very few people there: a few still trickling out from the flight I'd just been on and the employees at the café. No one was even at the service desk. I looked around, trying to locate anyone who might be able to help me, but a teenager at the café was my only option. I watched her for a few minutes, debating. She popped a bubble and gazed down at her phone, twirling her long, curly hair with her thickly-polished fingers. I had nothing to lose. I walked over to her and gave her my best Kaló apógevma – *good afternoon!* She didn't look up from her phone. I tried again.

"Excuse me, kaló apógevma!"

I had her attention. I explained that I needed to contact someone about picking me up at the airport instead of a bus stop, but the Wi-Fi wasn't working. Did she have any insight for the network? If nothing else, could I use the café's phone to call Yiannis? I tried to create a sense of urgency, but it was like talking to a brick wall. The girl stared at me, chewing her gum, and her fingers were now motionless, just holding on to the piece of hair she'd been twirling moments earlier. My heart sank as she started shaking her head.

"So sorry, I – no English."

I didn't know what to do; I'd never experienced a language barrier that I couldn't overcome before, and I didn't know if she was serious or if she just didn't want to deal with me. I pointed to my phone and showed her the "Not Currently Available" message the Wi-Fi was displaying. She shrugged and shook her head a second time. *You have got to be kidding me.*

I turned around, walked over to sit down in one of the chairs, and tried to connect to the Wi-Fi again. *Not currently available.* Wonderful. The few other employees I saw were a janitor, a small group of unapproachable flight attendants on their way out, and a woman working at a phone kiosk. To my horror, none of them spoke English. *This is an airport. Someone has to have a phone that I can use to call Yiannis!* Despite my efforts, no one was willing to help me. I was rejected by three different employees when I finally decided to ask the janitor, who turned out to be the only one remotely helpful. He walked with me over to the service desk and dialed a number on the phone. He covered the receiver and told me he was checking with the IT person to see what the issue is. Then someone started talking on the other end and they exchanged a few more words in Greek. When he hung up, he looked at me and sighed.

"Sorry, miss. The Wi-Fi is not functioning today. There is some problem with it, but they are trying to fix it."

I couldn't believe it. I had never had much luck with technology, but this was just ridiculous. When I got my first laptop in eighth grade, my parents didn't have wireless internet in our house. Instead, I had to shove my laptop into one corner of my bedroom and connect to an open network that was incredibly undependable. It cut in and out depending on the breeze, but it worked until I could have an internet cord wired into my bedroom. Then there was that entire semester my junior year of college when my laptop updated and with it, all of the firewall settings. It kicked me off of my home network and refused to recognize it when I searched, so I spent most of my evenings – for an entire semester – in the media center. I was no stranger to feeling frustrated with internet connectivity. But to be stranded in an airport in a foreign country on the very day when the free Wi-Fi network decided to stop working was more than just bad luck. It was a disaster.

I decided to start walking around the airport in hopes of finding a better signal for the Wi-Fi. I managed to connect at one point and sent a message to Yiannis: *Hi Yiannis! I am at the Chania airport, but I realized I have no money for a bus ticket. I am so sorry to inconvenience you, but is it possible for you to come pick me up?*

It seemed far too cheery for how I actually felt, but to properly convey my mentality through a message would have involved much more profanity and I wanted to make a good impression on my host. I stayed in the exact spot I had service (standing in the middle of the concourse, bag in hand) but a few moments after the message sent, my phone disconnected. I continued walking.

Nearly forty-five minutes went by until I was able to connect again and saw that I had received a message from Yiannis: *Sam! I am sorry to hear of your situation, are you ok? Of course I can come, I need to pick up my son from a friend's house but will be there afterwards. Please stay there until I arrive.*

I felt such a strong sense of relief flood through me that I almost started crying again. *He was coming*, I thought, feeling a smile on my face for the first time in hours. *Yiannis is coming and I will be safe.* While I had service, I decided it was time to share the state of things on Facebook, as most of my friends and family had asked that I keep them posted on things during my trip. Little did they know this would be coming. Maybe one of them would have some words of wisdom or advice to comfort me.

Wallet stolen at the bus station (or maybe on the bus?), unconfirmed flights because the bank closed international use of my cards, no money whatsoever, and shotty Wi-Fi here at the airport. Praying for the best... #AtLeastIHaveMyPassport

Yiannis finally arrived nearly an hour later, and I hugged him the moment he walked into the airport. The first thing I noticed was that he smelled like my dad. And while I highly doubted that any store in the entire country carried Old Spice, it was close enough. He took a step back after a moment and put his hands on my shoulders, looking me directly in the eyes. His were clear as crystal, with slight blue and green tints, lines forming in the corners. They were kind eyes. They were dad eyes.

"Are you ok? Are you hurt? Sam how did this happen?"

Yiannis was wearing a red and blue plaid button-down shirt tucked into blue jeans. He was fairly tall (from what I understood so far of Greek men) and was mostly bald with a five o'clock shadow. He looked thoroughly concerned and asked if I had my things. I nodded, lifting up the carry-on slung over my right arm and patting my very secure purse.

"This is it?" he asked, taking the bag from me.

I nodded. He laughed and shook his head as we walked out to his car, which was still running in the parking lot. There were two kids in the back seat, who Yiannis introduced to me as Milos (his seven-year-old son) and Elektra (Milos' friend). He explained that because of his business, he did not have much time to spend with his son. The brewery kept him very busy, from keeping everything running smoothly with the equipment and his team to visiting local restaurants and making sure his taps were fresh and in proper working order. He even said he'd be happy to show me his brewery at some point if I'd like, and I could give him an American's opinion on Greek beer. I had no point of reference; I'd never had Greek beer before.

Milos and Elektra were being shy in the back seat, so Yiannis tried to engage them in conversation with me. I picked up a few words: Ameriki (America), Thessaloniki, and Aerodrómio (airport), and sorted out that he was telling them why I was visiting. He must have told them that I was robbed, because at one point Milos got very animated and gasped.

We drove for about fifteen minutes and my stomach let out a loud growl. It was now nearly 4:00pm and I hadn't eaten anything since I was at the bus stop that morning. Yiannis told me that we would be going to dinner with Milos and Elektra and asked me if I liked pizza. Truthfully, I didn't: I had never been much of a pizza person but at that moment I might've even considered eating meat if it had been the only food available. Pizza would be fantastic. He turned and told the kids *Pítsa!* and they both started shrieking with delight. Not too long after, we pulled up to a small, gray stone restaurant with a large sign over the doorway, *Pizza Gustosa*. It was a very open restaurant, with an entryway so large there weren't even doors. Large white tables were set up both inside and outside, surrounded by blue-backed chairs with spindly legs. The delicious scent of *Pítsa* wafted from within.

We walked inside and who I could only assume to be the owner rushed over to Yiannis, letting out a big, hearty laugh along with something in Greek. He and Yiannis shook hands and embraced each other, and he motioned to a table in the very front of the restaurant. I sat down across from Milos and Elektra and looked over the menu. Everything looked phenomenal.

Yiannis and the owner spoke for several minutes near the bar while I did my best to entertain the kids. Having just spent the last several hours feeling like a child myself, it was easy to do. I spoke simple words in English, using big hand gestures to convey what I was trying to communicate. From the few words we exchanged, I got that Elektra really liked my earrings and Milos played soccer. For not having any way to really understand each other or communicate verbally, the kids and I got along just fine. Eventually the two of them started dancing around the table, giggling like only small children can. I envied their simple happiness. I would've given anything to go back to that morning and at least separate my cash from my credit cards or *something*. There had to be something I could've done differently that would have prevented the entire situation: something that would've allowed me to feel as happy and carefree as the two children now dancing around the table. Maybe I would have even joined them.

A few moments later, Yiannis returned with two large glasses of perfectly foamy, golden beer. He smiled and handed one to me as he sat down. Then he picked his up by the handle and clinked it against mine.

"Stin iyia mas!" He said. "Or Yiamas! It means, 'To our health!'"

"Yiamas!" I responded, smiling. Another word to add to my list.

Yiannis took a long drink of his beer and looked at me, expectantly. I took a swig. It was crisp, easy to drink, and had a sweet, light flavor to it. Being a wine person who typically only chose to drink beers like Michelob Ultra (not having much experience at all with craft beer), I was impressed.

"This is amazing." I told him honestly.

He seemed thrilled that I liked the beer. He told me it was his flagship brew: Χαρμα ('Charma') Lager. We talked and drank, eventually looking over the menu and deciding what pizza to get. We landed on one with olives, feta, mushrooms, tomatoes, olive oil, and peppers (for me and Elektra), and one for 'the boys' with green peppers, olives, and ham. While the pizza was being made, the owner brought us bread baskets generously filled with fresh, hot breadsticks and pieces of kristini like that I'd had in Thessaloniki. It tasted better than any of the breadsticks I'd ever had in America, especially with the accompanying olive paste and tomato sauce. And when Yiannis returned with the pizza, I learned that I never gave Greece enough credit for its food: it was incredible. We had another round of beers, I devoured three slices of pizza along with the breadsticks, and we sat talking and watching the kids jump around for another hour or so. I was a fan of Pizza Gustoso.

Afterwards, the kids wanted dessert, so we stopped at a small shop on the way home. Yiannis bought them ice cream and ordered black coffees for us, at which point I was asked if I wanted cream and sugar. I'd heard Yiannis use the expression Né! a few times in conversation, so based on context I figured that it was the Greek word for 'No'. I took a leap of faith and gave it as a confident response.

"You do want cream and sugar?" Yiannis asked. I shook my

head.

"Oh – I meant no."

From then on, I didn't try to use words until I had solid proof that I knew the definition. As it turned out, 'Né' actually meant 'Yes', or 'Sure' in Greek. Of course their 'yes' sounds like our 'no' – that's not confusing at all. Yiannis said something in Greek to the woman behind the counter (about me, I was sure – hearing 'Ameriki' was about all I needed to understand) and the two of them laughed. He smiled and handed me my coffee. The four of us left shortly afterwards and were on our way.

We dropped Elektra off first, and I let Yiannis and Milos have some father-son conversation (without interrupting) before he was dropped off as well. Soon it was just me and Yiannis in the car, making our way through the dark streets of Chania. He asked me to tell him once more about the morning and if there were any other issues the situation had caused. I told him yes, I had no way to get back to Athens because my unconfirmed flights got canceled when I canceled my credit cards. Then he asked if I had gotten ahold of my parents. Again, I told him yes – my mom would be going to Western Union that day. He said given the late hour (it was now nearing 8:30pm), we would have to wait until tomorrow when the Western Union in Chania reopened. In the meantime, he would give me the Wi-Fi password at his place and I could see what to do about the Chania – Santorini – Athens situation. He even said that if the UPS package containing my new debit card did not arrive from Germany in the proper time frame, I could stay an extra day or so if I needed. I thanked him – endlessly – for all of his help to that point and for being so willing to continue to help me. He told me the Χαρμα (Charma) had gotten to my head.

Yiannis was now the closest thing I had to a parent in Greece.

He had saved me from a truly awful situation: of being a lost foreigner, of being hungry, of being terrified, of not having a roof over my head. He could have easily left me in that airport when I couldn't buy the bus ticket to get to him, but he came to pick me up regardless. *And I'm Couchsurfing, of all things! I'm not even paying him to be such an incredible host!* It may have been a terrible morning, but whether it was in fact the Χαρμα, or the fact that I now had solid food in my stomach, or just the fact that I felt safe and taken care of, it was turning out to be an OK day. There were far worse ways things could have gone.

When we arrived 'home', Yiannis parked in the street in front of a large, white stone building. It seemed to stretch for miles in either direction, full of flats rising several stories high. He grabbed my bag and led me through a little gate, then up a stairway between two sections of the building. The stairs twisted around to a little wooden porch, and Yiannis held open a heavy, castle-style wooden door.

"Welcome to home."

I had been rather nervous about my second Couchsurfing home after experiencing the chaos of Olivier's flat. But Yiannis' was something entirely different: a beautiful main room (with actual bookshelves!) that doubled as an office and a dining room, a sunken living room with two large, clean, comfy couches, and display cases of trinkets standing along the walls. He ushered me off to a hallway on the right, and I saw a small kitchen with beautiful wooden cupboards, a matching wooden table and chairs, and the entryway out to the back of the porch. Down the hallway was a closed door ("That's my bedroom," Yiannis pointed out), a small closet, and the bedroom from the Couchsurfing website. It was exactly as I was expecting, right down to the Donald Duck books on the desk. The bed looked so clean and inviting. *Ok, thanks for everything. Can I just go to sleep now?*

Finally, at the end of the hallway was the bathroom (I was delighted to see a shower curtain and a proper shower head). I was elated to be in such a welcoming home and felt embarrassed that I had no money to pay Yiannis back for everything. He set my bag down just inside my bedroom door and returned moments later with a small slip of paper. It was the Wi-Fi password, and he told me I could spend some time contacting my family if I needed. Then he would take me for a short walk around Chania and we could call it a night. I thanked him (again) and set about connecting to the network.

The post I'd shared at the airport was now flooded with comments. Some mentioned Western Union, Olivier commented with ferry schedules and pricing, one of Papa's brothers tried to shed positive light on things by saying it would make the journey 'more interesting when you look back on it' (I'd always loved his optimism), and I had several people say they would pray for me. I called my mother again now that it was a more respectable hour back home, and she was as thankful as I was that Yiannis had turned out to be such an amazing host. She said she was on her way to the Western Union and would let me know as soon as she was able to transfer money to me. I promised to keep her posted as I called and emailed back and forth with my bank. (She had mentioned asking if they could send money from my account, which I thought was a great idea. It was the first email I sent once I was connected to Wi-Fi.) We talked a bit more, and then agreed that regardless of everything, I still needed to try and enjoy Chania as much as I possibly could.

Once I'd uploaded some photos, replied to a few friends who

said they, too would try to wire money to me, and managed to freshen up, Yiannis and I headed out. By that point, it was rather dark outside, but the city was alive and the stars were bright. It wasn't long until we were at the Venetian Harbor, where restaurants were bursting with people and the entire harbor was lit up with lanterns. It was nothing short of remarkable. As we walked along, he pointed out that many of the restaurants there carried his beer, so he'd formed relationships with most of the owners. They came out one by one, as if Yiannis was a beacon that drew them out of their restaurants. I laughed and asked him if there was anyone in Chania that he didn't know. He just smiled and shrugged.

"It's easier to meet people when you're the one with the beer."

We stopped at a place called το μαύρο πρόβατο ("To Mávro Próvato", *the Black Sheep*) and sat at a table outside. Yiannis went inside and brought out a few of his beers. We sat for what felt like hours, talking about everything from the beer making process and why he doesn't sell his beer in the United States to what brought me to Greece in the first place and some of the things I should see during my time in Chania. At one point, the owner came out to greet Yiannis and taught me how to say the name of his restaurant ("So now you can make fun of your colleagues and call them "To Mávro Próvato" when they do not fit in!") He and Yiannis started a conversation about taxes – in English, because they still pulled me into it every now and then – but it quickly developed into a fully Greek exchange that left me looking around the city.

Chania at night was beautiful. The Venetian Harbor, with all of its sparkling restaurants and gorgeous view of the Aegean, was understandably one of the top tourist sights on Crete. Each building had a different, brightly-colored awning, and the music – the music was absolutely phenomenal. I loved everything about Chania already – on day one – and if I'd still had my wallet, I would have even called it 'perfect'. Fortunately, I had an amazing host who was willing to show me around and help me until I once again had everything I needed and could continue on my way. I felt so fortunate. Even sitting there at To Mávro Próvato, still slightly uneasy about what would happen in the coming days and slightly buzzed from all the Charma, I felt like the luckiest person in the world. I was in a beautiful city, in a beautiful country, and there was so much more to be explored and discovered.

Yiamas! to that.

11

I had an email response from my bank the next morning. They were still working on processing the card from the mint in Germany but would not be able to send money from my account. There was some kind of security policy in play that prevented them from sending money unless someone was physically present in the branch to authorize the transaction. I felt my heart sink as I read the email a second time, not wanting to believe what I'd read. I had really been hoping there would have been a quick fix to the situation. This is not a great way to start the day.

I also had roughly a dozen missed messages from my mom, who had made it to Western Union. They started out full of excitement and as I read them, I could feel my mom's concern growing.

Ok, heading to Kroger now! There's a Western Union there and I'll send the money on my way out. Hold tight!

How much did you need again? There might be some kind of limit.

Sam, I'm not sure it's going to let me send the money to you today. It says there's some kind of issue with my credit card.

Ok – have to talk to Dad. The woman here told me I might have to use cash. I'll keep you posted.

The messages continued, and as I read them I felt tears once again forming in my eyes. I had cried more in the past two days than I had through college – exams included – and was not thrilled with this new round of bad news. I had really been hoping that Yiannis and I would have been able to go to Western Union that day, get the money, and I'd be all set for the rest of my trip. *An issue with her credit card? My parents are extremely responsible with finances...what the hell?*

The messages from my friends were similar:

SAAAAMMMMMM! I tried sending you money through WU but it said my form of payment couldn't be accepted. I'm sorry, I tried! Let me know if there's anything else I can do for you!

Hey Sam, tried wiring ya $50. It doesn't seem the system is accepting credit card information to transfer money. Is there some other way I could send you money?

Sooooo apparently Western Union won't take my credit card for wherever you are. I just used it last week to send my cousins birthday money, and it worked just fine for the US. Is it something with Greece?

I buried my face in my pillow. My friends were so kind, trying to send me money to make the rest of my trip a little easier, and for some reason it wasn't working. Did I do something to deserve this? Is this Karma for something? How could this possibly get worse? I Googled Western Union to see if I could find some kind of explanation, and it didn't take long to find the article. Apparently in Greece and other certain countries with struggling economies, credit and debit cards were not accepted. The country simply didn't have enough cash to hand out without solid money behind the transaction. *Only accepting cash at this time.* That explained it.

I took a screenshot and sent it to my parents and the friends who had messaged me. At the moment, it was only about 1:00am EST, so I didn't expect any responses right away. To my surprise, one came almost instantly.

Hey Sam. That's stupid, I'm sorry. Are you ok? Do you need anything? Seriously – anything? Call me.

It was from my friend Pat. Pat and I had been friends since the tenth grade. He went to my high school and occasionally sat at my lunch table. We'd gotten to know each other better when I started 'hanging out' with one of his friends. Naturally, the friendship I had with Pat long outlasted that relationship, and there we were – still friends – over seven years later. Pat was that responsible friend who always stepped in at a critical moment and helped his friends out of sticky situations. If a car broke down, someone needed money, a friend needed a ride (or even just a beer), or some other kind of issue came up, he was first in line to help. And more often than not, he was the only one who was dependable enough to actually pull through. I knew we'd be friends as soon as I met him; he was always genuinely kind and always asked how I was doing (even though he knew how I felt about high school – not my shining years). We'd kept in touch throughout college and had established the kind of friendship that was just as strong if we talked every two months as it was if we talked every single day. To see his response come back so quickly – and to know he would truly do anything he could to help me – was an enormous relief. Pat had helped me in tough situations in the past, and I hoped he'd be able to do the same now. I picked up my phone and called him.

We had a brief conversation about how my wallet had been stolen in the first place. He had me walk him through the events of the previous day, telling me to calm down when I started talking too fast or getting worked up over the reality of the situation.

"So…you're waiting on the money from your mom. And the card is coming from Germany soon?"

"Yes."

"Are they going to buy your flights back to Athens?"

It occurred to me that I hadn't told my parents about the canceled flights from Chania to Santorini and Santorini to Athens. I felt I had worried them too much with the entire situation, and as they were already sending me roughly $300 through Western Union there was no way I could ask them for flights as well. I told Pat all of this, and after a moment of silence he responded.

"I hate to break it to ya Sam, but if your bank is sending you a card and it's going to take around three days, you're not going to make it to Santorini. At least not on this trip."

Hearing Pat say it out loud made my heart sink. Santorini had been on my bucket list for years, and after spending so much time looking at pictures of the beautiful blue and white city, finding a host, and researching where to see the best views, I had really been looking forward to experiencing it. This realization was not how I wanted to start my morning. I talked to Pat a bit more, talking about any other possible options to make that trip possible. Could I have the card sent to Santorini and I could just pick it up when I get there? *No, Sam. Terrible idea. Think of what would happen if a host (who you'd never met, might I remind you) got a random American's debit card in the mail. Be smart*. And then came his magic words:

"Let me pay for your flight back to Athens."

"Pat, no – that's way too much. I couldn't ask –"

"You can pay me back later. You're not asking, I'm offering."

I had no other option. While I hated the thought of being so indebted to someone, I acknowledged that I was in a situation where I really didn't have a choice. I couldn't refuse such a generous offer, my only option so far. I had to let go of my "I'm completely independent and can manage everything myself" complex and just accept it. I was beyond thankful as we started discussing times and airlines, and he said as soon as I had my new card, he would book it.

I went into the kitchen, where Yiannis had set out a few things for breakfast: a package of Rusk (rough Triscuit-like crackers), a plate of sliced avocado, and a basket of oranges. I smeared some of the avocado onto the crackers and started peeling the orange. Yiannis joined me moments later, and I filled him in on the morning's news. We couldn't go to Western Union yet, but my mom was going to try again today. He stayed positive, repeating his earlier offer of letting me stay another few days if needed. Then we veered off topic and discussed what the day ahead would hold. He explained that there was a company in Greece – Safari Adventures – that operated Jeep excursions for tourists through different areas of Chania and its White Mountains. It was an eight- or nine-hour tour and went up through the town and surrounding mountains to explore different aspects of Cretan culture. He mentioned some of the stops it would make – a winery, a traditional Cretan restaurant for lunch, a shepherd's hut – and told me he'd been thinking about working with the company to add his brewery to the tour.

"So, the company invited me and my marketing person to go on this tour and see if it would be a good fit for my brewery," he said.

"That's a great idea," I said. "I'll be anxious to hear how it is!" I expected Yiannis to follow by telling me I'd be fending for myself that day. Maybe there's something in the fridge he'll let me have for lunch. Or maybe he's about to tell me we can meet up for dinner somewhere after the tour. His response was a laugh, and he shook his head, smiling.

"No Sam, I am not going on the tour. I can't – it goes through the mountains and my stomach does not do well. I will be sick if I go in the back of a Jeep, driving up those mountain paths. I'd like to send you instead." He looked at me, waiting for a reaction.

My mouth must have dropped open because he quickly continued by telling me that his marketing person, Mona, would be accompanying me. He thought we'd get along well: she spoke English fluently, had traveled quite a bit herself, and had just started working for him a few months earlier. Yiannis told me that we'd be leaving shortly, and that he would be at the brewery all day. Once the tour was over, Mona would message him and he'd come to pick me up. Everything was arranged, and the ticket was already in my name. I was speechless. Is he serious? This is going to be incredible! I had told him the night before that as a thank-you, I wanted to cook dinner for him, so I offered again to do so that evening. Yiannis nodded and said that he would take me to the supermarket after the tour. I could make dinner that night, try a bit of his homemade wine, and maybe the next day we could pick up my money from Western Union. I told Yiannis that I would pay him back for the tour and the groceries as soon as I had the money. As usual, he shook his head.

"You're doing me a favor; my stomach can't handle this rollercoaster of a tour. Just tell me if it's a fit for the brewery."

"Then let me pay you back for the groceries, at least."

"Sam don't worry about it. But hurry to get ready to go – the tour leaves at 8:45am."

I looked at the clock on the kitchen wall: 8:10. I hurried to finish my breakfast, then went to put on my jeans, a long-sleeved t-shirt, and my fleece. We were about to leave, but Yiannis told me it would be smart to bring my coat. Apparently as we rose higher and higher into the mountains, it would get much cooler than it was there in town. I didn't argue. I trusted my Greek dad.

By 8:25am, we were once again in his little car, zipping down the streets of Chania. It was such a beautiful city. The houses — mostly stone buildings with either individual residences or flats inside — rose four to five stories high and were painted various shades of white and brown. Most had fences or little gates in front (similar to Yiannis'), with various knick-knacks and decorations littered about the front lawns. The streets were similar to those in Athens and Thessaloniki, sprouting off from one another in different directions without any detectable pattern. However, Yiannis zipped along, turning sharply every few streets, and we eventually reached our destination.

We pulled into the parking lot of a small bakery. Who I assumed to be Mona had already arrived and walked over to greet us as soon as we parked. She stood a few inches taller than me, and I could tell she had a slender frame beneath her puffy white jacket. She smiled at me; her eyes and expression were that of a young woman but the strands of silver in her hair suggested otherwise. I noticed her blue jeans and tennis shoes and desperately hoped that we wouldn't be doing much walking up in the mountains. I looked down at my own feet. Converse. Why didn't I bring better walking shoes? The blisters from my first few days in Athens had almost healed, but the idea of spending a day walking – hiking, even – was not ideal.

"I'm so sorry to hear of your situation, Sam," Mona said thoughtfully. "Yiannis told me what happened at the airport. That must have been terrifying."

Is. It *is* terrifying. Still going on.

We talked with Mona for a few minutes before Yiannis said he had to be on his way. He handed me a €50 note and then pulled out another €20. The first was for the tour and the second was spending money if I needed anything until he picked me up that evening. I tried protesting, but he simply told me to have fun, told Mona to watch out for me, and went back to his car.

I felt like a preschooler who'd been left alone with their

teacher on the very first day of school. Yiannis' car disappeared around the corner, and Mona and I looked at each other, unsure. I had the sinking feeling that she'd rather be going on this expedition with Yiannis than with some Couchsurfing American girl she had never met. Regardless, I tried to make pleasant conversation with her until the Tour Jeep arrived. It pulled up slowly, painted black and white, with Jurassic Park-like writing painted along the sides: Safari Adventures. As soon as it arrived – at 8:45am sharp – a man jumped out of the front and came over to us. He introduced himself as Stelios, then had a brief conversation with Mona in Greek. She handed him her €50 note and instructed me to do the same. (I later found out that the tour actually cost around €90,00, but because Yiannis was a potential business partner with his brewery, we'd been given a discounted rate.) I handed it over and we each signed a waiver. *I'm signing away my safety in a foreign country where I have no money and will be spending the day with someone I've only known five minutes. In the mountains. In a* Jeep. *Smart.* Stelios led us to the back of Jeep and pulled opened a large door. We climbed aboard.

Two benches ran along the inside walls of the Jeep, facing each other. When we climbed in, I was surprised to see there were already three others in the back. Fortunately, everyone was fairly small-framed, so we had no problem finding room. Stelios slammed the door shut. Through the glass pane separating the back seating area from the front, we watched him take his place in the driver's seat. Another man – older, with light gray hair and wise features – was buckled in next to him in the front seat. He turned around to introduce himself as the Jeep lurched into motion.

"Seymour, nice to meet you ladies."

"Nice to meet you." Mona and I said in unison. She introduced herself, and I followed suit.

Soon everyone took a turn, and we were officially acquainted with our fellow travelers. Seymour's wife Linda — also older, white hair pulled into a neat bun at the base of her neck — was sitting across from Mona and me. Linda looked like she had money: small, fancy neck scarf, surprisingly dressy outfit for spending the afternoon in the mountains, and very dramatic sunglasses balanced on her petite nose. She explained that they were visitors from New York, and this was a trip they'd been looking forward to for quite some time. They had traveled all over the world and heard from a friend in Santorini that Chania was a 'must-visit'. So there they were, simply enjoying retirement. At the mention of Santorini, I remembered my conversation with Pat that morning. Inside, I fought the fresh wave of disappointment that I wouldn't get to see Santorini and tried not to let it ruin my mood. *Today is going to be a great day.*

Next to Linda was Lora, a busty woman with short brown hair and loud clothing. She was originally from the UK but had spent the last few years living in Crete, working in tourism with her partner Melissa. Melissa had also joined the tour and was sitting next to Lora. She excitedly chimed in that she, too, was from the UK but absolutely loved living on Crete because it was a "truly divine little place". I wondered if they'd ever been to Koutsouras or knew anything about the city where my great-great-grandfather's boat had taken off. I decided it wasn't the right time to ask.

We drove to the edge of town, where the buildings gave way to mandarin trees. The trees grew thicker and thicker, and soon even the air smelled like citrus. Stelios told us the exact amount that Chania exported annually, about the different recipes that locals made with them, and how they were very protective of their trees.

"Should anything happen to them," he cautioned, "a large part of Chania's economy would suffer."

We continued upwards into the mountains, making light conversation with each other about what else we'd seen on the island and our plans for the duration of our time there. As locals, Lora and Melissa were the chattiest. I quickly learned that their positions in tourism were heavily sales-focused. They had a 'give-you-more-information-than-you-want' approach to every topic. Seymour and his wife were from what part of New York? Lora and Melissa had been there once upon a time and shared every detail, from their cab driver's name to the color of the quilt on their hotel room bed. You'd walked around the Venetian Harbor? I received a mile-long list of must-see restaurants they'd been to, and they continued on with some story of how they'd once set up this one couple with a vacation package that included some kind of boat ride just outside the harbor. They chatted on. It was nice to have background noise while I looked out the window.

The Jeep powered along, and we noticed the mandarin trees beginning to look different. They transformed from being bushy and leafy, with trunks nearly buried under the fruit and foliage, to shorter and spindlier, somewhat akin to the Tree of Life. These new trees had far fewer leaves, and the trunks looked thick and twisted. We were told that we were entering the olive groves, where thousands upon thousands of trees grew (some of which had been growing for hundreds of years). Mona leaned over and told me that most people in Chania owned at least a few olive trees, and it was a sort of communal effort to keep the olive production alive and well.

"Even Yiannis owns a few hundred trees, I think around eight hundred?" I felt my eyes widen. *He owns a brewery* and *made his own wine* and *had eight hundred olive trees? Was there anything this man didn't do? Anything he couldn't do?* The Jeep tossed us from our seats and I snapped back to reality. We pulled on the seatbelts (or 'seatbelt' as it was one giant belt per bench) and steadied ourselves. I understood what Yiannis meant when he said it was a rollercoaster.

As we climbed higher, I expected the olive trees to disappear. Yet as we climbed ever higher, they just kept coming. It went on for at least another thirty minutes: the five of us in the back seat, bracing ourselves as if the Jeep would fly off-course any moment, everyone being jostled about as the road grew steeper and rougher. Stelios (seemingly unaffected) continued on about olive production.

"It starts with the employees out here – there, you can see some with their long broom-like tools – shaking the olives from the trees. Only the ones that are ready to be harvested will fall to the ground, and they put those tarps down around the trees to make for easy pick-up. Once they've collected the olives, they separate them. Not all olives can be eaten and not all olives can be used to make olive oil, you know!" He wagged his finger. I liked Stelios: he was animated and friendly, and even in his excitement his Greek accent wasn't too difficult to understand. "They are cleaned, crushed into a paste, and something called 'centrifugation' – say it with me, centrifugation – is used to separate the oil from the pulp. The oil then gets fermented and the pulp is animal food." He looked back at us as if he wanted to stress the point, "It actually is quite good for them."

We continued climbing as he finished the conversation on olives and olive oil, concluding that the best is from Greece, and the best in Greece is from Chania. I liked how proud he was of his city, of his country. From what he told us (and what I'd learned from Yiannis so far), most of Chania felt the same way. Everything made in Chania was the best: the olive oil, the olives, the mandarins (and all the fruit in general), and of course, the beer. Stelios told us that most farmers worked their own land, but in certain parts of Crete they had grown so large that they started to bring in immigrant workers from Africa. It was affordable labor and the job was done well. Our surprised looks at his words prompted an explanation.

"Well, if you look at a map, parts of Crete are actually closer to Africa than they are to Athens."

Not having a map with me, I didn't know if I believed Stelios or not. However, I did know the plants I was beginning to see on the sides of the mountains, barely visible in the dark green landscape around us.

Grape vines. We had reached the vineyard.

Before we reached the winery, Seymour convinced Stelios to stop the Jeep (when it was safe) and permit us to get out and take some pictures. We were incredibly high up, and the city below resembled little more than a pinhead in the distance. Mona pointed out the Venetian Harbor (also barely visible) and we talked about the vineyard, our favorite wines, and why we liked them. When I mentioned that there were over a hundred wineries in Michigan alone, Mona was surprised.

"I didn't know you had wineries in Michigan!" Oh so, so many.

Linda and Seymour asked me to take their picture, and somehow I became the photographer for the group: Linda and Seymour first, followed shortly by Lora and Melissa, then one of just Lora, and of course one of just Melissa. Seymour offered to take one of me and Mona, so we smiled, and he clicked away. Then we walked as close as we could to the edge without being in any real danger and took in the view.

It stretched for miles. Everything was dark green at the bottom, with blips of brown and white where the cities were. As my eyes scanned the mountains, the dark green transitioned to a slightly lighter, paler green where the olive groves were, and finally a yellow-green where the vines stretched across the steep hills of the vineyard. I turned around to see the mountains continuing upwards and couldn't imagine the Jeep handling the even more rugged terrain. The mountaintops themselves weren't even visible in the shrouded mist, and I wondered how high we'd go before we stopped and turned around.

We piled back into the Jeep after a few final pictures and headed towards the winery. I was mildly shocked that it took another ten minutes to get there, but the vineyard just went on and on for seemingly miles in any direction. Eventually, we turned down a little dirt path and knew we'd arrived. Stelios parked the Jeep off to the side and hopped out of the driver's seat. Moments later, the back door opened again and we all climbed out, ready for a wine tasting.

"Welcome to Manousakis Winery!" he said. "Enjoy!"

The winery was breathtakingly beautiful. It was a large, smooth, white building with colorful flower pots scattered all around the front porch and walkway. Parts of the building were made of various colored stones, and there was a sort of dining area under a large, wooden canopy at the end of the walkway. On one tree, a sign had "Wine tasting this way!" written on it with chalk and we followed it to the table where a woman was waiting for us. She had long, red hair and wore glasses, blue jeans, and a green polo shirt with the winery's name and logo embroidered on it. There was a huge smile on her face as we approached.

"Hello everybody, how are we doing today?"

She introduced herself as Heidi and explained that she was originally from Germany but had gotten into the wine business, fell in love with Manousakis Winery and the story behind it, and decided to move and completely change her life. So there she was some fifteen years later, still loving every moment of it, and was one of very few non-family employees working at the winery. She went on to share with us the history of Manousakis and how it was founded. According to her, the owner had been born in one of the bedrooms of the very house that now also functioned as the winery. When he was just a boy, Theodore Manousakis emigrated to America with just $2 in his pocket to support himself and his two sisters. They went through Ellis Island, attended school, worked in factories, and established good lives for themselves in America. As he grew older, he became very successful, and was even rumored to have been involved in the unveiling of Watergate. Eventually though, he decided to get back to his roots and made the decision to renovate his old childhood home into a winery. He flew in the best professionals from countries all over Europe to select only the best grapes and plan his winery. Then he started making his wine, which she assured us we would be trying shortly. It was an absolutely fantastic rags-to-riches story, made even better by the fact that it was true. We hadn't even tried the wine yet and I already knew I'd like it.

The winery's dog, Twix, followed us as we moved from the dining area to a large building: the production facility. Heidi motioned for us to follow her inside, and we were greeted by eight or so giant metal tanks. A few other machines were here and there, which our guide acknowledged as she walked us through the wine-making process. Depending on the type of wine, the process would be slightly different, but overall there was a general flow to things in a winery. She explained that grapes are harvested and the juice is extracted. Then, the skins are sometimes removed before everything is fermented (which is what the wine was currently doing in those giant tanks). After the fermentation is complete, the juice is pressurized, filtered, and put into regular barrels to be aged. Depending on the wood of the barrel and the type of cork used in the bottling process, the flavor could vary, even if the grape used was the same. It was all so fascinating to me that something as seemingly simple as wine had such an elaborate process behind it. From what she'd mentioned outside about Theodore Manousakis bringing in experts for grape and location advice to the fermentation and aging process she was teaching us about then, I realized that wine wasn't actually that simple. On the contrary, it was rather complex. There were so many factors that could affect the flavor of wine; it really was necessary to start at the source to fully understand it.

We made our way back to the dining area under the canopy and I decided to let my inner 'wine-o' take over. I pulled out my notebook and got ready to take notes on each of the wines we tried. They were served to us one at a time along with Rusk crackers, herbed olive oil, and a small dish of sea salt, all of which were meant to be palate cleansers. As soon as the server set the dishes in front of us, Melissa dove in with gusto. *Someone's hungry.* The rest of us waited for the wine.

First, we tried a dry white wine called 2 Mazi. Heidi said it would be rather dry, but my unrefined palate found it quite sweet. Typically, I didn't care for white wines, but it wasn't bad; I gave it eight out of ten stars in my notebook. The second wine (a red, my preference) was much better, and was the first wine that Manousakis had ever released. It was called Nostos Grenache and was a dry red whose name came from the ancient Greek for "nostalgia". Linda didn't much care for Nostos Grenache, and I watched, feeling almost embarrassed for her as she spit it back into her glass. Did that woman just spit out wine? Is that legal here? There was a pot in the middle of the table where we'd been instructed to dump any wines we didn't like. Linda just slid her glass containing her spit wine to the side and waited patiently for the next sample. I had to remind myself that staring would be rude.

Heidi continued on as the next wine – Nostos Alexandras – was brought out, followed by my personal favorite of the afternoon, a red blend called Nostos Blend. A few other samples came out, and the six of us had a wonderful afternoon of sipping, munching, and learning about life in each other's countries. Seymour and Linda had been to Michigan several times and encouraged me to travel to New York at least once in my lifetime. As the wine flowed, the story of my stolen wallet eventually rose to the surface and they were all so concerned for my well-being. I made sure that I gave Yiannis high praise, talking up his beer and brewery, then casually mentioned that Mona actually worked there as well. She smiled, becoming more relaxed and talkative as the tasting went on. She started to chime in about the beer, about its flavor, and about the brewery itself. The entire exchange resulted in an exchange of business cards between Mona, Melissa, and Lora, and even Seymour mentioned they might try to visit the brewery before they left to head back to New York. Mona thanked me later for my free publicity.

By the time we were ready to get back in the Jeep, I was worried my stomach might not make it too much further on the rollercoaster. I'd eaten nothing but Rusk, avocado, and oranges all day and had now had several samplings of wine on top of it. Fortunately, Stelios told us that our next stop would be at Taverna Leventogiannis, in Therisso Village. It was a very small, very traditional Cretan village but the food – Stelios could hardly keep from salivating – was absolutely phenomenal.

We reached Therisso Village a short while later. It was a very old-looking village, made of wood and stone and completely engulfed in foliage. A woman came out to greet us as we arrived, and ushered us into the large, stone building. It was cozy inside, with dark wood floors and heavy wooden tables. The walls were made of stone and there was a fire burning in the fireplace at one end of the main dining area. It was warm and smelled amazing. By the time we found our seats we were all much chattier, though verging on the edge of nauseous, and very hungry. The woman, who introduced herself as one of the owners, first brought out large jugs of what looked like apple cider. We poured glasses of it, unsure of what to expect, and she told us it was (supposedly) wine. Melissa smelled it, then asked for a Coke and Linda refused to drink it altogether. I decided I'd just sip on mine (it tasted very strong) and prayed the food would come quickly.

When it did, the best word to describe it was "feast". They first brought out plates with pieces of Rusk on them, topped with crushed tomatoes, a thick layer of goat cheese (from those very mountains), and herbs. Then they brought out a sort of Horiatiki salad with olives that had come right from the olive groves we'd driven through and more goat cheese ("From the shepherd's hut we will see in a bit!" exclaimed Stelios). Drizzled over the top of it all was locally made olive oil. It was unlike anything I'd ever tasted in the United States.

Then came a sort of potato stew comprised of giant chunks of potatoes, quinoa or red lentils (I couldn't tell the difference), tomato sauce, giant beans, and more olive oil all mixed together in a warm, sort of blissful dish I deemed 'Greek comfort food'. We continued eating and drinking, and at some point, more food arrived. I was already full, but Mona told me the next dish was actually the main course. *The stereotype of 'Big Greek Eaters' really isn't seeming too off right about now*. That would explain our family gatherings; there never seemed to be any shortage of food at birthdays or holiday gatherings.

Two waitresses arrived, each carrying an enormous tray of plates. Arranged on each was a large chunk of lamb meat, vegetables sautéed in olive oil and herbs, and a small mound of potatoes. Apparently Yiannis had managed to inform them that I was a vegetarian, so I was served the meatless version: no lamb meat, extra vegetables, and a large mound of potatoes. Everything was hot, incredibly well-seasoned, and was possibly the best food I had ever eaten. As the dishes were passed around, the subject of me being vegetarian became the focus of our conversation. Linda openly disapproved (I was even offered a forkful of her lamb because how could I resist?) and Melissa said she practiced vegetarianism every now and then for a few weeks to 'cleanse her system'. Mona seemed very intrigued in this new piece of information and asked me more about why I had become vegetarian and what Greek foods I had tried – and loved – so far that were meatless.

"Souvlaki is one of the best! How could you experience that if you don't eat meat?" she asked.

"I had one filled with vegetables in Thessaloniki – it was really good." Mona smiled and shook her head. I was reminded of Olivier; he had ordered Souvlaki nearly every time we ate out.

When the plates had been cleaned and we were all thoroughly satisfied (and feeling a very strong buzz from the Cretan wines), the waitress returned with a tray of what looked like the Terkelin pastries (as I'd had on the plane) and a round of small, clear shots of something that smelled very potent. Mona took hers almost immediately, then quickly took a bite of the pastry. She set it down after a moment and explained that the dessert served with a shot of *Tsikoudia*, or Raki, is a common practice in most restaurants on Crete. It was a sort of thank-you gift from the owners. They appreciated whoever came into their restaurant to eat and therefore gave them a free shot and small dessert. I thought it sounded like an ideal concept: owners thanking customers for coming in and spending money on their hard work.

Melissa turned her nose up at the Tsikoudia and ate both her and Lora's pastries. Seymour was the only other one who took the shot, and soon all eyes were on me. Mona clinked her water glass against my little shot glass.

"Yiamas!"

Oh why not, I thought. *How often will I visit Greece?* I threw the shot back like I was still in college and shoved the dessert in my mouth like a chaser. It was no Sunny D, but it helped to cut the incredibly awful, pungent flavor of the Tsikoudia. I remembered

that Officer Max had mentioned it at some point during my conversation with him at the airport in Thessaloniki, so as truly disgusting as it was (I likened it to drinking nail polish remover and
think I actually would have preferred tequila), at least I could say,
"I did it."

After the meal, Melissa and Lora announced they simply
could not continue. Their stomachs were far too uneasy to get
back into the Jeep and climb higher into the mountains, so Stelios
agreed that we could stop on the way back down and pick them
up then. He seemed annoyed that they were dropping out when
we were so close to the top, but they clearly wanted to stay at the
tavern and continue chatting and eating. Mona and I exchanged
glances that clearly read, 'how rude'. Those of us who would be
continuing thanked our host and the waitresses, then went outside and climbed back into the Jeep.

The rest of the trip was filled with fog (or were we in the
clouds?), steeper roads, and sheep. The path got bumpier and
bumpier, becoming so unbearable that I actually felt myself gag
once or twice. Admittedly the Tsikoudia had truly done me in: on
top of all of the wine at the winery and the apple cider-like drink
at the restaurant, I had consumed far more alcohol than an eight-
or nine-hour Jeep tour in the mountains permitted. I could tell by
their faces that the others felt the same, if not worse. Linda even
took out a small bag at one point to do some breathing exercises.
Or maybe she was going to be sick.

We climbed and climbed, nearing top of the mountain, and I
was glad to have followed Yiannis' suggestion to wear a coat. It
was at least fifteen degrees cooler there than it had been down in
the city, and I almost wished I'd brought gloves with me as well.
Stelios pulled the Jeep up one final, incredibly steep hill. We'd

made it. There, ahead of us, was the little stone shepherd's hut with a goat harness off to one side (to facilitate the milking process) and a little stone awning over some metal cheese-making supplies off to the other. The entire thing could have fit in my living room. We got out of the Jeep and Stelios showed us inside of the hut, where there were just two beds, one table, and a bible. Then he took us out to the goat harness, which almost looked like a child's swing. He explained that the shepherd would straddle the swing in such a way that the goats could pass underneath it quickly, and his knees wouldn't tire out as he milked the nearly 250 goats twice per day. He said that the shepherds had quite a difficult task to do up there in the mountain, but the simplicity of it all was what made it so enjoyable. *I enjoy simplicity, but I also enjoy civilization*, I thought. Though I did have a new respect for the goat cheese we'd just enjoyed at the tavern.

On our way back, we picked up Melissa and Lora, as promised, and the two didn't stop talking the rest of the way home. I fell asleep at some point, and Mona woke me up just as we were pulling into the very parking lot where we'd taken off that morning. She helped me into her car (I was half sleeping, half buzzing) and told me that Yiannis still had some things to finish at the brewery. She correctly determined that I needed a coffee, and we set off for her favorite café.

I let my eyes close again in her car, allowing my head to droop sideways against the headrest. I could not have imagined a better day in Chania. I couldn't wait to tell Yiannis all about the tour: the winery, the amazing food, and even the shepherd's hut. I made a mental note to ask him about his olive trees and what he made with his olives, then strongly advise he get his brewery onto the expedition. After everything I'd seen that day, I was certain; if my great-great-grandfather truly had been from Crete, he'd lived a wonderful life. As even Stelios had said, it was a simpler life there, so it was much more enjoyable. My mind started to wander to the rest of my family and where they might be. *If Leon had never come to America, would I still exist somewhere in Greece? Or could my soul even exist if my parents had never met? Would it be in someone in Germany? How exactly does God assign souls to bodies after all?* I felt the thoughts mixing and mashing together, making less and less sense as they did so. My head drooped even lower. *I am never taking Tsikoudia again. Never.*

And I fell asleep.

12

Mona nudged me awake as we parked in front of the café. I felt a headache coming on, so I hustled to follow her out of the car and get to the coffee as soon as possible. She pulled open a door tucked into the corner of a large black and white building and ushered me inside.

The café had high ceilings and a modern, sophisticated vibe. The floor was dark hardwood, contrasting sharply against the bright red tables. I looked around, taking in the different artwork on the walls (mostly newspaper headlines, black and white images of an older version of Chania, and a few colored cartoon images). It was just cool. There were different areas where the walls had been cut out to allow for a built-in bookshelf, with tattered copies of different novels stacked neatly inside. Mona and I took a seat at a small table near the front and she handed me a menu.

When a waiter approached, she ordered a hot chocolate and I ordered coffee. We then spent some time chatting about the brewery, at which point I learned that in addition to doing the marketing, she also gave tours and ordered supplies for Yiannis. She loved working there, and as she spoke both Greek and English, she was able to effectively show most of the tourists around. I casually mentioned that I spoke French, Spanish, and some German, and she gave me her business card.

"You should send me your CV when you return to America. Maybe there could be a place for you here in Chania!"

My heart skipped a beat as I stuck the card into my wallet. From what Mona told me, the brewery kept her very busy, but it was worth it. Working at Cretan Brewery allowed her to live in a beautiful place, work with a great team, and meet people from all over the world. I started thinking of how it would be if I ever did move abroad and was about to let my imagination run away with me when our drinks arrived.

Mona's hot chocolate looked delicious, with whipped cream spilling over the edge of the cup. My cup was set in front of me, empty, on a little plate holding a few small cookies. I was confused at first, but the waiter set down a mini French press next to it and smiled. Then came his thick, Greek accent.

"In five minutes, it ready."

I told Mona that in America, you had to specially order a French-pressed coffee and it wasn't very common in cafés. She informed me that this was the standard on Crete (and in most of Greece). Black coffee was never made in a pot; it was almost always served as a French press. She continued, telling me that the small cookies were also part of the Greek café experience. She turned her hot chocolate on its plate and I saw she had a small truffle. As a former barista, I found this small fact more interesting than most. We never gave away free sweets of any kind with our drinks. In fact, I couldn't think of a single place in America that did. Everything had to be purchased.

A few minutes went by and I pushed the top of the French press down, watching as the grounds swirled to the bottom. I poured my coffee, took the first long, delicious sip, and felt a wave of relaxation come over me. Mona and I continued talking, enjoyed our drinks, and just had a lovely evening winding down after our busy morning. As the caffeine hit me, I felt my headache start to disappear. When we'd finished, she drove me back to Yiannis' house and gave me a hug goodbye. Any reservations I'd had from that morning about her and how she thought of me were gone. In fact, I was actually quite excited when Yiannis said I might see her again if we had the chance to go to Cretan Brewery while I was there.

Once Mona had gone, Yiannis and I walked to the supermarket, as promised. It was less than a mile from his flat, and I told him about the day as we walked. I had in mind to make a roast vegetable dish for dinner, so we picked out zucchini, tomatoes, carrots, mushrooms, peppers, garlic cloves, and fresh parmesan, and fresh sheep milk yogurt. *Of course – Sam, you must try this, it is simply the best in all of Chania!* When he went to pay I gave him the €20 note from that morning.

He looked surprised but took it and handed me back the change. "You might need a coffee in the morning."

I couldn't believe how truly kind Yiannis was. As we walked home from the supermarket, groceries he'd bought in hand, I felt incredibly fortunate. Yiannis could have easily been a much less responsible, much less caring host. He could have left me at the airport, not wanting to deal with a stranded foreigner who had no money. He could have simply stopped responding and left me on my own. He could have, but he didn't. Instead, he was bending over backwards to make sure that I was safe, comfortable, and entertained. He'd told me he would take me to the UPS store when my debit card arrived and walk with me to the Western Union in town when my mom's money was ready for pick-up. He'd even given me spending money in the meantime. And now he'd bought groceries for me. *There's no doubt in my mind that angels are real*, I thought as we climbed the stairs to his flat. *And this one makes beer, on top of everything.*

Once inside, Yiannis set the bags down on the kitchen table. He told me he had an exercise class to get to but was looking forward to my cooking when he got home (or so he said). He showed me where the pots and pans were, which drawer the knives were in, and where he kept his spices. Then he pulled a cloth off a gravy dish sitting on his counter and slid it towards me. It was the most beautiful olive oil I'd ever seen. I asked him if he'd made it from his olive trees. He nodded, then pulled out an enormous jug – the kind that the Hawaiian Punch from my childhood came in – and it was completely filled. Yiannis smiled at the shocked expression on my face.

"I may not be the best with exercise, but I am certainly good at eating." He patted his stomach and laughed. "Ok. I'll see you later. Please don't burn anything."

He pulled the door shut as he left, and I turned to face the big, empty flat. I wasn't sure how long Yiannis would be gone, so

I set about preparing dinner. It would take a while, as I was planning to roast the vegetables, and I reasoned that if Greek exercise classes were anything like the ones we had in America I probably had about an hour. I called my mom, figured out how to preheat the oven, and set about peeling and chopping the vegetables while I filled her in on my day. She, too, was amazed by Yiannis' generosity. I told her about the amazing trip I'd taken into the mountains that day, filled her in on Manousakis winery – They even do weddings there, mom. Could you imagine!? – and started salivating as I described in detail the food we'd eaten at Taverna Leventogiannis. She sounded as excited as I was about it all.

I had really come to enjoy talking to my mom on the phone and was so glad that Facebook messenger made it possible to do so (eliminating the need to purchase an international phone plan). It just felt good to talk to someone familiar after spending a day or two with complete strangers. And while most of our conversations had unfortunately been because things were going wrong and I needed advice (and money), hearing her voice made it seem like she was close by. She was right there with me, not thousands of miles away. I'd felt the same way in college, during the summer I lived in Dublin, and when I was in Portland for my internship: hearing my mom's voice brought me home for a few minutes. Greece was no different.

"Also, Dad and I have the cash for you – we'll use the Western Union at Kroger to try again this evening when he gets home from work." To my parents, 'this evening' meant five or six o'clock, which was around midnight for me (Chania being seven hours ahead of Michigan). I was elated. Hopefully the transfer would work this time around and I would finally have money to continue on my journey. I just needed the debit card to arrive and I'd be good to go.

It wasn't that I wanted to leave Chania; it was actually one of my favorite places of those I'd visited since arriving in Greece. I still had to talk to Yiannis about getting to Koutsouras (I planned to do so that evening over dinner), but so far everything I'd seen on Crete had been beautiful. The food was delicious, the air was fresh and smelled of the sea, and Yiannis' flat was quite comfortable with my cozy bed and the normal shower. I had no complaints whatsoever. The worry and desire to move on stemmed from my fear of being stuck on the island. Prior to Pat's offer, no money meant no ferry ticket. No ferry ticket meant I couldn't get back to Athens. Not getting back to Athens meant I couldn't fly home. And beyond any of that was the feeling that I was completely at the mercy of Yiannis for everything. It was very difficult for me – someone who had always been very independent and liked to maintain control of a situation – to be entirely dependent on someone else. I had no way to buy my own food, no way to pay for things like museums (or the Jeep excursion), and the fact that he'd already given me so much made me feel guilty because I was unable to repay him. Yet. *But tomorrow I'll be able to repay him – double – and start to feel like I can truly enjoy Chania.* It was a very exciting thought.

My mom and I spoke for a few more minutes, then hung up as I tossed the vegetables in some olive oil and popped them into the oven. I decided to start writing. I sat at the kitchen table, notebook in hand, trying to remember the events of the day. Prior to coming on the trip, I had promised myself that I'd write as often as possible – daily, if I could – so as to prevent myself from forgetting any of the smallest, but often most significant, details. Today had been the perfect example of why it was important to do so;

there was just too much to reflect on. If I waited three days and then tried to write about the amazing Safari Adventure, there were undoubtedly several details that would have been left out.

I'd practiced this same concept the entire summer that I spent in Dublin. I was there from June to August, living with the other interns, spending our evenings exploring the city and surrounding areas. I didn't keep a detailed journal, but I did gain consistency on my blog (something I'd dedicated years to in college) and posted several times a week to update far-away family and friends of life in Ireland. My posts covered every topic from the food to random performers I'd seen around the city to the tour we took on a DUKW. I'd posted about the Guinness Storehouse and my weekend in Hannover with Cleo, the bus trip a few of us took up to Galway and back, and even the one crazy day another intern and I flew to Paris to see the end of the Tour de France. I blogged about all of it. It was a sort of 'online keepsake' of the summer, and one aunt even told me she'd printed each post so that she could share them with a friend. Ever since, I'd made sure that if I ever went anywhere new or did anything of particular interest, I'd write about it as soon as I could. I had a fairly good memory, but I wanted concrete words on paper. I never wanted to forget the places I'd seen or the people I'd met.

By the time I'd finished writing, the vegetables were done. I plated dishes for both Yiannis and myself, covering them with pot lids (like my mom always had) to keep the food hot. He arrived home shortly after, commented on how wonderful everything smelled, and took a quick shower. When he returned to the kitchen, he said there was a very good movie just starting so we relocated to eat our dinner in the living room. I was expecting it to be some popular Greek movie or something cultural, but I couldn't have been more wrong.

It was called *Rush*. And because we watched it, Chris Hemsworth, Daniel Brühl, and Olivia Wilde instantly became embedded in my brain as parts of my Greek adventure. I had never seen it before but was glad to have some time to get to know Yiannis better and talk to him about Koutsouras. I sat down and put my plate on the coffee table, and Yiannis joined me moments later with a plate of avocado slices and a dark green wine bottle.

"The best!" He smiled, and I knew what was coming before he even said it. "I made it myself."

The wine had a slightly brown, slightly orange color to it, and we drank it out of small brandy glasses. It could have been brandy, for all I knew, as it tasted nothing like any of the wine I'd had prior to coming to Chania. In fact, it tasted more along the lines of the apple cider-like stuff we'd had in Therisso Village that afternoon. I exaggerated how much I liked it, and he seemed quite content. We ate our meal (his suggestion to add the avocado made it taste even better than I was expecting), each had a few glasses of the wine, and watched the movie.

"Do you think it might be possible to go to Koutsouras tomorrow?" I asked. I had been more hesitant earlier, knowing that it was on nearly the opposite end of the island from Chania. But there, on the comfortable couch with a full stomach and plenty of wine, I took the shot. Yiannis shrugged, calculating something in his head. After a moment he turned to look at me directly.

"We could, but what did you say your grandfather's last name was?"

"Christopoulos."

"Then he's not from Crete, I'm sorry."

Yiannis explained that last names in Greece were very indicative of that family's origins. According to him, people whose lineage was truly Cretan or from one of the surrounding islands likely had "-akis" at the end of their last name. It was a demeaning, belittling suffix that had been imposed under the Ottoman occupation (like adding "-let" to pig for piglet"). The suffix of my grandfather's last name, "-opolous", had originally come from the Peloponnese meaning, "son of". Yiannis went on to explain that this was now quite common for last names in Greece, so it would be very difficult – if not impossible – to figure out exactly where my family had come from. It wasn't the answer I'd been hoping for. I couldn't just return home or pick up the phone and call Papa, asking if he knew which city Leon Christopoulos was from. Yiannis seemed to sense my disappointment.

"But dear Sam, you are still here. You are still seeing the country where your family is from and you even made it to Crete, where you know the boat departed all those years ago. There is nothing to see in Koutsouras, so I don't think we will go, but the greatest part of the culture here can be experienced in Chania. And you've been to Athens, as you know the main city, and learned about its history. And you even made it to Thessaloniki, in the north, which I'm sure you noticed is much different. Don't think of it as a wasted effort. Actually, you've probably seen more of the country than most of your ancestors did – than most Greek people do! And that is a great accomplishment you should be very proud of." He continued eating as if he hadn't just given me the greatest accolade I'd ever received for going on my journey. I stared at him for a moment, soaking in his words. "By the way, this is delicious. You are a very good chef."

I smiled, and we turned back to the movie. I *was* proud of

myself.

. . . . .

I had to hand it to them; the Greeks knew how to drink.

I woke up the next morning with a pounding headache. The wine at Manousakis, the even stronger wine at lunch (and the shot of Tsikoudia), and then that homemade, somehow stronger still wine the night before had truly hit me overnight. I felt terrible.

I realized what had woken me up was Yiannis, knocking on my door. I scrambled to get dressed, then went out to meet him in the kitchen. He had set out all kinds of food: the sheep's yogurt, a small jar of honey, a jar of nuts, the basket of oranges, and a container of cinnamon. He told me it was very common on Crete to top the yogurt with the nuts, cinnamon, and honey for breakfast, so of course I needed to try it. Then he looked at me as a worried expression crossed his face and told me that he had another Couchsurfer coming to stay with him that day. My first thought was that this was the end of my time with Yiannis. *Maybe this is his way of politely kicking me out. Maybe I've caused him too much stress.* Then he continued that he had some work to do at the brewery before picking her up. He'd already told her that I would be staying a few extra days, and she was actually looking forward to meeting me. He simply referred to her as the "Russian girl" and made a joke about hoping we got along (something about Americans and Russians — I often had trouble deciphering his humor). I was relieved, even slightly excited. *Another new person to meet? What else could today hold?*

Yiannis left, telling me he'd be back in about an hour and a half with "the Russian girl." I ate my truly phenomenal breakfast and scrolled through missed messages on Facebook. The very first one was from my mother.

"Sam, good news! Western Union confirmed the money has been sent – we're all set. Let me know when you get it."

I nearly fell out of my chair. *It worked? Was this possible?* I wanted to call her but knew it would be around 2:00am back home. I decided against it. Instead, I finished eating and pulled up Chania on Google maps. I made it my mission that morning to find the Western Union by myself and save Yiannis the trouble of taking me there himself. It didn't seem too complicated: down one main street, right on another, continue on for a few blocks, and it would be on the left. Okay. I can do this. I hadn't spent much time in the streets of Chania yet, but was excited to explore. Yiannis and I had walked to the supermarket the evening before, but that wasn't downtown. I was looking forward to just getting out and enjoying the fresh air. I figured that maybe I would even be able to find a café and get something to help with my terrible headache. Yiannis had foreshadowed I might want a coffee in the morning.

He'd left me a spare key, which was hanging on a little hook in the back of the kitchen. After I cleaned up my dishes from breakfast, I grabbed the key and headed out. The morning air was crisp and refreshing: the kind of air that could only be breathed in a harbor town. I followed the map I'd sketched out on a slip of paper, working my way through the streets, and came across a small open-air market. Just in front of a park, the tables and tents were set up along both sides of the road. My schedule for the day was light, and I decided to take a detour to browse through it. There were mountains of fruits and vegetables, trays of home-baked goods (*is it too early for baklava?*), and even books and knick-knacks for sale. Large signs hung from the tables, showing incredibly cheap prices for what was being sold, but people still bartered and haggled (loudly) trying to get a better price. One woman was talking with grand gestures, waving her hands as if physical intimidation would make the vendor reduce his price. Another man was picking through a pile of oranges. A small group of children were giggling over something in a book. The street was alive with noise, color, life. I could have pulled up a chair and sat for hours, taking it all in.

I continued into the heart of the town, walked past a few random stores (a bakery here, an Apotheke there, a few bookstores with tables outside covered in the newest), and thought of how nice it would be to live in such a place. The town was small but busy, and with the beautiful Venetian Harbor in one direction and the mountains in another, how could anyone not want to live there? I contemplated the discussion I'd had with Mona the day before, making a mental note to send her my resume when I got home. *Why not?*

It wasn't long before I saw the bright yellow sign sticking out from the side of a tall, stone building. Western Union: a beacon of hope. As I approached, I saw that it was more of a booth than an actual store, just a window connected to the row of stores stretching in either direction. I walked up to it and looked inside. The woman there – large, dark-haired, inattentive – was reading a book, and I knocked loudly on the glass.

"Kaliméra!" I said. She looked up and said the same without so much as a smile.

I found it to be a challenge to communicate to her that I was there to pick up money from the United States. Her English was very broken, but as we worked our way through the transaction she grew friendlier, asking me how I liked Chania. I told her I loved it, which brought a smile to her face. As she processed my passport, she asked me what I wanted to see next and recommended a great café just down the street where the pastries were fresh and the coffee was strong. Then she handed my passport back to me, along with my confirmation document, and an envelope containing €258,97. I nearly squealed with excitement as I put everything in my purse, excited to finally have my own money again. I thanked her and headed off in the direction of the cafe. I had my independence back.

It was called "13" Sweeties & Salties, just a short walk down Skalidi. Inside, there was an enormous pastry case filled with everything from sandwiches to desserts, and a small restaurant was buzzing off to the side. It had a wonderful aroma of freshly baked bread and coffee. As I browsed along the different options, a small round of Kaliméra!'s came from behind the counter. I ordered a coffee and a Kalouri, paid my own €1,50, and headed home. I was ecstatic. I arrived back to Yiannis' house about twenty minutes later, properly caffeinated and in very high spirits. He was in the kitchen peeling an orange and looked up as I entered.

"She has returned! I wondered where you'd gone."

I couldn't help but smile as I reached into my purse and pulled out one of the €50 notes from my mom. I handed it to Yiannis and thanked him again for sending me on the Safari Adventure the day before. It felt good to repay him: letting me stay with him for free was one thing, but to pay €50 for me to go on that excursion was just too much. He looked very surprised.

"Ah, your mother was successful! And you found the Western Union, that's great! Oh — the Russian is here, hold on."

I watched as Yiannis leaned into the living room and motioned for someone to join us in the kitchen. As I had come in through the kitchen door, I hadn't seen anyone but Yiannis since entering the house. But just moments later, there she was: timid, but a smile breaking across her face when she saw me.

"Sam, this is Elena. Elena, meet Sam." Yiannis introduced us like we were the new kids in class. He looked from Elena to me, then back to Elena. "Ok. I have to go to work. You two have a nice day and just message me on WhatsApp if you need anything." A few moments later he was out the front door and we heard it shut behind him. I turned to Elena.

My first impression was that she looked like a doll. And not like a scary Russian nesting doll, but like one of the beautiful, painted porcelain dolls that people collected on their mantels. Elena was very pale, with reddish brown hair that was brushed into a perfect chin-length bob. Her face was strong, with expressive brows, dark but bright eyes, and rosy cheeks with high cheekbones. She wore red lipstick and had on a floral blue button-down shirt, black jeans, and thick wool socks. She smiled and said a soft 'hello.' We sat down in the kitchen and talked for a while, eating oranges and telling each other about our current travels. I was instantly intrigued by Elena. She was passing through Greece and would be continuing on from Chania to the city of Heraklion the next day. She'd heard that Chania was beautiful, and as she'd never been there before she wanted to see as much of the city as she could before a bus took her on her way. As she told me some of the things she was hoping to see, part of me felt guilty that I had gotten to go on the White Mountain excursion the day before. If only she'd come a day earlier!

Elena and I decided not to waste the day sitting at Yiannis' flat, so we headed out to explore the city. She mentioned something about the "Old City" – a historic part of Chania with narrow streets and lots of different locally-owned shops – and before we knew it, we were on our way to find it. It didn't take us long. The buildings of the Old City rose up high on either side of the cobblestone streets, and dark, twisting vines decorated the sides of the buildings, climbing nearly to the roofs. There were lots of colorful flower pots with different kinds of flowers in them all along the streets, some on the ground and some sitting on little wooden chairs just outside the doorways. Elena and I walked along, popping in and out of a few shops as we went. As we exhausted our usage of, "Kaliméra!" we realized that no one spoke English in the area. We didn't buy anything (though there was one shop selling traditional, handmade children's clothing that I was very tempted to buy something for my nephew), and wandered slowly through the city. The only word that came to mind was *whimsical*. Stray cats were everywhere, and I was taken back to when I explored the "Upper Town" of Thessaloniki. *Had that really only been a few days ago?* The trip was going by far too fast. While I was looking forward to getting home and sorting out my stolen wallet situation, I also wanted to slow down time and just stay there, enjoying the beautiful towns and their history.

Elena and I left the Old City, walking along the water, then around the Venetian Harbor. We found a small passageway behind the shipyard, and eventually climbed up along a high stone wall that led out to the lighthouse. The sky was bright blue, the water sparkled, and people all around the harbor were busy going about their day. Some performed music in the streets, others sold things like roasted chestnuts and trinkets, and some were just enjoying the good weather on the restaurants' outdoor patios. At one point, we were even approached by a group of students from America doing a research project during their summer abroad. Not wanting to fall victim to another theft, we pushed past them before they had a chance to interview us. I had a hard time trusting anybody at this point.

We started getting hungry and decided to stop into a small grocery store to buy snacks and wine. There was a cheap bottle Elena found in the back called Vin de Chania (a Syrah/Cabernet blend) and I picked out a bag of mixed crackers, a few Kinder Eggs, and a package of pretzels. It felt so good to be able to purchase something with my own money, especially now that I was not the only one staying with Yiannis. And while I knew I had to be careful to save enough for food and small souvenirs over the next few days, it was still nice to have the freedom to buy whatever I wanted in the moment.

Elena led the way back to Yiannis' flat, following a map he'd left for us on his kitchen table. We shared stories about everything from our families to our past travels to boys (naturally) and entertained every tangent the other went on as we spoke. I found her incredibly interesting; Elena had even spent two years living in India! She seemed equally intrigued in me, surprised that an American would actually take a trip to discover their roots. When I asked what she meant, she said it didn't seem like most of "them" cared where their ancestors were from. She was blunt, but I unfortunately knew what she was trying to say. I had received the same response from many people I'd told prior to coming on the trip. *Why? It's not like it's your actual parents or grandparents who came over on the boat. You're talking about your great-great-grandparents. That's not the same.* Except it was, to me. Elena seemed to understand.

By the time we returned to the flat, we had successfully established the foundation of our friendship. We set our purchases on the kitchen table, opened the wine, and continued chatting. We were just two old friends, day-drinking delicious Greek wine. At one point Elena laughed and asked me if I was sure I wasn't Russian. I nodded.

"Well you drink like a Russian."

We talked, laughed, munched on the snack mix, excitedly opened some of our Kinder eggs, and after a short while Yiannis came home. He was pleased to see that we were getting along so well, again cracking a joke about having a Russian and an American in his flat. He sat down, poured himself a glass of our wine, and joined the conversation. It was a truly amazing afternoon. Yiannis told us that he had some business to attend to but invited us to join him for dinner that evening at his family's restaurant on the Venetian Harbor, Aroma. We accepted.

Yiannis left and the rest of the afternoon passed quickly. We went out in search of coffee, coming across a small ice cream shop/bakery near the Old City. It was bright and colorful, with every kind of ice cream imaginable on display. There was chocolate and vanilla with honey, orange sherbet, and even a bright blue kind with little plastic Smurfs stuck into it. Elena got an ice cream and a small coffee, and I ordered a latté, and we thoroughly enjoyed them as we did a bit more exploring before dinner. We came across a little bookshop, where I bought The Little Prince in Greek (I already had the English and French versions), and we both bought postcards from another small boutique nearby. Elena told me that she also sent postcards when she traveled: just another thing the two of us had in common.

We finally rested when we reached the Venetian Harbor. I felt certain that my blisters had reopened from walking so much, so we took a seat on a bench looking out over the water. She took out one of her postcards and started writing, so I followed suit. Who to write first?

As we sat there, writing, time finally seemed to stand still. It was all just too good to be true. From the absolute nightmare just a few days earlier to now, my world had changed in so many ways. I had experienced the complete mercy of a total stranger and the extreme generosity of a close friend. I was reminded how fortunate I was to have parents that cared about me and were willing (and able) to send me the money I needed. I had been high into the mountains of Chania, bonded with my host over food I cooked, and met another traveler who was arguably even more adventurous than I was. There was no way that I could have foreseen any of the past few days' events prior to coming on the trip. In fact, I had imagined it unfolding in a very different way (and would have been in Santorini, had everything gone according to plan). Regardless, I had been forced to make the best of the situation. And it had somehow managed to become the best situation possible.

13

It wasn't long before the sun started to set over the harbor. Elena and I decided it was probably time to find Aroma and walked along the stone street as the sun bounced off the blue and green water beside us. It was only a short distance away – just on the other side of the harbor – and soon we were walking through the gate at the front of the patio.

The outdoor seating area was covered by a thin, white tent, with dozens of round tables scattered about covered in matching white cloths. There were candles in the center of each, with place settings waiting for the impending dinner rush. Along the edges of the patio, long, rectangular tables were set in the same manner, with couch-like benches on either side. The restaurant certainly lived up to its name, Aroma; as we passed the tables on our way inside, we were met with robust, savory smells suggesting that we were in very close proximity to delicious food.

The atmosphere and smells of Aroma took me back to my college years. There had been one summer in particular – between my freshman and sophomore years - when I came home to work in a Mediterranean restaurant. I had found the position when I was home for Easter: it was a brand-new restaurant, just finishing up construction, getting ready for its grand opening at the beginning of June. When I got home from college that May, it still hadn't opened. Nevertheless, the owner told me and the three other servers-to-be that we had to come in for training, so we spent hours sitting around a folding table among the dust and boxes, learning menu items and how to describe them to customers. He repeatedly told us that we would be paid as soon as the restaurant opened, so we naïvely continued going. The kitchen was done first, and our meetings were soon accompanied by all kinds of delicious foods: homemade hummus and pita bread, falafel, stuffed grape leaves, roasted vegetables, tabbouleh, and – for the meat eaters – shawarma. The smells were so powerful and absolutely amazing: garlic, herbs, lemon, and more in each and every dish. By the time we were ready to open, I knew every item on the menu and could describe it in my sleep. Unfortunately, that time came just two weeks before I had to move back to school. The owner told me he wasn't going to be able to pay me by the time I had to return to school because of some issue with setting up payroll, and instead told me to focus on the great tips I'd made. I was, of course, furious, but was perversely thrilled to see the restaurant had closed the next summer when I returned home for a visit. Ever since, the smell of Mediterranean food instantly took me back to my experience working there. Now, after having visited Aroma, I would have a new memory to associate with it; I would instantly be brought back to Chania.

I wondered what Yiannis had in mind for us. *More traditional Cretan food? Are we ordering ourselves? Where is Yiannis anyway?* We didn't see him in the restaurant, so we took a seat at a table near the kitchen. The inside of Aroma was just as beautiful as the patio. The tables were covered in white cloths as well, but the floor and ceiling were made of fresh, light wood and the bar, of stone. It was rustic, but sophisticated. It was unlike any restaurant I'd seen before; we didn't have too many completely open restaurants like Aroma in Michigan (or at least I'd never been to one). And we certainly didn't have any with such a beautiful view just outside.

Elena and I looked around, not wanting to look suspicious and not entirely sure what we should do while we waited. We sat talking for a bit until a white-aproned waiter came over and greeted us. We told him we were waiting for Yiannis and he nodded, saying he would go check to see if the meeting upstairs was nearly finished. He disappeared up a stairway in the back and re-emerged not two minutes later.

"They are not done yet. But he said he would like to offer you a drink while you wait."

Elena and I looked at each other, and I knew we were both thinking the same thing: starving. The last time I'd eaten anything was that afternoon at the flat, when we had the snack mix and Kinder eggs. It was now nearly 8:00pm. *Can we have food instead of drinks?* I perused the menu and pointed out the Charma beer to Elena. She ordered the light lager and I chose the dark. A few minutes later the waiter returned, drinks in hand. He also put down a few small dishes of a nut mix and told us to enjoy. I heard Elena's stomach grumble and felt mine do the same. *Beer has never tasted so good!*

Yiannis finally came downstairs around 8:45pm and greeted us with a giant smile on his face. He apologized for taking so long but told us our dinner would be worth the wait. We followed him out of Aroma and were glad to be on our way. It wasn't terribly far, and Yiannis took the opportunity to tell us about his family and how Aroma was not the only restaurant they owned. One of his brothers owned a fish restaurant – Elena and I threw each other looks at the mention of it – and it had done much better than they were expecting it to. It was now a high-end restaurant, he told us, and had become a sort of 'stomping ground' for food critics from around the world. I was intrigued. And then, when we finally reached a small, light-blue restaurant with no sign, but a fish painted above the door, I knew we'd arrived at our destination.

Our host disappeared to find his brother, leaving us standing in the doorway. The restaurant wasn't much bigger than a coffee shop, with long, wooden tables painted white squeezed into the middle. A group of boys was sitting at one – roughly the same age as Elena and me – loudly discussing something in what sounded like Swedish. All around the outside of the restaurant, a ledge stuck out from the wall (also white) with high stools underneath. There was a spindly black iron staircase in the back, next to which were two giant, iron doors I assumed to be the bathrooms. Then the kitchen was off to the left, from which Yiannis re-emerged several moments later. He seemed to captivate the attention of the rowdy Swedish boys as he came over to us.

"Ok ladies, welcome to *Thalassino Ageri*! It means, 'Sea

Breeze'. Our host said our table is ready. We feast upstairs!"

I'd come to appreciate how animated Yiannis became when he spoke English. I'd heard him speak to Mona and a few others in Greek, which he spoke without any sort of enthusiasm. But the moment he switched to English he was completely different and much more energetic: I half expected him to add, "Opa!" at the end of his sentences. It was actually something I'd read about: depending on the language being spoken, people could sometimes have different personalities. It had something to do with the emphasis placed on different words and people's individual interpretations of that emphasis and the language itself. Whether that was true or not, I had never known. Until I met Yiannis. He excitedly ushered us to the back of the restaurant and we made our way up the staircase.

As it turned out, the upstairs was a sort of balcony that overlooked the small restaurant below. Our table was against the far edge, with nothing preventing us from falling but a low wall with a glass divider on top. It had a polished wood top, with candles and a pitcher of wine in the center. They had already delivered a bread basket, and I wondered what kind of food we'd be having with it. My stomach growled again. Elena and I took our seats at opposite sides of the table, and Yiannis took his place at the end.

"So ladies, tonight we feast. It is not often I have two adventurers stay with me, so my brother has made a very nice meal for us." He smiled and turned to me. "And since you are missing your Thanksgiving tomorrow, I hope that you enjoy our feast tonight instead."

It hadn't even occurred to me that it was the day before Thanksgiving. I was somewhat touched that Yiannis remembered and felt yet another wave of gratitude come over me for his hospitality. If I was being honest, I didn't even realize I'd be gone for Thanksgiving prior to booking my trip. Thanksgivings in our family meant a large gathering with my mom's sisters and their families...at Papa's house. Everyone would bring something – different pies, Jell-O with fruit inside, butter and rolls, mashed potatoes – and spend the entire afternoon talking and cooking. The cousins would play ping pong in the basement or watch episodes of The Office in the den while the "grown-ups" cooked dinner, usually a giant turkey, stuffing, and my step-grandmother's specialty: Bacon Noodles. It was a simple dish: egg noodles cooked in lard with fried onions and bacon pieces. But (in my pre-vegetarian days) I loved them. I wondered what my family would be doing back home. Papa wasn't there. He wouldn't be enjoying the pecan pie or the bacon noodles. Would a family gathering – could a family gathering – even be worth having without him? I felt a pang of guilt as I realized I was actually thankful to be away from my family for the holiday. I couldn't imagine a Thanksgiving that didn't include our Papa.

I was just about to say something to Yiannis about Thanksgiving when a waiter appeared out of nowhere. He introduced himself as Louie, then gracefully lifted the pitcher of wine and poured us each a very full glass. Elena and I watched, amused, as Yiannis grabbed his arm just as he was about to leave. He said something in Greek, then poured a swig of wine in an empty glass, handed it to Louie, and held up his own.

"To a night of good food, and good friends, and to Greece and to America and to Russia." He nodded to each of us as he spoke. "Yiamas!"

"Yiamas!" We responded in unison, clinking our glasses. The

waiter stood near our table for a short while, speaking Greek with Yiannis and drinking his wine. They periodically mentioned something about me or Elena and Yiannis clarified in English. The two of us started gnawing at pieces of bread, starving and slightly buzzed from our beers and now the wine. It was delicious. At that point anything would have been delicious.

Louie disappeared for a few minutes when he and Yiannis finished their conversation and returned to the balcony a few moments later with a large platter. There were three dishes arranged on it, and Louie grinned widely as he started to set them down in front of us. This first dish was a pea green soup that smelled as strange as it looked. There were large chunks of a thin, white something floating in it and I just stared as Louie placed it in front of me. Yiannis explained that this was a very traditional fish soup - something his family loved - and handed us each half of a lemon. He squeezed his over the bowl of soup and took a big spoonful. It was accompanied with an exaggerated "Mmmmmm".

"Fish soup. I told him you were vegetarian, so there you go."

I didn't want to tell him that in America, vegetarian meant completely meat-free. (As in, fish included.) But apparently in Greece, fish was not considered meat. I decided that I had to at least try it out of respect for Yiannis and his family. I squeezed my lemon over the soup and stirred. Without it, the soup would have been rather bland. With it, I decided it wasn't too bad. I had no intention of eating the slippery white chunks of fish, but the soup itself was thick and had a somewhat fresh taste to it, almost like a cucumber purée. We drank, slurped, and talked for nearly twenty minutes before the next course arrived. Or rather, courses: Louie had five enormous plates of food balanced on a tray, and each looked more mouth-wateringly delicious than the next.

The first platter had a thick layer of what I assumed to be hummus on it, with bits of dark reddish-purple squid and bright green capers neatly arranged on top. It was generously drizzled in olive oil, with herbs sprinkled over the top. I wonder if his whole family owns olive trees? Or is that Yiannis'? I was anxious to try it as I had always been a complete enthusiast for anything involving hummus (squid aside). The next plate looked like fish and chips, but Louie told us that it was actually fried cuttlefish. It was served with a white sauce and French fries and smelled heavenly. I was beyond ready to 'dig in' but restrained myself, instead taking another swig of my wine. Then another plate was set down. This third dish – *Boureki* – was a layered, giant piece of what looked like some sort of Greek lasagna. Yiannis walked us through the layers: phyllo dough, olive oil, feta cheese, ricotta, sliced zucchini, sliced potatoes, repeat. And it was topped with butter and sesame seeds, cooked to a crisp, golden brown color. I can't let myself start drooling! I looked up to see Elena already taking a scoop of hummus as Yiannis took the next plate from Louie. It was an assortment of stuffed cabbage rolls, of which he told us half were stuffed with spinach and rice and half had some sort of shellfish in them. Then finally, he set down a bowl of stew made with chestnuts, onions, and potatoes, all swimming in a delightfully fragrant tomato sauce. We'd been told we would have a feast, but neither of us had anticipated quite so much food!

Yiannis told us that there was only one rule during dinner: we had to try everything. I wasn't so sure. At the Mediterranean restaurant I'd worked at, the cabbage rolls were my least favorite thing on the menu. There was something incredibly off-putting about eating slimy leaves that were normally crisp, if not sweet. I took one to "follow the rules" and make him happy, but let it sit on the edge of my plate for the remainder of the meal.

The Boureki was without a doubt my favorite. It was piping hot, creamy from the cheese, and savory from the vegetables. The phyllo dough was cooked perfectly: not too flaky, not too mushy. I could have eaten an entire tray by myself if they'd let me. I did get the waiter to write down the recipe for me, and he even offered to show me how they made if I had time to come back the next day. I cautiously told him "I'd see", knowing full well that we'd both forget the conversation by the time we left.

Elena, Yiannis, and I sat there, eating and talking, for what felt like hours. Elena told us about her family and some of their favorite foods in Russia. She went into greater detail about her trip to India, about how she stayed there much longer than she'd originally intended, and how she'd even had a relationship with a boy she met while she was there. The subject changed quickly when Yiannis pressed for details and she started blushing too hard to carry on. Then it was my turn. I told them about my first trip to France, about my internship in Dublin, and not remembering if we'd talked about Germany already, I re-told the stories about my first few trips there, including my efforts to find my family. Even Yiannis chimed in, telling us about his trips to different countries and the different people he'd met and most unique places he'd seen. It was an absolutely wonderful experience. I'd come to hate that when speaking with friends and family who never traveled much, talking about my own travels sometimes felt like bragging. As unintentional as it was, it was all too easy to get carried away about the beauty of the Eiffel Tower or the rolling hills of Ireland. It was like people who never learned how to play the piano asking a seasoned pianist to play. I wanted to share my experiences, but apart from a select few, I'd never found anyone so genuinely interested in the places I'd been to. That is, apart from the two people sitting across from me right there at that table. Elena even asked me to share some of my hosts' information with her from my time in Thessaloniki. It felt so good to be able to just talk and hear each other's stories. We were all on an equal playing field.

Elena seemed amazed. She told me how she had to have a special visa to travel to Europe, and an entirely different one to travel to America. According to her, some were only good for one year; some for three. I felt very fortunate to only need one passport for all of my travels, and it was valid for ten years. I was about to express the unfairness of it all when Yiannis interrupted with a story of a past Couchsurfer he'd had from America. His stories weren't as awful as Olivier's, but he also mentioned that he screened everyone he allowed to stay. Some basic requirements were: having a verified profile, excellent past host reviews, and some communication prior to visiting. Apparently some people on the Couchsurfing website withheld as much information as possible to avoid being rejected. I didn't see the point; *the person was going to meet me in person anyway, so why allow room for surprises?*

As we began to clean some of the plates in front of us, Yiannis' brother came upstairs to check on us and see how we enjoyed the food. I was shocked when he introduced himself as Yianni and wondered how their mother even kept them separate when they were little. Louie came back upstairs to join them, and the three men spoke for quite some time. They occasionally asked Elena and I questions – what our favorite dish was, where were we from, what is our favorite part of Chania, etc. – and then returned to their own conversation. We finished the wine, leaned back in our chairs, and waited for Yiannis to walk with us back to his flat. I was done; I was ready for bed.

But then there was dessert.

I had forgotten what Mona taught me at Taverna Leventogiannis. So when Louie disappeared without so much as a nod of acknowledgement and returned with a small tray of Tsikoudia and what looked like upside-down crême brulée, I instantly remembered her words. *Dessert served with a shot of Tsikoudia is a common practice in most restaurants on Crete. It is a sort of thank-you gift from the owners: it shows their appreciation for whoever came into their restaurant to eat.* Restaurants typically gave visitors a free shot and small dessert. *How could I forget?* My stomach churned as I looked at the shot glass. Elena picked hers up without hesitation and I looked at her, genuinely concerned. *Poor dear doesn't know what she's about to do.* All I could do was shudder and remember how awful it had been at the tavern. There was no way I could do another shot of it.

I failed to underestimate the potency of peer pressure. Somehow, more shots of the stuff appeared and soon Yiannis, Yianni, Louie, and Elena were all holding theirs up, looking at me expectantly. I wanted to vanish on the spot. Instead, I picked mine up, echoed 'Yiamas' when they said it, and clinked my small glass against theirs. Down it went, and I felt my eyes snap shut as the taste memory came rushing back. Nail polish remover, tequila, really bad tequila; all in one. It took everything I had to keep down the monstrous amount of food we'd just eaten.

I tried to cut the awful sensation in my mouth and throat by shoving a spoonful of the crême brulée-looking stuff into my mouth. Unlike the small pastry we'd had during my first encounter with Tsikoudia, this did absolutely nothing. In fact, it amplified the pungency of the shot. It was nothing like crême brulée at all; instead it was a thick, milky pudding with the slightest aftertaste of honey. I wanted to spit out the bite I had taken. It felt like I had just eaten curdled milk. I set my spoon down, trying not to make a face. I was gagging. Yiannis let out a laugh and patted me on the back.

"I think Sam is not loving the Raki!" His bubbly imitation-American personality was in full swing. He had thrown his back without so much as a shudder. How is that possible?

"It's awful!" I said, still reeling. Even Elena seemed to be having some trouble with it; her eyes were still pressed shut in anguish. After a few minutes, we'd regained composure. It was now after midnight and between the late hour and the alcohol, we fought to keep our eyes open. Yiannis told us we needed to take a picture before we left, so I stood among the three Greek men as Elena snapped a photo for us. I did the same for her, then offered to pay for dinner as a thank-you for everything (but Yiannis only let me pay for the wine). We were soon on our way home, ready for a short walk and fresh air. Yiannis told us a friend of his was coming to give us a ride, which we were very thankful for as even going down the stairway was a difficult thing to do. Fresh air would have been nice, but not nearly as nice as actually making it home and not drunkenly falling into the harbor. We opted to accept the ride. When the car arrived, Elena and I giggled and climbed in the back. We buckled our seatbelts, listening to Yiannis and the driver begin an animated conversation we couldn't understand.

I leaned against the window and looked up into the night sky. My head was absolutely spinning; two glasses of wine that afternoon with Elena, a lager at Aroma, and an impressive amount of wine at Thalassino Ageri. And then that God-awful shot. I closed my eyes and smiled. I'd just had an amazing evening with two complete strangers, who were quickly turning into friends. My stomach was absolutely stuffed with good food, and perhaps just a bit too much alcohol. I had at least another day in this beautiful city, which now seemed a blessing instead of rushing off to Santorini on a ferry boat. It was all just too good to be true; Chania was too good to be true. I re-opened my eyes as the little car flew through the streets. Elena was in the same zoned-out state as I was, so I let my focus roll back to the window. *How is the sky so much more beautiful in the nighttime than it is in the day? Why can't it always be like this? Why can't we always be like this? Just travelers spending time and sharing stories with one another. This should be a more common thing. My God, those stars are beautiful.*

· · · · ·

When we got back to the flat, I couldn't even bring myself to shower. I took my shoes off by the front door, thanked Yiannis again for a wonderful evening, gave Elena a hug goodnight, and went to my bedroom. I climbed into the soft, white bed and closed my eyes. I was beyond ready for a good night's sleep.

My phone buzzed a few times and I ignored it. I was thoroughly exhausted, and I didn't necessarily trust myself talking to anyone in my current state. However, when it began to buzz again a few moments later, I answered. It nearly 1:00am in Greece and I wondered who would be calling me at such a ridiculous hour. It was my bank.

"Samantha, hi – I just wanted to let you know that your card will be arriving to the UPS store in Chania tomorrow and you will be able to pick it up first thing in the morning."

Is really happening right now? It seemed like it could be, but my mind was not in the right place for a proper phone call. I thanked the woman on the phone and asked her to send me an email confirmation, then hung up. *If it's there in the morning, I'll get excited about it then. I need to sleep.* And then I closed my eyes drifted off.

. . . . .

The next morning, I woke up in a haze. My mouth was uncomfortably dry, my mascara had crusted in the corner of my eyes, I still had on 'last night's clothes', and my legs were very sore from all of the walking Elena and I had done around town. I laid there for a few minutes, wondering if it would be more beneficial to fall back asleep and hope I woke up feeling better, or to pull myself out of the comfy bed, brush my teeth and hair, and take a shower. It was an agonizing decision that I couldn't make, so I flopped onto my other side. My phone was on the floor, and I stretched one arm over the side of the mattress to grab it. I couldn't help but to wince as I looked at the painfully bright screen. It was going to be a rough morning.

And then I saw the email:

Dear Samantha,

This is an email to confirm that your replacement card has been approved, processed, and will be available for pick-up tomorrow: Friday, November 25th at the UPS store provided – they had asked, and Yiannis told me which location I should share with them – Please note this parcel will only be available for 48 hours or it will be returned. There will be information included to activate your emergency replacement card. Do not hesitate to inform our team if you need any further assistance. Thank you for your patience and correspondence through this process. We understand the inconvenience this has caused you on your trip and hope our service has met your expectations.

Kind Regards,

I flew out of bed, ignoring the soreness, headache, dry mouth, and crusty eyes. *My card was coming!* I felt ecstatic. I would have it the next morning; I would have it in just one day. My first move was to tell Yiannis. He was nowhere to be found, so I sent my mother a message despite the fact that it was the middle of the night in Michigan. Then I sent Pat a message to let him know the card was almost there. Miraculously he was still up, so we talked for a while about what I'd be doing next. Eventually, he concluded that he would book my flight for some time early afternoon on Friday. I would have a good portion of the evening in Athens and could meet up with Olivier, spend all of Saturday looking through the museums I'd skipped and of course visit the Parthenon, and then find a bus back to the airport on Sunday to head home. It was exactly what I'd been most looking forward to; it was a plan. *Everything is coming together,* I thought, my heart pounding with excitement. *Just one more day!*

Elena was still sleeping on the couch, so I took a shower, brushed my teeth, re-organized my bag, and sat in the kitchen writing until she woke up. It was nearly 9:00am when she finally joined me, completely zombie-like as I had been just a short while earlier. I made a cup of tea for each of us (though I would have done anything for coffee, there was no way to make it), and we sat at the table each writing in our own notebook. We ate more of our salty snack mix and the oranges on the table for breakfast, occasionally asking the other about some small detail from the night before for clarification. It was a great feeling to be sitting there with another traveler, each recording a different version of the same story from our night in Chania. It just felt *right*.

I told her about my card being ready and asked if she'd noticed Yiannis sneak out earlier. She shook her head. As if in response, both of our phones buzzed at the same time. It was Yiannis, through WhatsApp. He told us we should be to Aroma by no later than 10:00am. He was currently at the brewery with Mona, and had sent one of his employees, Apostolos, to fetch us. We were finally going to see where Yiannis' amazing beer was made.

We were going to Cretan Brewery.

14

Elena and I made our way to Aroma, taking in the morning hustle and bustle of the city. The sun was shining, and people were out walking their dogs and riding their bicycles, stores were selling things outside, and children were playing outdoors at the small preschool on the corner. We heard the occasional car horn, people shouting to each other from the streets to the windows above, and bits of conversations coming from groups of teens huddled on the sidewalks. As we walked, I thoroughly enjoyed the fresh air and the occasional whiff of citrus from all of the trees. It did absolute wonders for my headache. This was the perfect morning.

We reached Aroma right at 10:00am and took a seat outdoors, at one of the rectangular tables with the sofa-like benches.

As if we both knew we'd be there awhile, we each ordered a coffee and took out our notebooks to write. I couldn't help but people watch. The morning crowd at Aroma was so different than the crowd we'd witnessed the night before. Families came in for brunch with their little ones, a few teenage girls came in and ordered nothing but iced beverages, and a few older women came in with their knitting. There were no classy-looking couples sharing wine, groups of gentlemen doing business, or large groups of teenagers. It had an entirely different atmosphere and we rather enjoyed it.

Our hunch was correct in assuming Apostolos would be late. He didn't arrive until nearly 11:30am. He paid for our coffees and apologized for running so late, and then we climbed into his little red car to head out. The drive to Cretan Brewery took about thirty minutes from the time we left Aroma. I was surprised to see that the freeway from Chania to Zounaki (the small village where the brewery was located, roughly 16 miles west) was incredibly similar to those in America. Apart from distances being in kilometers instead of miles and towns written in Greek, the roads themselves reminded me of home. Was I expecting it to be much different? Why is this so surprising? During the drive, Apostolos pointed out different buildings and areas and told us about their significance in the history there. Some of the buildings were quite old, and most were churches. He explained that 'back in the day', the way families contributed to a church was by buying the bricks or windows or roofs, and because so many religious people came to Crete, there were a ton of churches built. If the family wanted to buy the bricks for a church and they'd already been purchased, they would just build another church. According to Apostolos, this happened frequently, and yet most of them now stood vacant. It was interesting and sad at the same time. I wondered if my great-great-grandparents had once helped to build a church.

The conversation changed as we drove, and Apostolos told us about his role at Cretan Brewery. He explained how he'd met Yiannis and how he'd come into the picture as a salesman for him. It was clear to me, after hearing him talk about Yiannis and having had a similar conversation with Mona, that his employees thought very highly of him. Yiannis was clearly an exceptional individual and a talented businessman. *How did I get so fortunate to find him as my host?*

The buildings grew further and further apart, giving way to fields and patches of orange trees as we distanced ourselves from Chania. When we finally saw the large sign with the brewery's symbol – the head of a mountain goat – Apostolos smiled and announced that we'd arrived. Elena and I looked at each other, very excited for the day ahead. I had never been to a Greek brewery before; I didn't even know such things existed. If this is half as amazing as the Greek winery though, it's going to be a fantastic day! We parked, got out of the car, and looked around. It had to be the most beautiful brewery I'd ever seen and was only slightly larger than Manousakis Winery. This building, however, was very modern: it was a simple, square shape with exterior walls that were painted solid red, white, and black. There was an enormous patio off to one side, with a dozen white picnic tables waiting to seat the brewery's visitors. In view of the patio were rolling hills covered in orange trees, which Apostolos told us were used in some of the beer they made. They stretched as far as the eye could see. I could only imagine working there and enjoying that view every day.

He ushered us inside, where Mona was waiting for us in what

seemed to be the gift shop. It was full of boxes. She explained that they had just started carrying a wider selection of inventory, and it was still in the process of being unloaded. She opened a few of the boxes, showing us the keychains, pint glasses, and other branded knick-knacks they would soon start selling. There were two men in the store as well, waiting to meet with Apostolos about carrying the beer in their restaurant. We were all introduced, then headed off down a hallway for a tour. Mona led the way.

She first showed us the large, metal vats in which the malts were mixed. There was a small, glass door on the vat that we could look through and see the contents within it. She explained that each type of beer had a different combination: overall it took five weeks per batch. As she spoke, I could tell that she was enthusiastic about the beer. She had told me that she'd been giving tours since the opening of the brewery, and yet it didn't seem like she was just rattling off information. She kept us interested; I thoroughly enjoyed hearing her explain the process. We climbed down a metal ladder into a room full of enormous silver vats, with pipes running every which way. We saw Yiannis looking at a gauge on one of the vats, scribbling something down on a small clipboard. He nodded to us, then continued going about his work. We followed Mona to the entryway of the room, where she continued.

From the mixing vats, the malts were ground and mixed with water. She explained that the water they used at Cretan Brewery came from the White Mountains of Crete; Yiannis wanted his beverage to live up to its slogan, "All of Crete in a glass". She went on to say that they were an incredibly environmentally friendly brewery, requiring only 5L of water per liter of beer compared to the usual 10L. On an unrelated note, she also mentioned they burned olive pits and used solar panels for heat and used leftover ingredients for animal feed and bio fertilizer. If something could be done to reduce environmental impact, they were sure to do it.

Once thoroughly mixed water, the batch was heated. Apparently different types of beer required different temperatures, so the brewery could only produce so much in a given period of time. From the heating vats, it was sent through a vessel that separated the ingredients, eventually making its way into a boiling tank where hops were added. In the final stages of the process – and the most time consuming – the mixture was spun to allow centrifugation to remove the remaining solids of the hops from the rest of the 'beer must'. Then it was cooled and allowed to ferment for nearly five weeks.

Mona showed us each machine or vat as we went, including the water purification room and the kegging room. At one point she even ushered us into the room where giant burlap bags of malted barley and hops were stored. She explained the origin of their ingredients: France, Germany, and America for the hops, Belgium and Komotini (in Greece) for the malted barley. Yiannis was very specific about only having the best ingredients in his beer.

The two men speaking with Apostolos smelled some of the hops and gave approving nods, then followed us as we continued. Our final stop was a small kitchen, where the four of us sat while Apostolos and Mona prepared a small lunch for us. We were offered a few samples of beer - Elena and I choosing the blonde lager and the two men choosing an IPA and the dark - and they set out oranges and small pieces of Spanikopita for us to eat. From the beer to the amazing food and fresh fruit, I was very impressed with the brewery. It was so neat to see the brewing process, especially because I'd seen how passionate Yiannis was about the end product.

He came to join us there in the kitchen and asked us what we thought of his brewery. Elena and I were both at a loss of words. Mona's statement from just a few days earlier was resonating through my head: send me your CV. *Could that even be a possibility to move to Greece and work here? With this awesome team, in this amazing place, and that beautiful view? Seriously?* Yiannis seemed thoroughly content with how much we liked it. He told us that we would have to come back, as he was planning to make a winter dark lager with Carob and have seasonal offerings as the brewery grew and expanded. They were also planning to eventually open a proper restaurant, not just the picnic tables we'd seen earlier. The two men sitting near Apostolos perked up at that, and from their tone of voice I could tell they'd made up their minds to carry Charma in their restaurant. *Leave it to Yiannis to really drive the sale home.*

Mona told me and Elena that she would meet us later for coffee, and Yiannis followed by saying he'd be home for dinner. We offered to have it ready for him, and he happily accepted. Originally Elena was going to leave that evening for Ritima – a nearby city – but changed her plans to have one more night in Chania. So, we decided to make the most of our last night together there. We would spend some time at Yiannis' flat, then head out for coffee. Afterwards, we'd shop and cook dinner for our host. It would be a fun but relaxing evening. Apostolos drove us back to Aroma, and we waved out the back window as we pulled away from the brewery. It was an odd feeling leaving Cretan Brewery; whether it was because I'd had such an enjoyable afternoon or because I considered the founder to be a sort of father figure in Greece, I felt like I was connected to it in some way. I didn't want to leave.

When we got back to the restaurant, we expected Apostolos to let us get out of the car, then drive off. Instead, he offered to take us on a tour of the area of the Venetian Harbor that had not yet been overrun with restaurants and tourist shops. Intrigued, we followed.

He led us to what looked like a gravel parking lot around which were situated many tall, dilapidated old buildings. Apostolos explained that they weren't functional buildings: they were simply taken over by inhabitants who stole the electricity and lived inside without paying rent.

"It's best not to look in the windows." he warned. Elena and I raised our eyebrows in unison.

Off one side of the parking lot (against the edge of a cliff), we could see the Aegean stretching into the horizon. Apostolos told us that it was one of the best views of the Venetian Harbor and he'd brought many dates here to impress them. It was breathtaking; dark blues and greens swirled, stretching into the evening sky. *I would love for a man to bring me here!* Apostolos talked a bit more about how locals didn't like that tourists were taking over the historic Venetian Harbor, and how they liked to keep this spot separate from the rest. He said that if the spot ever became too overrun with tourists, the town's culture would start to be lost. I tried to imagine what it must be like living in such a historic place, finding balance between keeping the culture alive while staying in-tune with the rest of the world. That was a problem we would never have where I grew up in Michigan: we only had a few hundred years of history to preserve, not thousands.

Apostolos walked with us back to Aroma, where we headed home to relax. The evening atmosphere had returned to the city, and in the place of the children, walkers, and bikes were couples holding hands, older gentlemen dressed in suits, and – further away from the harbor – groups of teenagers, still huddled on the sidewalks but now with cigarettes. When we finally made it back to the flat, we decided to finish our wine. Before we drank it, Elena taught me how to properly 'cheers' in Russian.

"Za tvajo zdarovje!" she said. "It means, to your health."

I tried (unsuccessfully) to repeat her, and almost had it by the fourth try. We clinked glasses and sat at the kitchen table for a while, just talking. We decided we'd make a potato-vegetable dish with avocado for dinner and stop at the grocery store on the way home from our coffee date with Mona. Then we took out our phones, took a few pictures, and caught up with family and friends back home. She showed me her family members and I showed her mine, and we shared stories about foods our moms cooked and things we loved about our home countries. It was so nice to just sit and chat with Elena, and before I knew it I was thinking about a trip to Moscow. We had only had two full days together and there we were, already making plans to visit each other in the future.

Mona picked us up around 6:00pm, and said she wanted to take us to her favorite café on the Venetian Harbor. Her small car could only hold one passenger, so I folded in half and squeezed into the trunk while she and Elena took the front seats. I chimed in on the conversation on the drive, shouting through the seat to be audible. I would have never imagined that one day I'd be riding around an island in Greece in the trunk of a car. *The things you do when you travel alone.*

We reached the café before long, and I was surprised to see that it had been constructed in one of the old ship repair buildings.

The front was nothing more than a counter built into the wall, and most of the tables were outdoors. Everything about the café said sophisticated. The tables were white with glass tops, on which sat small vases holding flowers. The chairs were made of black metal and had smooth, white cushions. And all around us, men and women were dressed in high fashion, fitting in with the clean lines and sophisticated atmosphere of the café. Even the menus were fancy: each offering was written in both Greek and beautiful English cursive. A waiter (also dressed in a sophisticated manner) came over to greet us and take our orders. As Mona had predicted, my black coffee came in a small, individual French press with a small biscuit on the side. Elena got a cappuccino with a small cinnamon cookie, and Maria got a tea served with olives. The three of us sat enjoying our beverages, talking about everything from the morning at the brewery and what we thought of Yiannis' work to poor Elena's hiccups (she contracted quite a case of them while we were sitting there). We were just three girls on a coffee date. No one would have known we were from such different countries and had met under truly unique circumstances.

Elena told Mona about her upcoming plans to go to Ritima and Heraklion, and I told her about mine to return to Athens and fly back to Detroit. She wished us the best of luck, telling us she used to travel the same way we did and was very proud of us for being such strong young women. We finished our coffees, she gave each of us a business card with her contact information on it, and we hugged her goodbye. As we turned to walk home, I realized how wrong I'd been about her the first day I met her. It was hard to believe that there we were just two days later, and I already considered her a great friend.

We managed to get turned around on the way back to Yiannis' flat. We tried to find Carrefour – the grocery store I'd been to with Yiannis my first day in Chania – and ended up down some street with nothing but flats in either direction. Fortunately, we saw a girl our age walking towards us and she was able to help us. Clea (from Athens, she shared) helped us find the store and even walked with us until it was in sight. We walked through the store, picking out everything we'd need: peppers, tomatoes, feta cheese, tomato sauce, and onions. (I thought I'd seen potatoes on Yiannis' counter, and I knew he had a basket of avocados in his fridge.) We paid and started walking home just as it began to get dark outside. *Where did the day go?*

When we returned to Yiannis' flat, we set our groceries on the kitchen table and went about preparing dinner. As one of the first steps was to get the potatoes into the oven, we pulled the bag out from the corner of the counter. I pulled out the first potato.

And then I screamed and let it drop to the floor. *Worms!*

Elena burst out laughing as I shook my hand violently, feeling like it was crawling with the little white worms. It was covered; I had never felt something so disgusting in my life. *Did I not realize they were bad when I saw them? How could Yiannis not know he had a bag of wormy potatoes on the counter? Is that one wiggling under my fingernail? It's Olivier's apartment all over again!*

I shook my hand again and threw the bag in the garbage. We decided one of us had to go back to the store to buy a new bag of potatoes (our minds were set on making the dinner for Yiannis), so I volunteered. I nearly sprinted through the street to get there as soon as possible, not knowing how late the store was open. I'd noticed things closed rather early in Chania (in all of Greece, really), and fortunately Carrefour was still open when I got there. The woman at the till gave me the, 'Weren't-you-just-here?' look and watched me as I bee-lined towards the potatoes. I set a bag down in front of her and barely had time to get out an *efcharistó!* (thank you) before she waved me out the door.

I power-walked home, not feeling entirely comfortable in the dark streets of Chania with nothing but a bag of potatoes to defend myself. Elena was busy chopping vegetables when I arrived and smiled as she poured another glass of wine for me. I raised an eyebrow, seeing that she'd gotten into Yiannis' wine – *He said we could, remember?* – and we cheers'd in Russian and Greek before taking a drink. She told me that she had her plan figured out for the next day. Her bus would leave at 9:30am for Ritima, and she would pack her things in the morning. I told her that Yiannis and I would probably go to the UPS store early since he had to work, but that I'd walk with her to the bus stop. It was a solid plan, and we could enjoy one last coffee together at the bus stop before heading our separate ways.

We wrapped the new potatoes in tin foil and put them in the oven (now properly pre-heated), then finished chopping the vegetables. I thought back to the night with Cleo when we were making curry with her friend, dying laughing from the sting of the chopped peppers. Was that really a week ago? How is that possible? We then tossed them in herbs and olive oil, then put them in a pan to turn on fifteen minutes before the potatoes were done. I sat at the kitchen table and checked my messages while Elena busied herself with something on her phone as well. I had a confirmation message from my next host in Athens – Tamara – that everything was set for my last few nights there. I also had a screenshot of the confirmation page for my flight, sent by Pat earlier that day. My flight was scheduled for 7:00pm, so I would have the entire morning in Chania. I had a few things in mind that I wanted to do once I had my debit card, including buy the Greek All Seeing Eye Pandora charm for my mother and a few other souvenirs for my family members. I also wanted to have one more beer at Aroma and take a nap before the busy evening began. I planned out a few things for the morning, and before long it was time to finish preparing dinner.

Yiannis came home and quickly changed before heading to his exercise class, telling us how wonderful it smelled in his flat. He told us he would exercise better knowing that there was a delicious dinner waiting for him, thanked us, and headed out. Elena and I enjoyed our dinner without him, hungrier than we realized after our busy day. We sliced open our baked potatoes and piled the vegetables, avocado, and feta on top. It may not have been anything remotely similar to an American Thanksgiving dinner, but it was absolutely delicious, and I was thankful for a friend to enjoy it with.

After dinner, we fixed Yiannis a plate and cleaned up the kitchen. Then we took what was left of the wine into the living room and sat on the couch, taking care not to spill any on the white fabric. We found Sex and the City on T.V. – in English, thank goodness! – and watched it until Yiannis returned. He showered, then heated his dinner and joined us on the couch, pouring us each another huge glass of wine. God help my liver, I thought, clinking glasses with them. The three of us spent the rest of the night enjoying one another's company, drinking our wine, and entertaining Yiannis' guesses as to what the "secret ingredients" were in our amazing dinner. He wasn't used to having someone cook for him; as he ate, he couldn't stop smiling.

And it was in that moment that I realized he was as thankful for us as we were for him.

. . . . .

The trip was passing by far too quickly. It was hard to believe that just two weeks earlier, a coworker was picking me up to drive me to work, wallet and card intact. Just two weeks earlier, I had still never met my family, I hadn't slept in Olivier's tiny flat, I hadn't met Lena or Dimitria or Marilena, and I hadn't yet known how incredibly kind Yiannis and Mona were, or that I'd be going up into the White Mountains of Crete. It had evolved from a trip to discover my roots into an adventure I would never forget, both the good and the bad. There wasn't a single point during the entire trip when I'd wished I was home; even at the worst, I only wanted to find my wallet and get back to Athens for the security of having a way to get home. Waking up to my last day in Chania made everything sink in. I had become so comfortable with Yiannis and Elena. Spending the day with them felt like spending the day with family. I wasn't ready to leave.

I woke up at 7:00am as Yiannis and I had discussed going to the UPS store at 7:30am. He had to get to the brewery but would be back by 4:00pm to say goodbye (I was planning to head to the bus stop by 4:30pm). I had only a slight headache when I woke up, but knowing it was my last day in Chania put me in a sort of funk as I sat at the kitchen table with my breakfast. I ate the rest of the sheep's milk yogurt drizzled with Cretan honey and cinnamon. It was delicious as always, especially as it was the last morning I'd be able to have it. The 'bummed out' mood I was in quickly disappeared when Yiannis came into the kitchen with a huge smile on his face. He asked if I was ready to go, so I grabbed my passport, shoes, and purse. Then we were in his car, zipping through the streets on the way to the UPS store.

When we got there, it didn't seem like a store at all. It was completely different than the UPS stores we had in the United States, with only a few shelves of boxes and a row of envelopes behind the counter. It was tiny. In fact, if Yiannis hadn't pointed it out, I wouldn't have even seen it on the side of the road. I told the woman I had a package to pick up and handed her my passport. She looked up something on her computer, then disappeared through a door behind the desk. Moments later, she returned with a large, hard envelope and handed it to me. The moment I had it in my hands, I felt an enormous wave of relief come over me. I had it. *I finally had it.*

Elated, I thanked the woman over and over again until Yiannis ushered me out the door. My head was buzzing so loudly with relief and excitement that I barely understood what he was saying as we drove back to his flat. He was excited because there was a group of kids going to the brewery that day to learn about the ingredients and brewing process. I didn't quite understand how that worked – the drinking age in Greece was lower than in the U.S. but it was still only 18 – but was glad that he was so happy talking about it. Before I knew it, we were pulling up to his flat and he told me he would be home at 4:00pm to say good-bye.

"And maybe have one more Charma, yes?"

He drove off and I climbed the stairs to his flat. Elena was there, packing her things, and I excitedly showed her the envelope I'd been given at the UPS store. I went into my bedroom to pack and sat on the bed to open the envelope. I nearly ripped it open, flipping through the small instruction booklet that came with the replacement card. It wouldn't work in an atm machine; the card could only be used as credit cards were normally used and not to withdraw money. *Ok, not a problem*. I looked at the card and noticed it didn't have a three-digit code on the back but thought maybe that was because it was an emergency replacement card – not a standard card – and had its own set of rules. There was nothing in the booklet about it, so I put it in my purse and went about packing my things.

Elena was ready to go at 8:45am, so we left early and walked to the bus stop. We were glad to have a few minutes together before her bus left. I ordered a tea and a piece of Spanikopita and she ordered a cinnamon roll-looking pastry and a coffee. We sat enjoying our brunch until it was time for her to go. It was quite sad, giving my new Russian friend a hug goodbye with no solid future plan to see her again. We gave each other that 'last look' as I'd given Cleo when I left Germany – that infamous, unsure half smile – and hugged again. Then she turned and climbed aboard her bus and drove off moments later. I tried not to get emotional. It was something I'd come to learn about travelling: oftentimes the friends made abroad can be some of the best, but of course the hardest to spend time with. *I'll see her again. I'll make sure of it.*

I decided to head to the Venetian Harbor for a final afternoon of aimless wandering, enjoying the beautiful view and one more beer at Aroma. But first there was something I had to do. I'd passed it with Elena the day before on our way to the harbor to meet with Apostolos and made a mental note to come back before heading to Athens.

I had found a fish spa.

I'd first read about fish spas in a magazine article several years earlier, and thought it was the most disgusting thing ever.

Having little fish nibble the dead skin off your feet? Not for me, thank you very much. And after that, it had been in social media posts and even one of the articles I'd found online about Chania titled, Top 10 Things to Do in Chania. So there I was, standing outside the fish spa, wiggling my toes in anticipation. A large sign outside advertised, "€8/15min". *Is this really going to be worth it?* I had to find out.

"Nervous" couldn't even begin to describe how I felt as I looked at the tanks of fish situated beneath the chairs. A woman started talking to me as she came out from the back. She was a small woman, with massive amounts of brown curls pulled back with a clip.

"Kaliméra!" She said, smiling. "You'd like to do fish spa?"

"Kaliméra — and yes, very excited to try it!"

She introduced herself as Katharina, the owner. We got to talking about what I was doing in Chania, where I'd been, where I was from, etc. — the usual traveler chit chat — and she seemed elated when I mentioned I'd been to Bielefeld. She told me that she had a friend studying in Bielefeld, and she'd learned a bit of German to 'get by' when she visited her. I instantly started speaking to her German, and she responded the best she could. I could tell she'd been taken off guard as she was instantly surprised but excited to hear me speaking German. She led me to the back of the shop, where she had me remove my shoes. Then she washed my feet in a wash bin, dried them, put some kind of lotion on them, and led me back to the row of chairs with the fish tanks underneath them. She explained that she had to wash everybody's feet because actual dirt was bad for the fish; they were meant to eat the dead skin instead. I cringed, and my nerves returned. I looked down at my now-clean feet, appalled that another human being had just touched them. They were red, with calluses and ripped blisters (which no longer stung, thank goodness) on the tops and sides. Thankfully I'd trimmed my toenails before leaving for the trip, but still. My feet had seen better days. As if she could read my mind, Katherina laughed and put her hand on my shoulder.

"Don't worry, I've seen much, much worse feet. Yours will be fine."

Lovely, mine will be fine for the fish to eat. Why was I doing this again?

She set a timer next to my chair and placed my feet into the tank. It was like sticking a magnet into a bowl of iron shavings; the fish instantly swarmed my feet and I almost yanked them back up out of the tank. It tickled so much for the first few minutes that my nails were digging into the seat. I leaned over the tank and watched as they gnawed away at my toes, my ankles, and even the part of my leg that was submerged in the water. I wanted to burst out laughing and crying at the same time. Katharina told me to try to relax. Apparently I would get used to it.

"And actually, they don't have teeth, so it's like they're giving you small kisses to pull off the dead skin particles," she said. I just stared at her, nails still firmly embedded into the cushion beneath me.

Ok now you're just going to make me throw up. She went on to tell me that it was actually an amazing therapy for poor circulation and many senior citizens come as her 'regulars' to help with their different ailments. As if that wasn't surprising enough, she continued by saying that some places submerge the entire body in a tank of the little fish. From the neck down, people literally let the fish eat the skin from their entire bodies to improve circulation and treat different skin issues. *Nope, nope, nope*. I thought. *My feet are enough, thank you.*

After a few minutes, Katharina was right; I was used to it. It felt more like little bubble jets on my feet, and I was finally able to relax. It was actually quite soothing. I continued talking with her as the fish feasted, talking about the different people she'd met from all over the world and how odd she found it that I was traveling in November. We were still talking when the timer went off, and for conversation's sake she gave me an extra ten minutes free of charge. By the time she helped me lift my feet out of the water, I could barely feel the fish anymore. But my feet felt fantastic. It didn't hurt to put my Converse back on, and any tenderness I'd had that morning was completely gone. I was very glad that I'd be able to walk around Athens without having to stop for sore feet.

I paid Katharina and went on my way. I found a little Mediterranean Bookstore on one side of the Harbor, where I bought a book called Learn Greek Without a Teacher, which at the time I fully intended on doing. *I already learned six words, and what's another language?* I also still had in mind the idea of sending Mona my resume to work at the brewery. If it miraculously worked out, I would need to have some foundation of Greek. The book was cheap, so I bought it and headed over to Aroma. I ordered the dark Charma lager and enjoyed people-watching and writing for a few hours, fully taking in Chania for the short amount of time I had left to enjoy it.

I stopped into a market on the way back to the flat and bought tomatoes and cucumbers with the idea in mind to make a homemade Horiatiki salad while I packed. I used the leftover feta from our dinner the night before, drizzled some of Yiannis' home-made olive oil over top, and enjoyed my delicious salad. Then I cleaned up the kitchen, packed my bag, and took a nap. My alarm went off at 4:00pm, and I waited for Yiannis.

By the time I wanted to leave – at 4:30pm – Yiannis still hadn't arrived home. I was getting nervous about finding my bus stop on time (it was different than where Elena and I had been that morning), so I wrote him a very nice note, a wonderful review on the Couchsurfing website, and headed out. I didn't enjoy the feeling I had as I walked down the stairs from his flat one last time, through the gate, and off down the street. I wanted to turn around and head back. Instead, I got lost on the way to the bus stop and had to ask for directions. I had managed to go quite out of the way, so by the time I reached the bus stop (running), I had two minutes to spare until the bus took off for the airport.

Despite my desire to stay in Chania, I did feel relaxed to finally be on the bus heading back to the airport. After all, I had found the right one after a small panic that I'd miss it, and the majority of my stress during traveling was figuring out the public transportation in other countries. From there I just had to get to the proper gate at the airport, then take the metro from the airport in Athens to the station Sygrou Fix to meet Tamara. I leaned my head back against the seat. I still had cash from my mother's Western Union transaction. I had my replacement debit card. I had my flight back to Athens. Everything had been resolved.

When the bus pulled up to the airport, I got in line to check in behind a group of English speakers from California. They were extremely upset because their upcoming flight had been cancelled due to a Lufthansa strike. *Please God don't let that happen to me on Sunday when I fly back to the U.S.!* I got my boarding pass, passed through security quickly, found my gate, and only had to wait about thirty minutes before boarding. There were about thirty of us on the plane, and somehow I managed to get stuck between two large men emitting strange noises. Fortunately, the flight went by quickly (I was thrilled they gave us more Terkelin pastries and coffee), and I managed to doze off. Before long we were descending into the airport in Athens, and as we touched down I was pulled out of my half-sleeping daze. I smiled as I leaned over and looked out the window.

I made it. I made it back to Athens

15

For 8:00 in the evening, Athens' airport was buzzing. I was still half asleep but managed to push my way through the crowd waiting at the gate. I was scheduled to meet Tamara at Sygrou-Fix at 9:00pm, so I set out to find the metro. Fortunately, everything at the airport was very clearly marked. I found it in no time, bought my ticket, and waited for the train to arrive.

The lights flickered on the platform. There was a periodic shaking and the 'whooshing' sound of the trains echoed in the tunnels. I felt like I was in a movie. All around me, people were shuffling about, some nervously checking their watches, others digging through their backpacks or purses in search of something. And the people there were so incredibly diverse. I guessed they came from all different countries, given the different languages, fashions, and personalities. It seemed strange to me that there could be so many people in one spot who I'd never met before. The world could seem so small sometimes, but sometimes – in moments like this – I remembered just how big it was.

I boarded the train when it arrived and spent the next forty-five minutes jotting down notes from the morning. I made sure to keep my purse directly in front of me, balancing my notebook on top as the train rumbled along. People got on and off as we made our way, and I noticed a man in the center holding what looked like a marionette. About twenty minutes into the ride, he hit a button on the back of the puppet and rock 'n roll music started playing. *Is that Alice Cooper? Really? On the metro in Athens?* The man was a metro performer; as the music played, he made the puppet (dressed like a rockstar) "play" his guitar. A few people were amused, a few looked annoyed, and I watched with wide eyes this strange thing that I could never imagine seeing in Michigan. Not only did we have limited public transportation, but people kept to themselves far too much. No one would be so bold.

We pulled up to Sygrou-Fix and I made my way up out of the metro. It was dark outside, and I emerged in the cool night air surrounded by the familiar buildings and stores I'd gotten to know just a week or so earlier. I recognized the area around the metro station, realizing I was quite close to Olivier's apartment. *I wonder where we'll go for dinner tomorrow?* I was thankful for his friendship but looking forward to staying with Tamara this time around instead. I looked around the platform for her, but still had a few minutes until it was 9:00pm. I sat on the top step and waited. I managed to find a Wi-Fi network and connected just in time to receive a message from her:

Running late at a shoot, be there shortly!

Tamara had mentioned that she was a freelancer but never went into much detail about her work. A shoot? Is she a photographer? I couldn't help but wonder. And then – nearly fifteen minutes later – she arrived, and it hit me: *model.* She was absolutely beautiful, with long blonde hair and bright green eyes. She had a black hat on, and as she approached I could see pink highlights in her hair. A dark green jacket (though not in the style of the anarchists), leather pants, and high black heels: even her outfit shouted model.

"Sam! I am so sorry, I hope you weren't waiting long!" She seemed out of breath in that glamorous way that only models can, gave me a hug as soon as she reached me, then kissed me once on each cheek. I reciprocated without hesitation. *She even smells like strawberries. Jesus, can I just be her?* Tamara smiled and took my bag. I half expected her heels to snap in half at the weight of it, but she managed it with ease and ushered me to follow her. I took notes as we went, remembering street names and landmarks so I could find my way back later on. We finally passed a petrol station and reached her flat moments later. It was a tall, pink building on a corner, at the very top of a hill. I couldn't imagine wearing the heels she had on and successfully walking home from work without falling flat on my face. The girl was skilled.

When we reached the door, she reminded me of the German couple staying with her as well, then said there was also another boy staying there just for the night. I could use the kitchen, help myself to whatever cooking supplies I needed, and use the Wi-Fi so long as I was sure to lock the door as I came and went. Unlike Olivier's and Marilena's flat buildings, Tamara's had an elevator. I sighed in relief as we ascended to the fourth floor. The doors opened, and we made our way down a narrow hallway with a rough wooden floor and white walls, turning to a door at the very end.

"Welcome to my home," she said, pulling open the heavy wood door.

I was surprised to see how empty her flat was. Given her personal style – chic, clean, modern – I expected her flat to be the same. Instead, it seemed like no one even lived there. There was a small television set up on a table off to one side, a large, suede sofa facing it on the other. There was also a small coffee table set up with a magazine on top between the two, but that was it. No knick-knacks, pictures, or personality. The wood floor was bare, and the white walls were empty, save for a few wires that disappeared under what I imagined were the bedroom doors.

She showed me the kitchen – also empty, white, untouched – followed by the bathroom. I was thrilled to see a shower curtain in the bathroom (also white, but at least it had panda bears on it) and even more excited when she told me there were clean towels for me on my bed. She led me to my bedroom and set my carry-on down inside. After asking if I needed anything, she said she had to run off to meet someone. She handed me a key, told me to enjoy the evening, and left. I waved, then turned around to take in the room. Unsurprisingly, the bedroom had white walls. However, there were a few pictures hung there – mostly cartoon sea creatures and bubbles – and a small white nightstand next to the bed. The comforter was brightly colored and matched the lamp shade on the nightstand. On the floor was a small rug (placed 'just so' to prevent my feet from hitting the cold floor when I woke up in the morning). It was very simple, but cozy. For two nights, it would be just fine.

I decided to head into the city for a final night out before heading back to America. It was Friday, and while I still had another night in the city ahead of me, I knew I'd have to go to bed early to catch the first bus to the airport on Sunday. I organized my purse, locked the door as I left, and set out for Syntagma. I walked the route I planned on taking Sunday morning (the bus left from Syntagma at 6:00am) and arrived after about 30 minutes of walking. By the time I reached the Square, my feet were starting to hurt again. It was already 11:15pm, and surprisingly very few places were still open. I didn't dare try to find the area Olivier had taken me the first night, when we'd seen the bar with the witch above the doorway. Instead, being a creature of habit, I found Piatsa and was glad to see they were open until midnight. It had been a very busy day; all I wanted was to sit on the balcony overlooking the Square and enjoy a glass of their red wine with my favorite salad. *There's still plenty of time to explore tomorrow.*

It was as delicious as I remembered. The wine was bold and fruity: not too sweet and not too dry. The salad was fresh and the feta was creamy, but the olive oil was nothing compared to Yiannis'. Regardless, I thoroughly enjoyed it. At 11:55pm, the waitress told me they were closing and that I had to leave, so I asked for the check and pulled out my new debit card.

"Ma'am, I'm sorry, but it says this card is declined."

"Excuse me?"

"I can't process this card; there is an error. I'll try again."

She ran it through her handheld machine once more, and it let out a sad beep. I stared at it, mentally willing it to work. You have got to be kidding me. My blood started pumping and I felt my face grow hot. *This is the replacement card! It's supposed to work! I waited three extra days in Chania for this!* The waitress shook her head and asked if I could pay in cash. Fortunately, I still had about €40 left, so I unfolded a €10 note and handed it to her. She thanked me and I left.

As I walked back to Tamara's flat, my mind was racing. *The replacement card doesn't work. It doesn't work. It does not work. I tried to use it, and it got declined.* I felt the petrified sensation I'd experienced in Chania creep back over me as I thought about how many euros I had left and if it would be enough to get me through until Sunday. I had enough for food and would be sure to save money for the bus ticket to the airport, but that was it. *But what about the Pandora charm for my mom? What about the other souvenirs I want to buy? Thank GOD I already bought my Starbucks mugs!* Between the failed card, my sore feet, and the late hour, I finally broke. I felt tears rolling down my cheeks and didn't bother to wipe them away. My excitement of having the card was gone; it was nothing but a useless piece of plastic. My bank had told me it wouldn't work at an ATM, but at a *restaurant*? Had there been some mistake?

Maybe it was just the restaurant. Maybe tomorrow it'll work just fine at Pandora and the other souvenir shops, and I can just use my cash for food. But then I remembered there was no three-digit code on the back of the card. *Did that have something to do with this? Did they send me a dud card?* I tried not to panic, but as I walked I realized I was moving faster and faster and my palms were beginning to sweat. I tried to find the petrol station Tamara and I had passed earlier that evening but couldn't seem to find it anywhere. I thought I had done a good job of retracing my steps. *Had I possibly missed it? Had I walked right past the street in my panic?* My first night back in Athens was certainly not going as I'd hoped.

I saw the sign for Sygrou-Fix metro station across the street and went over to the steps where I'd sat only hours earlier, again taking a seat on the cold concrete. A few people stared at me, sitting there on the top step of the metro station with my tear-stained cheeks, and others just continued about their business. There was a surprising amount of people around, as there were a few late-night bars open nearby. I found the Wi-Fi network and messaged Tamara asking for help. *Please respond soon!* To my delight, it was only a matter of minutes before a response popped up: a map, with the route from the metro station to her flat highlighted. I got up to head home and felt my stomach growl. (As delicious as it had been, the salad at Piatsa was not very filling considering the amount of walking I'd done.) I saw a street cart selling pastries, candy, and drinks, and debated how much I could spend while still having enough for the rest of my trip. There was a cheap bottle of wine for only €3,50, and a box of cheese-filled pastries that were €1,50. *I could afford to spend €5. Right? Down to €25 for tomorrow. Totally doable.*

By the time I did finally reach Tamara's flat, I was exhausted. I barely had enough energy to shower but forced myself to do so as I couldn't bring myself to get in my clean bed covered with the dirt and grime of the day. I had managed to acquire a brand-new set of blisters, so ss I pulled my socks off, I winced as the fabric pulled open my fresh wounds. The shower water was absolute murder on my feet, but it felt good to get clean and crawl into bed. It was so comfortable, and after a day of walking, traveling, and more walking there was nothing better than getting cozy. I turned the lamp on and spent about forty-five minutes writing, enjoying a glass of the wine I'd bought, and eventually drifted off. I had just one more day in Athens, and despite the debit card situation, I was determined to make the most of it.

．．．．．

Not three hours later, I woke up to hear a loud banging coming from the living room. I shot bolt upright, instantly thinking the flat was being robbed. I didn't want to leave my bedroom, but the banging continued. *What the hell is that?*

I walked out into the living room and saw two people standing there in their pajamas looking equally confused and annoyed. The girl was about my age, with tight curls and sleepy eyes. The boy was maybe a year or two older, with long brown hair and lots of facial hair. As soon as they said hello and I heard their accent, I identified them as the German couple Tamara had told me about. We briefly introduced ourselves, then looked back to the door as the banging grew more desperate. The German boy – Peter – walked over and looked through the peephole. Then he pulled open the door, and a scrawny black-haired man pushed his way inside.

"Goddamit I've been knocking forever, what took you so long? I'm going to be late!" He rushed past us to the third bedroom. I saw him drop something onto the bed before rushing back towards the door. "Forgot the bloody key. Seeya." The door slammed shut behind him.

"He was going to stay longer, but something happened and he had to go home this morning," the girl said. She'd introduced herself as Rosie, and I instantly liked her. Rosie seemed very easygoing and nonchalant, as if the banging on the door in the middle of the night didn't bother her in the slightest. The three of us had a brief discussion on who we were and where we were from, then said our goodnights and went back to sleep. *Just another night in an AirBNB.*

. . . . .

Despite the late night (or was it early morning?) interruption, I slept wonderfully. I woke up the next morning around 10:00am feeling well-rested, refreshed, and ready to take on my final day in Athens. I found bandages in the bathroom cupboard and did my best to 'fix up' my feet before putting on my socks and shoes. There was instant coffee in the kitchen, and I made a cup to help me wake up fully before heading out.

I made my way to Attika, where I decided to get one last piece of Spanikopita and a coffee for the walk into the city. It was warm, cheesy, and absolutely phenomenal. When I turned to walk out the door, I ran into someone and almost spilled my coffee, but they managed to dodge me as I literally fell out of the bakery. I recovered quickly, mildly embarrassed, and continued along the street. And then – just as soon as I had regained my composure – I was almost hit by a car turning out of a side street. The morning was far from perfect. But I had slept well, was in a great mood, and couldn't wait for my first destination: the Parthenon.

It took me a decent amount of time to walk there, and by the time I reached the entrance to the Acropolis it was already after noon. There was a line of people waiting to get in, filing one by one past the ticket booth. A few dogs roamed about, tourists clicked away on their cameras, and a few little girls ran in circles around their parents. And then there were those who, like me, couldn't stop glancing up at the magnificent structure at the top of the hill, standing proud and full of history. I love this city, I thought. Athens was just unlike anywhere I'd ever been in the United States.

It cost €10 to enter but was well worth it. The path wound its way up the side of the hill, passing different sculptures and monuments as it went. First, I saw the sanctuary of Dionysus, a few large stone pillars with carvings of grapes and vines in them. I remembered the sarcophagus I'd seen in Thessaloniki, which had similar carvings on it. I admired the passion the Greeks had for wine: a passion which had clearly existed for centuries and which, undoubtedly, I had inherited.

I continued along the path, eavesdropping on conversations I heard along the way. One couple was marveling at something off in the distance, another was reciting the history of a sculpture off to the right, and a mother was yelling at her son not to run off too far ahead. But my favorite was a couple with a new baby just ahead of me. The man was pointing at the stone theatre just around the corner, and his partner craned her neck to see.

"And that's where my Papa proposed."

The woman cooed and my heart melted. Oddly enough, it wasn't because of the romantic gesture or the beautiful hillside where it happened. It was because he said, My Papa. I instantly thought of my Papa and realized I knew nothing of his relationship with my grandmother. I had no idea how they met, how he proposed, or how (or where) they were married. All I knew was that she was a great Nana who sometimes made Spamburgers and passed away when I was one. I wanted to call my mom right then and there to find out more.

The couple walked on, and I followed them along the path. It led right up to the stone theatre, which was revealed to be a rather enormous structure as I rounded the corner. A sign at the bottom read, *Theatre of Dionysus*. I walked past a group and was surprised to see people sitting on the stone benches. Naturally, I climbed halfway up and took a seat among them.

It was in that moment that I experienced an overwhelming sensation of both reverence and pride. I was in one of the most historic sites in Greece, possibly in the entire world. I was literally sitting on a bench where some of the most influential philosophers may have once sat some two-*thousand* years earlier, enjoying the performance down below. My head rushed. There I was, visiting the theatre on vacation in my blue jeans and a t-shirt, when back in the day people would be dressed up to come and see the show. I couldn't bring myself to move; I just wanted to sit there on that bench and take as much time as I could to appreciate the beauty of it all. It was simply unreal.

I continued after spending some time at the theatre, climbing what felt like thousands of stairs to the continuation of the path above. I walked along, and eventually came to the next major 'attraction' tucked into the Acropolis. The sign read, Odeon of Herodes Atticus, and I heard a guide tell a group of people that it was built in Roman times and was "the place to be" when it came to seeing live, classical performances. It was huge: just a giant, semi-circular amphitheater nestled into the base of the Acropolis. The stone wall behind the stage rose at least three stories high, and the seating facing it seemed to go on forever. I continued listening to the tour guide nearby and learned that it could seat nearly six thousand people back in the day. Six thousand! The benches were roped off and we all gathered around the edge of the amphitheater, trying to get the best picture possible. From the different conversations around me, I heard random bits of information about it, including the massive amounts of wine that usually accompanied performances. *Do you see those large indented spaces in the walls? They used to house large jugs of wine that would fuel the actors between scenes. It was always a riot: every-body had a good time.* It sure sounded like it.

From the auditorium, I saw the Propeleia – honoring the gods of health – and eventually made it to the top of the Acropolis. There were a few dozen more stairs to climb, and it was absolutely swarming with tourists. I had to push my way through the crowd at the entrance just to make it into an open area. The Parthenon was in the process of being renovated, but it was still amazing to see it up close (despite all of the tourists). I had nothing to compare it to; I had never seen such a large, ancient building before. The columns towered above the platform, so much more massive up close than they had been from any of the views Olivier had shown me. I just didn't think it was this impressive! And then I overheard a tour guide tell her group that not a single drop of water was used to cement the pillars to the rest of the Parthenon: everything was based on the science of balance and pressure. I remembered my step-grandmother telling me about how winded she and Papa had been upon reaching the top (thanks to all of the stairs) and tried to imagine him breaking through the crowd of tourists to see such a magnificent structure. The look I saw on his face made me smile.

I walked around the Parthenon, exploring some of the other sites on the Acropolis as well. The temple of Athena and a few outlook towers were also constructed nearby, and I spent plenty of time taking photos and walking the perimeter. I just couldn't get enough of that view! At 3:00pm, I decided to head down and continue through the city. The path leading back down the hill brought me to many more busts and sculptures. I found it incredibly odd that some of the sculptures were nothing more than giant blocks of marble with men's genitalia carved out – in full detail.

Did they start with that and the rest was unfinished? Why are these on display? At one point there were five of these blocks gathered together, with a few Greek letters on the bottom and the same part of the body chiseled into each one. It was the strangest sight I'd ever seen: five Greek penises all in a row.

Shaking the image from my mind, I turned and continued along the path. It turned into a descending stairway, and I took them two at a time as I made my way to the base of the Acropolis. I concluded that the ancient Greeks must have had amazing legs; there was no way they could've done those stairs otherwise.

I made it down by 3:20pm and headed in the direction of the shopping district. I couldn't wait to buy the Pandora charm for my mom and truly hoped that the emergency replacement card worked. On the way, I saw a currency exchange and stopped inside to give it a try. The woman inside was very helpful and processed my request for American dollars. As she ran my card through the system, she crinkled her nose as it was rejected. I wasn't surprised, as I'd been told it wouldn't work in an ATM. Still, part of me had been hoping it would magically work at the currency exchange. I thanked her for her time and left, disappointed.

The shopping area was only a short walk from the currency exchange place. I had located the Pandora store on a previous walk-by as I explored Athens and felt a rush of excitement as I pushed the door open. A small bell jingled, and three women dressed in black all said "Kaló apógevma" in unison. I reciprocated and stepped up to the glass display case. There were charms of all shapes sand colors inside, each more beautiful than the next. Flags, bears, castles, characters from books...the options seemed endless. *But where is the All-Seeing Eye?* As if in response to my thought, one of the women walked over to me and asked what I was looking for. Before I'd even finished describing it, she pulled out the dangling, light-blue eye charm and I knew it was the one. She put the display back in its case, pulled another one out of a bubble-wrapped package, and boxed it up for me. Then we went over to the counter (my heart was pounding) and she rang it up: €55. *Please work, please work, please work.* I handed her my card and she swiped it through her machine.

It gave a sad beep.

She tried again, then shook her head and handed the card back to me. "It was declined, ma'am." At that point, I told her I needed to check something and sat on a bench off to one side of the store, pulling out my phone. *Here goes nothing.*

The next hour was spent being passed back and forth between Mastercard customer service representatives. I spoke with about five different people before my call was flat out disconnected. One of them had told me to have the saleswoman punch in the card's number manually, and she seemed thoroughly annoyed when that still didn't work. I can't go home without this charm. It has to work! I checked my phone for the time. In order to call my bank, I had to wait until they opened at 8:00am (Central Time). *Still one hour until my bank opens and I can call them. Hopefully they'll be able to straighten this out.* I was frustrated and upset but forced a smile and thanked the ladies at the Pandora store for their assistance before I left.

I went back to Piatsa when I realized how hungry I was, remembering that I'd seen some very cheap pita sandwiches on their menu. I only had €15 left and needed €6 for the bus ticket in the morning. I spent €5,50 on food at Piatsa, where I connected to the Wi-Fi and messaged my parents to fill them in on the new situation. My mom couldn't believe that the emergency replacement card wasn't working. In fact, her exact words were, "You really do have the worst luck." I couldn't disagree.

After Piatsa, I went back to the currency exchange place to try again, telling the woman there to try punching the numbers in manually as the Mastercard people had told me. She seemed optimistic, agreeing that yes, sometimes that did the trick. However, it once again failed to go through. She tilted her head to one side and apologized, but I could barely keep eye contact with her. I was so unbelievably frustrated. It was the last day of my vacation and it was turning out to be the worst. My good mood from earlier had evaporated: almost spilling my coffee and almost being hit by a car were nothing compared to the current situation. I sulked and tried to clear my head by walking around outside.

I went back to Piatsa so I could take advantage of their Wi-Fi one more time, looking up the contact information for my bank as I sat down inside. The bank was finally open, so I called them and was instantly connected with an associate. The woman told me that she activated the replacement card, sent me a new one that would be waiting back at my apartment, and everything should be all set with the card I currently had in my hand. I felt remarkably better by the time we hung up, and I marched back to the currency exchange place to try again.

"The bank told me it is now activated. That was the problem with it last time we checked."

The woman tried to process an exchange. Again, nothing. But she reassured me by saying that if the card wouldn't work in an ATM, then perhaps that was why it wasn't working in her system, either. I wanted to believe her, but part of me had a sinking feeling that the card just wasn't going to work. Nevertheless, I made my way back to Pandora.

I felt the women's apprehension as I walked in. I tried to smile and told them that everything should work now that I got ahold of my bank. The one who'd helped me before took out the small parcel she'd wrapped and motioned for me to meet her at the counter. I handed her the card.

"I'm sorry ma'am, it still isn't working."

I was furious. I sat back down on the bench where I'd called Mastercard earlier and pulled out my phone once again. When I got a hold of the credit card company, the customer service representative said she couldn't see why my card wasn't working. She sounded clueless. I explained to her that I'd just talked to my bank and they said the card was activated, then told her that it kept being rejected by the restaurants and stores where I tried using it. She asked me if it had come with a pin number. *No.* She asked me if there was a three-digit number on the back. *No.* I was put on hold for a short while, and when the woman returned she told me that there was an error message in her system regarding my card. It read, "damaged card." I laughed out loud, causing all three Pandora associates to look my way.

I left the store, even more upset than before. *What good is an emergency card that doesn't even work? What kind of customer service is it to send a damaged replacement card? What good is that? What if I had more than one day left in Athens?* It was the first time during the entire trip that I just wanted to be home. I felt myself break into a nervous sweat and didn't know what to do. I didn't have any food and I had a grand total of €3,50 left (keeping enough out for the bus ticket). The trip had been so incredible until that moment; even when my wallet was stolen, my experience with Yiannis completely made up for it. I would even say it was a blessing in disguise, because I wouldn't have had the same amount of time with him in Chania if everything had gone as originally planned. But this? Having the emergency card fail me? It was too much. I wanted to be on the plane home. *Short of physical harm, I truly believe having your wallet stolen is possibly the worst thing that can happen while traveling abroad. This is an absolute nightmare.*

There was nothing more I could do. So with no Pandora charm for my mom and only a deck of philosopher-themed playing cards for my dad, I headed home. I messaged Olivier that I could now only meet him to chat and not for dinner, as I'd been planning to take him out. He told me not to worry, then instructed me to meet him outside of Attika later that evening. Then I messaged Tamara and told her the same: we'd messaged briefly about meeting for drinks that night after my dinner with Olivier. She seemed disappointed but understood when I explained the situation. Great, now I'm letting down new friends as well. My mood managed to sink even lower.

I found Tamara's flat with no problems and poured myself a glass of wine. I spent some time charging my phone, writing about the day's awful events, and recoiling at the thought that I'd have to pay huge international phone charges for calls that proved useless. Then I set my alarm for my meeting with Olivier and fell asleep on the end of my bed.

Just fourteen hours left in Greece.

16

The first time I ever traveled alone – the summer of my internship in Dublin – I spent the majority of my free time by myself. It wasn't that I didn't get along with the other interns, or that I was being 'left out' in any way, but there was just something about being completely free to explore a new city without having to depend on anyone else that I thoroughly enjoyed. It was the first time that I realized how much of an introvert I was, and I began to thrive when I had time by myself to just reflect and recharge. And it wasn't just me; one of my flat mates took a weekend trip to London by herself, and another went for a multi-day hike and nearly got lost without anyone there to help her (but took some truly beautiful photos). Of course, there were some intern "excursions" planned for the group and we did occasionally all meet for after-work drinks or movies, but the majority of the time I preferred to be alone. Some of my greatest memories of the summer were from my solo outings: roaming through St. Stephen's Park, shopping at Dunn's Market, and even doing an interview for my then-blog with the owners of a new bar. I loved being on my own and taking everything in at my own pace. The only person I depended on was me.

So when I met up with Olivier just outside of Attika, I wasn't sure how to react when he told me he was treating me to dinner. I was incredibly hungry and knew the next time I'd be able to eat wouldn't be until the flight home. Part of me wanted to give him a hug and accept his offer right away. But the other, independent side of me wanted to tell him that it was simply too much and that I couldn't go to dinner with him. It took only a minute for my stomach to growl in protest and hunger won. I gave him a hug, we gave each other les bises, and off we went to find dinner.

He led me to a little café behind the Sygrou-Fix metro station called Kalamaki Bar. It was beautiful inside: everything from the floor to the furniture to the walls was painted white, with wicker seat coverings and a candle in the center of each table. The ceilings were high, and the walls were decorated with modern artwork and large geometric shapes. Olivier and I were seated by a tie-wearing waiter at a small table near the front window. Next to the table was a beautiful stone waterfall with real water cascading from top to bottom. It took me a moment to take it all in. There was an undoubtable ambiance about the place.

Olivier handed me the large, brown bag he'd been carrying, and I was surprised I hadn't noticed it earlier. It was my Starbucks bag, and I was thrilled to see all four mugs inside, still perfectly intact. I took his keys out of my purse and handed them across the table. We exchanged a few pleasantries and then the questions began. *So your wallet was stolen? How did that happen? Where were you? How did you manage since then? Did you make it to Santorini? How will you get home?*

A waiter came over and we ordered our 'usuals': a Horiatiki salad and red wine for me, a chicken Souvlaki, French fries, and white wine for him. I tried my best to fill him in on everything that had transpired since I'd left Athens: the train ride to Thessaloniki, the girls I met there, the crowded bus to the airport, realizing my wallet was gone, and the amazing Yiannis who completely rescued me from what was a truly awful situation. The more I talked, the more animated I became. In retrospect, I realized how insane it all sounded, and wondered how I'd managed to have such terrible luck on a trip that had been so carefully planned. I continued, telling him how sorry I was that I couldn't treat us to dinner because of the damaged emergency card. Olivier's eyes watched intently as I spoke, both intrigued and concerned. He told me there were truly awful people there, who didn't care for anyone's well-being but their own. *I'd known that there were pickpockets in Greece, but weren't they everywhere? Hadn't I been careful to keep my things in sight at all times?* We talked and ate, and our dynamic felt completely different than it had the last time I was in Athens. I wasn't annoyed anymore and told him I was genuinely sorry for snapping at him the one night at his flat. In true Olivier fashion, he shrugged.

"Ne t'en fais pas. Ça, c'est dans le passé." *Don't worry about it. It's in the past.*

We spent another hour or so at Kalamaki Bar before deciding it was time to finally head out. To our misfortune, it was raining.

Olivier and I hugged, gave les bises one more time, and I thanked him again for dinner. We agreed to keep in touch, and then he was gone, off into the rainy, dark streets of Athens.

I trudged home, successfully finding the petrol station as I made my way back to Tamara's flat. The brown bag began to rip from the moisture of the rain, but I managed to catch it before the mugs could hit the ground and break. By the time I reached the front door to her building, I was clutching the soaked bag to my chest. I had been through too much in the past few days to deal with broken mugs on top of everything else. Being careful not to drop them, I pushed open the door and made my way to the elevator. It rattled viciously as it ascended. When I got to the flat, I showered and set about packing my bag for the next morning. It took nearly fifteen minutes to fit all four mugs, my clothes and shoes, my Greek copy of <u>The Little Prince</u> and <u>How to Learn Greek without a Teacher</u>, and the few other small souvenirs I'd purchased inside. As I tucked one of my Kinder egg prizes into the front pocket of my bag, I felt something razor sharp against my finger and pulled it out to see a fresh papercut. Then I reached back in and pulled out a crisply folded bit of blue paper.

It was a €20 note, tucked inside and forgotten. *Did I put that there in Germany? Where did it come from? I can eat tomorrow!* I was overcome with excitement; I'd been under the impression that the only food I'd have between the time I woke up and the time I landed in Detroit at 10:00pm would be airplane food. And I had a six-hour layover in Toronto. Finding the €20 note was the best stroke of luck I'd had in days. I didn't even care that I couldn't remember when I'd put it there in the first place; I had it now, and I was elated.

When I finally managed to get everything into my bag, I

zipped it closed and felt a huge sense of relief. I was packed, I had a small but sufficient amount of money, and I'd soon be on my way home. I set my alarm for 4:30am and crawled into bed, already wearing my clothes for the next day. It wasn't incredibly comfortable, but it was one less thing I'd have to do in the morning. I finally drifted off, listening to the rain against my window, and prayed that it would stop in time for my walk to Syntagma in the morning.

. . . . .

I'd had a hunch that wasn't going to happen.

When my alarm went off the next morning, the rain was still coming down. I flew about the flat getting ready, trying not to think about the fact that I needed to walk roughly three kilometers in the rain. I brushed my teeth, pulled a comb through my hair, and packed my cell phone charger into my purse. Then, I gave the room a 'once over' to make sure I had everything, locked the door behind me as I left, and slipped the key underneath (as instructed). I was mentally prepared for the rain, but when I left the building I realized it wasn't just a bit of rain: it was a torrential downpour. I walked quickly along the street, eventually breaking into a sprint down the hill. I quickly made it to the awnings outside of the shops below, thankful that so many were there to shield me from the rain. To my surprise, I saw that Attika was open and I stopped inside for a Spanikopita and a coffee. *I still can't believe I found that bill in my bag. Thank God!*

I only sat in the bakery for a short while, not wanting to waste too much time before heading on my way. The walk was laughably awful. Sloshing through the rain for two miles first thing in the morning was not exactly how I'd wanted to start my day. But I moved as quickly as possible given the circumstances: my bag was heavy with all the mugs inside, my blister-ridden feet were killing me, and the rain had gathered in large pools in the sidewalk. It was miserable. I powered along, determined not to miss the bus. By the time Syntagma came into view, I was once again full-out sprinting. I was completely soaked to the bone and therefore freezing by the time I got there, with my hair, clothes, and bag drenched (though fortunately my bag was waterproof). I bought my €6,00 ticket and was the first one on the bus when it arrived. Once on board, I found a window seat, still out of breath from the morning's walk (or run, rather), and set both my purse and my carry-on on my lap. *Phew.*

My head rested on the rain-coated window as I watched the city pass by outside. I saw some of the places Olivier had taken me, remembering my first night in Greece and how excited I'd been. I remembered the tavern we'd gone to, the beautiful Greek music, and all of the amazing food we'd enjoyed. It seemed like a lifetime ago; I couldn't believe it had only been twelve days earlier. Where did this trip go? The bus continued, passing by groups of people huddled under store awnings, people sleeping under tarps and cardboard boxes on the sidewalks, and the usual morning flurry of people darting to and fro. I closed my eyes and breathed. At the end of my summer in Dublin, I'd needed to take a bus back to the airport as well. Thinking back on that morning, I remembered it had also been raining that day; I truly had the worst luck. However, as I'd been there for nearly ten weeks instead of just two, I had both my carry-on and a large suitcase (not waterproof) to wheel through the cobblestone streets. It was a twenty-minute walk from my flat in Dublin to the bus stop for the airport, and I was completely soaked by the time I reached it. I would never forget that great sense of relief as I rounded the corner and saw the bus stop, bus already there and waiting for me. I handed my suitcase to the driver, who stowed it in the storage compartment, and climbed on board the bus. It had been an unforgettable, though very long, summer and I was ready to head home. I was drenched, exhausted, and overwhelmed with the memory of my trip. I opened my eyes. Same exact feeling.

After forty-five minutes, the bus reached the airport. I felt an odd sense of déjà vu as I made my way inside, praying that no wallets were stolen on the ride. I wondered if I'd ever be able to arrive at an airport without the thought crossing my mind. *Or ride a bus, for that matter*. I would never wish that experience on anybody.

Once inside, I found the airport was rather difficult to navigate given that a large portion of it was now under construction. There were large barricades set up around the building, and there seemed to be no organized flow to anything. Had it been like this when I got here? I got turned around and finally decided to ask for directions, and soon had my boarding pass in hand. I found the line to go through security and watched as they waved down nearly every person who walked through. Except for me. I must've looked so innocent with my wet hair and clothing, bags under my eyes from being up so early, and vacant, fatigued expression. Either that or they just feel sorry for me. Then I found my gate, sat down on the hard, blue plastic – seriously, every single airport! – and waited for boarding to begin.

The flight from Athens to Munich was rather enjoyable. I sat between a man from Germany who'd been traveling on business and a student from Cyprus heading back to his school in Philadelphia. His name was Alex, and he was nice to talk to but slept nearly the entire flight. I managed to stay awake just long enough to get a few caramellos from the flight attendant, then fell asleep as well. I woke up ten minutes before we landed, disappointed that I missed the free Milka bars and coffee. Alex was staring at me, snickering.

"What's so funny?"

"Sleep well?" He pointed at my neck. "You've got a little something –" I reached up and felt my neck, and found that there was my sticky yellow caramello, all tangled up in my hair. Damnit. I could only imagine how ridiculous it looked and tried to laugh as I pulled it out. How early in the flight did that happen? Did I seriously drool out a candy? Oh well. I'll never see these people again.

When we reached Munich, Alex and I collected our things and went our separate ways. He said goodbye and good luck, then turned to head on his way. As he walked down the hallway, he passed a small group of people my age huddled together just outside the gate. I overheard them talking about their next flight to Toronto. That's my flight. Recalling my excellent track record over the previous few weeks with making transportation on time, I approached them. I was far too tired to be shy and had no desire to miss my flight, so I figured it couldn't hurt to ask them for help. When I reached their huddle, I asked if they knew where the gate was. They seemed excited to meet another fellow traveler, and we were soon introducing ourselves. Claire, James, and Nick were also on their way to Canada and after the standard pleasantries (and the excitement of realizing we didn't have to navigate the airport alone) we decided to stick together.

Claire was a beautiful Asian woman with long, black hair and high-end clothing. She explained that she and James – tall, Asian, also very well dressed – were from Dallas, and had taken advantage of their Thanksgiving break to travel abroad. In the last few weeks, they'd been to Italy and Greece, and had even managed to make it to Santorini as they island-hopped. (I was only slightly jealous.) Nick - a short, American techy with glasses and a gamer hoodie – had been on a solo trip to Europe. He shared that he was from Chicago, and had visited Barcelona, Berlin, Paris, and Santorini – in just one week. It took a great deal of effort to hide the "You're crazy, how could you possibly enjoy all of those cities in one week?" look I felt coming over me. Instead, I just smiled and told him that it must have been a nice trip. Apparently the three had met in the airport in Santorini and were very open to accepting a new member to their group. I felt like I'd just been asked to sit at the "cool table" in high school.

We got through the passport check and found our gate. Claire and I went to find food, and I bought a mini baguette, an apple, a Kinder egg, and a pack of Ferrero Rocher Küsschen. As we moved through the line, she told me about her job in Dallas and how she'd always loved to travel. I told her about my mine in Michigan, and that I'd been bitten by the travel bug as well. We gave each other brief overviews of our trips (I left out the part about my wallet for the sake of time) and found seats together at our gate. James and Nick joined us shortly, and the four of us continued talking and exchanging stories. Claire mentioned that she'd love to visit Egypt one day. I told her I'd always wanted to visit Cairo, so naturally we exchanged contact information and decided that maybe one day we could go together.

We had to check in at the gate and get our boarding passes stamped before they started letting people on the plane. It was packed. The line wrapped around the waiting area and even then, every hard, blue chair was occupied. Eventually we made it. I handed the service associate my passport and boarding pass and climbed aboard. Nick disappeared into the crowd without so much as a wave, but Claire and James hugged me goodbye before finding our seats. I was near the back, and saw her bouncy black hair disappear as everyone found their seats. We were off to America.

· · · · ·

The flight back to Toronto went exceedingly well. I sat between a friendly gentleman from Germany and a bald man who ate nothing, drank nothing, and didn't speak to anyone the entire flight. I managed to sleep for a few hours, then watched The Choice and Blue Valentine (neither of which managed to keep my attention as I drifted in and out of sleep). Finally, I put on Le Petit Prince, and loved it. It was the first time I'd ever seen the movie and given that I'd bought the Greek version of the book, it seemed only fitting. It ended just as we began our descent into Toronto, and I made a note to buy it when I got home.

Once we arrived, I was amazed at how smoothly and efficiently my trip through customs went. Everything was streamlined and there were no bottlenecks in the line: from start to finish, it took just twenty minutes. Then I was on my way, into the massive airport. I had six hours to go. *Where to start?*

I found the currency exchange first and traded in my leftover euros for American money. The woman there smiled as she handed me a grand total of roughly $12. I did my airport walkthrough, visiting a few of the small shops and then just finding a comfortable spot to do some people-watching. I watched as travelers went in and out of the stores, leaving with giant bags full of new purchases. I never fully understood the concept behind shops at airports; there were boutiques selling watches and lingerie, outlets with high-end suitcases and purses, and all sorts of great gifts from alcohol to cultural knick-knacks. *But who actually buys this stuff? Who would buy a suitcase at an airport – wouldn't your things already be packed? And who wants to deal with the hassle of those giant teddy bears?* I usually limited my airport purchases to food, trail mix, or Kinder eggs.

There was a bright green sign ahead of me with a white "W" drawn in the center, and as I got closer I recognized it as a Wahlburgers. I'd heard of the restaurant on the news, when Mark Wahlburg visited the one in Detroit, but hadn't been expecting to see one in the Toronto airport. I was curious. And while I wasn't in the mood for a burger (though they did have a vegetarian one), I did stop in for a beer. A pint was $7.50, so I ordered one called a Walbrewski and sat at the bar for a while, watching the sports network on one of the giant T.V. screens. A few people filtered in and out, making small talk with me at the bar. Miraculously, the time I had left to wait at the airport flew by. Before I knew it, there was just one hour until I had to be at my gate, so I paid my tab and headed out to find it.

Miles later – at gate F90 (the very farthest gate from the main concourse) – I flopped into one of the chairs outside the gate. I was thoroughly exhausted. Just one more flight until I was home, safe and sound. I couldn't wait. I bought a water bottle from one of the convenience stores and returned just as they began boarding. I handed over my passport and boarding pass. Then I passed through the gate and was on my way to Detroit, with just $1.50 in my pocket.

· · · · ·

By the time the announcements came on to prepare every-one for landing, I was ready to be home. I had a massive headache from the day of travel, my blistered feet hurt after walking around so much in the airports, and I felt like I smelled awful (having the grimy combination of Athens' rainwater and the airplanes' stuffi-ness embedded in my skin). I just wanted to shower, crawl into bed, and sleep as long as I could. Unfortunately, I'd made the mis-take of planning to be back at work the very next day (Monday) and still had lots of driving to do before I was home. The last leg of the journey was always the hardest.

I felt like a zombie as I walked off the plane at DTW, over-come with the horrible mix of fatigue and dizziness, with just the slightest bit of relief of having finally arrived. I made my way through the airport, eventually reaching the top of the escalators by baggage claim. I saw the small bar where Marisa and I had stopped for drinks before my trip and couldn't help but to smile. *Was that really seventeen days ago?* I felt like a completely differ-ent person now that I'd met my family in Germany and had my adventure in Greece. I'd learned so much, experienced so much, and just felt entirely changed as a person. That's the best thing about airports; they make you realize how much you change be-tween the time you arrive and the time you return. Despite being a grown, 23-year-old woman, there was no greater feeling than being home.

I texted my friend Leslie, who had offered to drive me home, and she responded quickly that she would be there momentarily. I walked around the airport to stretch my legs after the flight, eventually sitting down just inside the door. I watched as people hurried about, collecting their bags from the conveyor belts. I wondered where they'd been; I wondered if any of them had their wallets stolen. A few minutes later, my phone buzzed to let me know that Leslie had arrived. I picked up my bag, slung it over my shoulder, and headed out.

In her car, I didn't know where to start. She asked me how my trip was, and I had a hard time getting out much more than, "Amazing!" There was simply too much to tell. It was almost overwhelming trying to recall it all at once, remembering small memories from each part of the trip as I tried. I attempted to tell her about meeting my family and the small amount of history we discovered, the architecture workshop I got to see while Cleo worked and the small owl I'd made out of foam, and the tavern that Olivier and I had visited my first night in Athens. I fast-forwarded to Thessaloniki and meeting Marilena and Dimitria, Lena, and her traveling friend who'd sold everything to just go. I had barely gotten to telling her about the moment I realized my wallet was gone when we pulled into our apartment complex. The two of us sat in her car for another hour or so as I continued, finally heading inside around 1:30am. It was so great to be back around a familiar friend; as much as I enjoyed adventuring and meeting new people in foreign countries, it was comforting to be around someone who knew me so well. I checked my mailbox on the way in and there they were: a brand-new Discover card and shiny, new Mastercard waiting for me. I almost cried. I had never felt such relief.

Work was rather rough the next day. It felt strange to be back in the office after visiting such a beautiful place, back to the gray carpet, blue-walled environment where I spent the majority of my waking hours. I tried to get back into a routine. I snacked on some almonds during the morning, drank coffee from the breakroom, and couldn't help but wish for a fresh cup from Attika and a piece of Spanikopita instead. I found it was very hard to focus. Hadn't I been in that exact spot just a few months earlier, receiving the news about Papa? And now, there I was again, having been to the country where his grandfather had been born, where part of our family had begun. I was in the same spot but felt like a new person. I had an entirely new perspective on life and appreciation for my family's history. As I spent most of the morning catching up on emails (I had well over three hundred waiting for me in my inbox), it felt like time had stood still while I was gone. The same candidates I'd been working with prior to leaving were still there, still waiting for an interview confirmation or an update. My coworkers sat in their same spots. And the conversations we'd had on a daily basis only shifted slightly to incorporate the details of my life-changing trip. Everything felt surreal.

The first evening after coming home, I went to my parents' house rather than returning to my apartment after work. As soon as my car pulled into their driveway, my mom's face appeared in the front door. I nearly ran to the porch and hugged her. We were both so relieved: all the panic and concern from the past week simply evaporated. I was back in the United States, safe and sound, and everything that had happened was now just a story. My new cards were safe in my wallet, I could go to Secretary of State to get a new driver's license (I was currently keeping my passport with me for identification), and everything else I'd stuck in my wallet was just irrelevant. My mom and I stood there hugging for several minutes before heading inside.

As I told her and my dad about my trip over dinner that night, it felt like I was talking about something that had happened years ago rather than in the past two and a half weeks. I edited my story as I went, not wanting to sound too rehearsed as I'd now repeated it about ten times since arriving home the night before. As I went, their expressions were full of concern and disbelief, and I could tell that all of my calls and messages had thoroughly worried them. I tried to imagine myself in their shoes; their youngest daughter, abroad, alone, with no money and few options to get home safely. I realized where I'd gone wrong, calling them at the early hours of the morning to let them know my misfortune at the airport in Thessaloniki. But I thanked them profusely for all of their help with Western Union and gave them a check for the amount they'd sent me. I gave my dad his philosopher playing cards and told my mom how I'd been planning to give her the Pandora charm. She smiled and told me not to worry (though in the end I did manage to find it online and ordered it for her). Despite all of the worry, I had a feeling that they were proud of me. I had left for Europe in hopes of finding family and discovering the cultures we'd come from. And I had succeeded. The idea that had come to me out of mourning – out of desperate research and with the small, blue bracelet my grandparents had given me – had turned into a truly phenomenal trip.

We spent the rest of the evening in their living room, small details coming to mind as we continued talking. My mom and I enjoyed a few glasses of Red Heron, our favorite Michigan wine, and I thought back to my afternoon at Manousakis Winery. I had learned so much about wine; about the process behind it and the significance of all the different kinds. I remembered the thought I'd had as we walked through the winery after learning about Theodore Manousakis and his family: Wine wasn't actually that simple. It was rather complex. There were so many factors that could affect the flavor of wine; it really was necessary to start at the source to fully understand it.

I looked at the bright red color of the sweet wine in my hand, then set the glass down and curled up on my parents' couch. It was my favorite spot to be: comfortable, warm, home. The two of them were both relaxing in their armchairs, occasionally asking another question about my trip or sharing some bit of news from while I was gone. They told me about their Thanksgiving, and I shared the details of the Greek Thanksgiving Yiannis had organized for me and Elena. Even they were grateful for his kindness. I made sure to send him a message when I got home, letting him know.

From my spot on the couch, I looked over to the pictures on my parents' mantel and remembered what it had been like to live there, five years earlier. I'd spent my days playing with my three siblings, spending hours in the basement building cities out of K'nex or entire afternoons baking with my mom, playing hockey with the neighbor kids outside in our rollerblades, all of the family gatherings for birthdays and holidays, and of course those visits with Papa. It stung, but I realized how lucky I was and how great my childhood had been. Even afterwards, in the years beyond my time at home – the years I spent in school out in Minnesota, the summer in Dublin, the first trip to visit Kristina in Germany – I had experienced so many wonderful things. There was just so much history in my own short life. There was so much that had contributed to the person I'd become.

EPILOGUE

"Travel isn't always pretty. It isn't always comfortable. Sometimes it hurts, it even breaks your heart. But that's okay. The journey changes you - it should change you. It leaves marks on your memory, on your consciousness, on your heart, and on your body. You take something with you... Hopefully, you leave something good behind." - Anthony Bourdain

My experience in Germany and Greece was not the first time I'd traveled. It wasn't the first time I'd flown internationally, or the first time I'd been in a country where they spoke a foreign language. (Fortunately I did speak a bit of German and got to spend my days with Olivier discovering Athens in French, but otherwise

I knew a grand total of only six words in Greek.) Needless to say, traveling was not a foreign concept to me; I just never expected that I could experience such an overwhelming change in heart, mind and soul more than once.

When I had traveled to France in high school, my eyes were opened to so many things. That was the first time I'd ever left the United States, and I had no idea what to expect. I never experienced "culture shock" in the general sense or any kind of severe language barrier, but there were definitely things I found remarkable that I couldn't imagine existing in America. And it went well beyond the Eiffel Tower, the Louvre, and the Seine. The other American students and I spent a day with our pen pals in their school, where we learned that everyone was required to take both English and another foreign language. In America we only needed two years of one foreign language. Late students were either not permitted in class or made to stand at their desk until the teacher deemed it a sufficient punishment. Groups of students would gather outside to smoke, which was forbidden at our high school. And perhaps most surprising of all was the food in their cafeteria: a dairy station with several options, a salad and baguette station, a 'main course' station with omelets, meat dishes, and cooked vegetables, and even a dessert station. All "bio" (organic) and not a Bosco stick in sight. Later, we took the métro, and had our first experience with busy public transportation, something most of us had never experienced in America. Public transportation doesn't abundantly exist in Michigan. After all, a huge part of its economy depends on the automotive industry. All of these things, along with the nightly home-cooked, traditional meals and three-hour-long dinner conversations I had with my pen pal and her family amounted to a 10-day experience I would never forget. It was the first time I realized the importance of traveling: the first time I felt truly changed by it. I wanted to learn more about my country's own history after visiting so many beautiful, historic places in northern France. I wanted to go out and try new things, visit new restaurants, and even adopt some of the habits I'd noticed during my trip. I wrote more, I read more, and I started having an occasional afternoon coffee and a small treat, just as I had in France. I remember returning home from that trip wanting to go back as soon as possible; the travel bug had bitten.

That sensation of change that I felt after just 10 days in France was nothing compared to how I felt after my summer in Dublin. I learned more that summer – about myself, about interacting with people of other cultures – than I did in any communications class I had in college. My internship was in a small office (nestled in the back of an antique shop) and my coworkers were from countries all over Europe. There were occasional language barriers of course, but the stories and customs we shared over lunch were eye-opening. The internship required me to spend a huge amount of time putting myself in uncomfortable situations. I wasn't used to the way my boss conducted business, I'd never had a desk job requiring near constant email communication, and even going out with other interns – a group of people I wasn't completely familiar with – took some getting used to. On one occasion, I even had my first professional conversation on the phone in a foreign language (French). It was my proudest moment of the summer. I experienced my first happy hour with coworkers, and even learned how difficult it could be to do business with so many countries. Coordinating schedules to fit time zone requirements and editing business proposals to address cultural needs were also huge learning experiences.

Similarly, I also experienced a huge shift in priorities in my personal life. Prior to going to Dublin, I'd experimented with being vegetarian. But after visiting stores like Nourish and Lush and noticing that foods and other products at the grocery stores were labeled as either 'vegan' or 'vegetarian', I started researching veganism. Outside of my internship, I began to focus on transitioning to a vegan lifestyle. I even blogged about it as the summer went on. It was incredibly difficult at first, but the more I learned, the easier it became. There were tons of vegan options in Dublin's grocery stores – Tesco and Dunn's – and of course I spent quite a bit of time in Nourish as well. By the end of the summer, between my professional development and the changes I'd made to my personal habits, I was a completely different person. My family wasn't entirely thrilled that I'd transitioned to a vegan lifestyle, but it was a way that I continued my Dublin experience even after being back in the United States. I liked the person that I had become.

Being vegan lasted about a year, and for financial reasons I eventually switched back to a vegetarian lifestyle (vegan products were much more expensive in America than they'd been in Ireland). I continued my blog, sharing my reflections on the summer and talking about future travel, and soon I'd begun to plan the next trip I wanted to take. Some of the other interns from my office and I had kept in touch since the summer in Dublin, so when I graduated college I decided to go back to visit them. I learned that I could have an incredible work ethic when I was properly motivated and picked up so many extra shifts at my part-time job that management switched me to full-time (while still taking a full load of classes). Finally, a few days after graduation, I went back to Germany to visit Kristina and her family. I was there for just six days, and from the time I arrived until the time I left, we'd transformed from simply being former coworkers to being as close as sisters. We still Skype often, planning trips to visit each other when possible, and consider each other to be best friends. I may not see her nearly as often as I see some of my friends in the United States, but I couldn't imagine a better friend than my dear Kristina in Germany. After I celebrated New Years' with her, I headed to Austria to visit Theresa and her family. We also grew quite close, and she managed to get me outside of my comfort zone – way outside of my comfort zone – taking me to different events in the Alps. In November. We spent half of the time I was there absolutely freezing (or maybe that was just me), but it was still an unforgettable experience.

I had thought the trip to France was a once-in-a-lifetime adventure. Everyone had told me so. And then the internship in Dublin, another 'once in a lifetime' experience. And then I started planning my post-grad trip back to Europe and had a phenomenal two weeks in Germany and Austria. I didn't want any of these to be 'once in a lifetime' experiences: I wanted to make friends there and truly invest in becoming a part of the culture. It wasn't just me wanting to go 'see cool places' and 'do new things': I wanted to be fully immersed and become a woman of the world. I had every intention of returning each time I came back.

Travel is truly one of the most challenging things someone can do. Beyond the planning, the coordinating, and of course coming up with the money to even afford it, it can be quite difficult to adjust. For me, some of the most difficult things I had to adjust to were those outside of my control: things like seeing the large amount of homeless individuals on the streets of Dublin and Athens and hearing how rude some English-speakers could be to shop owners or to the wait staff in restaurants. But by far the most difficult adjustment I had to make as a traveler was accepting just that: the fact that I was just traveling. I wasn't permanently staying and therefore couldn't very well plant roots of any kind. I realized how difficult it was to leave friends in foreign countries. To this day, I keep in touch with and consider my friends in Germany and Greece to be some of the best I've ever had. Fortunately, I've had the opportunity to visit them on subsequent trips and each time, leaving becomes more and more difficult.

As Anthony Bourdain said, *"It (travel) leaves marks on your memory, on your consciousness, on your heart, and on your body."* I couldn't agree more. I've only been to six countries outside of the United States (Ireland, Germany, France, Austria, Greece, Canada), and can say with confidence that my mindset has completely changed since the moment I boarded my first flight. The cultural differences and history of each country are unlike anything I've ever come across in the United States. Even in a textbook, it's hard to fully understand the impact of history and understand the culture just by reading about it. Spending time in those foreign countries – being the foreigner – is a completely different experience. It's like being a child. Everything is new, everything is confusing (at first), and sometimes nothing is understandable. The first time I ordered coffee at a café in Paris, I managed to order straight espresso instead of coffee. The first time I ever crossed the street in Dublin (I even waited for the crosswalk sign), I almost got hit by a car. And then that first time I went to the bathroom in a restaurant in Greece and realized they put their used toilet paper in a wastebasket next to the toilet rather than flushing it down the pipes, I was just disgusted. But to them, that's standard protocol. (The pipes in Athens are incredibly small, and certainly not designed to

support the massive metropolis above.) It was strange to me, finding the smallest of things so incredibly different in each country.
Their norms were in some ways like ours, and in some ways entirely unique. Even national holidays, like when I was stuck in Piatsa with the policemen, watching the riot going on outside, that
was the norm for that particular day of the year. Again: eye-opening.

As for the relationships I started with my German family, I'm
glad to say we still keep in touch. I even had the opportunity to go
back to Germany recently, where I spent a few days with them
before visiting Berlin for the first time. I actually stayed with Rosie
in Berlin – the curly-haired German from Tamara's flat – and we've
since grown to be great friends. On that same trip to Berlin, I
reached out and met Lena (from Thessaloniki) for drinks one evening. She had finished her internship in Greece and was back in her
hometown, just living her life and enjoying the city. It was amazing
to see her again, and when I saw her, we hugged like old friends
even though we'd only spent two days together in Thessaloniki.
I've come to realize that the friends I've made abroad have given
me a new way to connect to the culture, and just add to the reasons that I will continue to travel.

Obviously being robbed in a foreign country was not what I
had in mind for my great adventure. It was an enormous inconvenience that – fortunately – I have been able to move past and
now see as a blessing in disguise. I'm not sure what I was expecting
to find in Germany and Greece, but it certainly wasn't a pick-
pocket. I knew I wanted to go to discover my family's history, and
I did get to meet our relatives in Germany. While it wasn't the cut-
in-stone, here's-the-connecting-link discovery I was hoping for,
the relationships I made with my family members were well worth

the trip. My mom even seemed to think that Jürgen looked similar to one of my uncles in the United States. Maybe.

As for my family in Greece, I was mildly disappointed that I didn't learn more. I made it to Athens, and that was a start. After what Yiannis had told me about Papa's family not likely being from Crete, and after speaking more with my step-grandmother and Papa's brother, I learned that Leon was likely from Athens after all. I'd walked all over the city; as different as it was sure to be between the time I went and the time that Leon lived there some hundred years earlier, I still saw it. I still experienced it. I still saw the people, experienced the culture, and of course ate the amazing food. I regretted nothing. (Except perhaps missing out on Santorini, but that's another trip for another day.)

Despite the frustration, despite the exhausting layovers and all the painful blisters, my time in Germany and Greece was an experience I will never forget. It was different than the trips I'd taken in the past for many reasons, but most importantly because of how personal it was. Everything that happened in those seventeen days made me a stronger person – a more adventurous person – than I could have ever become otherwise. As for what I left behind, I may never know. Yet if it's anything like what I took away from my experience, then I know that it was good. Travel can be uncomfortable and heartbreaking, and at times is definitely not so pretty. In each new voyage to the unknown, there are inevitable highs and lows. There are always lessons to be learned. But travel can also be one of the most wonderful, life-changing things in the world: anywhere in the world. Mine was a journey to discover my roots and the places my family had come from. I wanted to experience the cultures first hand and gain a better understanding of the factors that made me, me. And I did just that. I may not have found exactly what I was looking for, but I discovered more about myself than I could have ever imagined.

www.ingramcontent.com/pod-product-compliance
Lightning Source LLC
Chambersburg PA
CBHW020916060726
47591CB00004B/1276